miracle Valley

**the story of
Hollybush Christian Fellowship**

**Jim Wilkinson
with Chris Spencer**

HARVEY WILKINSON

Harvey Wilkinson, Publishers
235 World's End Lane, Orpington,
Kent BR6 7SS, UK

Cover design and illustration: Spring Graphics, Saintfield, N.I.
Cover photograph: Ian Leck

© 2001 Jim Wilkinson and Chris Spencer
Part I first published in Great Britain
by Marshall, Morgan & Scott in 1984
All rights reserved

ISBN 0-9540718-0-8

Printed and bound in Great Britain by
Omnia Books Ltd, Glasgow

Contents

Part I
1. Voice in the dark — 9
2. Adventures in faith — 19
3. Winds of change — 35
4. Last stand — 54
5. Under new management — 69
6. Miracle Valley — 85
7. Naturally supernatural — 99
8. Mountains and valleys — 118
9. Battle stations — 136
10. On holy ground — 153
11. In His time — 168
12. Only the best — 185
13. Celebration — 204
14. The secret — 217

Part II
15. First harvest — 225
16. Come rain, come shine — 235
17. Home and away — 243
18. Getting it right, getting it wrong — 252
19. Sending out smiles — 258
20. Family matters — 264
21. Constant change is here to stay — 279
22. Spadework — 289
23. In search of revival — 299
24. Milestones and memories — 309
25. The greatest miracle of all — 314
    Postscript — 317

From the author

I dedicate this book with joy and gratitude to all my relatives and friends who have had an influence on my life from its formative years until this present time.

Above all to my wife and daughter, Cynthia and Joanna, whose love and support mean so much to me.

My thanks and gratitude for the dogged determination (at my request) of Vic and Sheelagh Harvey to bring the story of the Lord's dealings at Hollybush up to date, and for their practical upholding.

My gratitude also to every member of the fellowship, past and present, who has been a big part of our lives, whether blessing or shaping and honing this servant of God, and to everyone else, Christian or not, encountered on life's journey.

'I don't mean to say I am perfect. I haven't learned all I should even yet, but I keep working towards that day when I will finally be all that Christ saved me for and wants me to be.' (Phil. 3:12, The Living Bible)

My desire is that everyone who reads this book will become acquainted with the one who is the author of miracles – the Lord Jesus Christ, who is the same, yesterday, today and for ever.

Jim

Foreword

My longstanding association with the ministry that goes on at Hollybush Farm is one I deeply cherish. My mind reverts often to the first camp meeting there, at which I preached – the lively services, the beautiful countryside and the atmosphere of double devotion – openness to the Holy Spirit and the Word of God too. Indeed, that first camp meeting will remain as one of the golden memories of my life.

Central in my thoughts, however, as I write these lines, is my friend Jim Wilkinson – large in everything but his own estimation – and his truly gracious wife Cynthia. The thing that impressed me during my first meeting with Jim was his simple and quiet trust in God. I am not surprised, therefore, that the ministry of Hollybush Farm has come to be known as 'Miracle Valley'. When faith and trust are in evidence then God delights to work miracles.

Those who know nothing of the power of God in these modern days and think that miracles are a thing of the past, may regard this book as far-fetched, but I assure you the things recorded in these pages really happened. At Hollybush Farm I have seen, with my own eyes, the miraculous power of God at work, plucking fears out of people's souls, filling them with faith and confidence, touching the sick into health and, of course, the greatest miracle of all – Christian conversion.

My prayer and hope is that this book will not only fascinate you with its stories of modern-day miracles, but that it will expand the horizons of your own faith. And if you can pay a visit to Hollybush Farm some time, then do so. You will be driven to say, I am sure, as have hundreds of others – 'We never saw it on this wise before.'

Miracles do happen today. Maybe as you read this book one will happen to you.

Selwyn Hughes

Part I

1/Voice in the dark

About a week ago I was driving north on my way to a meeting where I was due to share some of the great things God had done for us at Hollybush Farm. The occasion, an outreach dinner organised by the Full Gospel Business Men's Fellowship, was geared to working men and my role as guest speaker that evening was to tell how I had met Jesus Christ, and how that encounter had changed my life and work.

It was a familiar routine. Over the years I'd been privileged to tell my story at more than 30 Full Gospel meetings, as well as on countless other occasions, and I was looking forward to the evening ahead.

Yet somewhere at the back of my mind there was a niggling little doubt about the line I'd planned to take in my address. I never used notes, but all the same I knew more or less the thoughts I wanted to share with the folks at the dinner. I'd told the story so many times that I could do it in my sleep.

But not tonight. Tonight, it seemed, I was to include a fresh emphasis in what I shared. It had begun at around eleven o'clock the previous night. Cynthia and I had been about to turn in when the telephone had rung and I'd lifted the receiver to hear the voice of a young man telling me he was on his way out to commit suicide.

We knew this lad; he'd been to several meetings at Hollybush and on almost every occasion we'd spent an hour or more talking through his problem with him. But now, he said, he'd had enough. He was going to end it all.

'Don't do that,' I urged him. 'I'll meet you and we'll talk this out.'

'There's no point,' he insisted. 'I'm just a hopeless case.'

'No, you're not. Listen, in God's eyes there's no such thing as a hopeless case. Now, where can I meet you?'

Reluctantly, he agreed to see me and I drove out to pick him up. For over an hour we sat in the car, and with God's help I talked him down. When I dropped him off at his house just after one o'clock in the morning he was calm and stable. His problems hadn't disappeared, of course, but he at least was able to face them again.

'We'll win through,' I assured him as he got out of the car. 'Remember, God has no hopeless cases.'

Now, as I motored through the early evening, that phrase kept coming back to me - 'no hopeless cases' - and I somehow felt that those words were to play a key part in what I was to tell those businessmen. That was fine by me. The story of our Yorkshire farm was, after all, a story of changed lives, and among those we'd been privileged to see transformed were plenty of folk whom the world had regarded as without hope.

As I turned on to the motorway I let my mind run back over some of the names. Who, I wondered, among all the 'impossible cases' that had come our way, was the greatest testimony to the power of Christ? One stood out above all the rest: Barbara Elenor.

We first heard of Barbara back in February, 1980. A manic depressive, she'd been in and out of mental hospital for seven years and was now home again after yet another course of treatment. As so often before she seemed little better and now we were being asked if we could help. The request had come independently from two sources familiar with Barbara's case - a social worker and a member of the hospital's nursing staff - and so we took it that the Lord wanted us involved. Of ourselves, of course, there was nothing we could do for someone with so serious a mental condition, but when a miracle was called for we knew the one who could help. In that confidence Cynthia and I drove up to the Elenors' home that same afternoon.

The family were market gardeners and at that time were living in a run-down caravan on the land; even before we'd stepped inside the van we sensed the depression. But nothing could have prepared us for the shock of coming face to face with the pitiful, unkempt woman who sat huddled in a corner chair, her face set like stone, her vacant eyes staring into space.

To make matters worse we were not welcome. Mrs Elenor would not speak to us, apart from acknowledging who she was, and her husband was openly hostile. But we'd been asked to help.

'Mrs Elenor, please may we pray with you?'

'You can do what you like,' she snapped. 'I couldn't care less.'

So we laid hands on her and prayed. We prayed that she would come to know the Lord as her own personal Saviour and that the Lord would set her free from whatever was tormenting her. And then we left.

Two days later her husband telephoned. There was no hostility now. 'Hey, she's different,' he said. 'My wife's beginning to live again.'

'Well, it's nothing to do with us,' I told him. 'It's the Lord.'

We kept in touch, both Cynthia and myself as well as other members of the fellowship, and as we prayed with them and for them we watched Barbara come alive beneath the touch of the Holy Spirit. Gone was the sour, cringing wreck of a person we'd first set eyes on. Greeting us on the caravan step now was a smiling, welcoming face that said it all. Christ had set her free!

But the experts were sceptical. The doctors and psychiatrists, the atheists and humanists voiced their doubts and said it was only a matter of time before the patient collapsed into depression again. Manic depressives, they said, could never be regarded as cured.

But the Lord proved them wrong. Barbara Elenor was a new person in Christ, and so dramatic and complete was the transformation that within three months the whole family - mother, father and four sons - were coming to the meetings. A year or so later they had all committed their lives to God.

The following year, still rejoicing in her new liberty, Barbara telephoned me to ask if I would choose a Bible text to go in the porch of the new bungalow they were building.

'And we're going to have a little dedication service,' she said, 'to commit the new place to the Lord. Will you and Cynthia come?'

'We'd be delighted,' I said, but we hadn't realised just how much of an occasion this was to be. For Barbara wanted everyone who'd known her as a manic depressive to come and see what the Lord had done for her, and she'd sent out invitations to the gathering at the bungalow and afterwards in the village hall.

About 70 people turned up, including two doctors, three social workers and six psychiatrists, and together we listened to Barbara's own story and then gave thanks for all God had done for her.

And the critics? Those who said it wouldn't last? They could stand and consider the text which the Lord had given me for Barbara - a text now etched in stone and cemented in prime place within the bungalow's porch: 'The Lord will perfect the things concerning thee.'

Theirs was an ideal story to share at a Full Gospel Business Men's dinner because at our own local chapter in Northallerton it was always people like the Elenors who brought others in. Those who have known what it's like to be written off are always first to tell other 'hopeless cases' the good news!

I glanced at the car clock and moved into the fast lane. Who else should I mention tonight? Who else had been beyond hope?

A memory stirred within me and a laughing face passed before my mind's eye. Yes, if ever there'd been a hopeless case, physically, it had been that man from Coventry who had caused quite a stir at one of our camp meetings a couple of summers past. I smiled to myself as I remembered the commotion.

Like so many others that evening, this man (I didn't catch his name) had come forward for prayer and was being ministered to, at the side of the platform, by one of our visiting speakers. The same thing was happening all around the front of the dais and there was plenty of prayer and rejoicing going on. But all at once this man let rip. One moment he was on the floor, laid out by the power of the Spirit and the next he was up and shouting and hopping on one foot as he tugged at his boot on the other.

All eyes were on him as he leapt up and down, crying out and laughing in the same breath.

'What's going on down there?' I called out over the microphone.

'It's his foot!' someone replied. 'His foot and his leg. They're growing!'

Apparently the man had a short leg and withered foot, requiring a special brace and a shoe with a four-inch heel. The commotion had started when he'd realised that the leg was growing so fast that he couldn't get the caliper off.

But then, after a struggle, he was free! Off came the brace, the special shoe and even his sock! Up he jumped on to the platform, laughing and whooping with joy, and then he leapt back to the ground, landing firmly on that once-withered leg.

A hopeless case by medical standards, he had been made whole by the Divine Physician.

There were plenty like him, I mused; plenty for whom the doctors and specialists had done all they could. But if I should choose just one other . . .?

As I slowed for the motorway services and turned off for petrol a name presented itself from that same camp week: Hilary Zoe James. Sure enough, she'd been another 'hopeless case' - a classic example of increasingly severe back trouble.

Hilary's problems had begun back in 1970 with pains in the lower part of her spine. Two years later this was diagnosed as arthritis, and after a further two years of suffering her condition had deteriorated to the extent that she was unable to walk. On Christmas Eve, 1974, she was admitted to hospital where doctors told her she had a slipped disc.

An operation, delayed by four months because of complications with a severe thrombosis, left her much improved but still in a great amount of pain. Visits to two specialists and a further three operations did little to relieve the condition, and in 1981 Hilary was forced to give up her job as a secretary. She seemed completely without hope.

But then she met the Lord! In July, 1982, she gave her life to Christ, and a month later her brother, a Christian for many years, brought her to Hollybush.

'I was so able to feel God's presence in that place,' she wrote to me later, 'that I wanted more.' But on her fourth visit to camp that week she received far more than she'd ever thought possible.

'Someone in this tent has severe back problems,' came the word from the platform. 'If you will stand we will pray for you.'

Hilary hesitated - in a crowd of more than 1,500 people there had to be many people with back trouble - but then she was on her feet, her arms raised before the Lord.

'But after that prayer of healing I didn't feel one bit better,' she wrote. 'In fact I felt foolish and resigned myself to the fact that the prayer wasn't for me after all.'

But the following morning, at her home in York, Hilary was hanging out washing in the garden when she heard someone call her name.

'I turned to see who it was, thinking it was one of my neighbours, but there was no one there. Then I moved further down the garden and the voice came again, calling my name so clearly. But still there was no one to be seen and I wondered if someone was having me on.'

The third time the voice came, said Hilary, it sounded as though it was just behind her shoulder:

'Your back's not hurting any more.'

With that she had almost dropped her washing. It was true! For the first time in years she had no pain. Back inside the house she prodded her back and her legs - nothing hurt. And then she tried a high-kick . . . and succeeded!

God had done it again. A year later, when Hilary wrote to me, she was still free of pain.

Back on the motorway, I slipped quickly through the gears into the fast lane again.

But what about myself? This was *my* story I was supposed to be telling, and in a very different sense I too had once been a hopeless case. There were certainly many folk in the little village of Snape, where I was brought up, who would vouch for that.

'Jim Wilkinson?' I could imagine them saying. 'Why, we never knew such a little terror.' Though, if they were fair, they'd admit that I wasn't alone in the pranks I played on them. It took more than one mischievous youngster to stuff a chicken down someone's smoking chimney, or to roll a five-gallon drum of water to someone's door, leaning it so that the water would flood into the hall when the door was opened. Jim was a hopeless case, all right.

With such a reputation I suppose it was understandable that a wave of relief swept the community along with the news that at 14 years of age I'd been converted. It happened in the summer of 1944 when a jolly, silver-haired evangelist by the name of Rev. Tom Butler came to take a week's mission at the little Methodist chapel where I went each week with Mother and Dad and my brothers, Alan and Derek. Perhaps the villagers took this as their chance to see the little terror reformed and prayed extra hard that week. Or maybe it was the result of years of prayers from Mum and Dad and the folks at the chapel that I'd follow them in committing my life to the Lord. Either way, on the Friday of that week I was one of the first out of my seat when the Rev. Butler invited us to step to the front if we wanted to receive Jesus as our Saviour.

Unfortunately for the victims of those pranks, however, this 'conversion' was short-lived. I'd meant it at the time, of course, but looking back I think the decision to become a Christian had come from my head and not my heart. So there was no real change, except that I now had a different sort of reputation to live up to and my practical joking had to be rather more discreet.

Outwardly, though, the signs must have encouraged them. In order to keep up the pretence of having been 'born again' I became increasingly involved with chapel activities, particularly the weekly Methodist Guild youth meetings, and at 17 I even joined one of the Mission Bands that went out on alternate Sunday evenings to take services at other chapels in our Methodist circuit.

I thoroughly enjoyed these outings, and so bold did I become - or perhaps I'd even begun to believe that I was a Christian - that on many Sundays I was the one asked to deliver the sermon. But these sermons were never my own; I'd stumbled on a useful supply of sermon outlines in a Christian periodical, and with someone else's thoughts and interpretations to hand I would hold forth from the pulpit like a seasoned preacher.

The trouble was, just as the words were another man's, so was the conviction behind them. Yet no one ever challenged me about this - until one crisp November evening in 1948.

We were on our way home from Ellingstring, a little village that sits tucked under the hill on the edge of Wensleydale. As so many times before, we'd taken the service in the little tin chapel that sits high off the road in the village street, and we'd enjoyed a good supper in the home of one of the chapelgoers. Now we were bowling home in the car, spinning through the twisty country lanes and laughing together at the memory of our host's face as we'd devoured every scrap of food laid before us.

But then, for me, the mood changed. As the laughs ran out and we began to motor down through the farms of High Ellington, the five of us in the car fell silent. And it was in that pause, just as we rounded a bend between the high hedges and dry-stone walls, that I heard the voice.

'You've been preaching about me tonight, haven't you?'

I was seated in the middle of the back seat and glanced first to my left, but it wasn't Lilian Donaldson speaking to me. Then to my right, but my cousin Carl was looking the other way. Leonard Abel was at the wheel; perhaps they were his words? But Leonard was concentrating on keeping his Dad's little Ford Eight on the road.

And then it dawned on me. It must be the Lord!

I'd never realised that God might sometimes speak to us with an audible voice - audible to me, anyway, if not to those around me - and all at once that sure knowledge brought a leap to my heart. Then, sitting there bumping along on that back seat, I thought I'd better answer the question.

'Mmmm,' I said. Almost immediately the clear, gentle voice came again.

'Do you really know me?'

I had plenty of time to think on that. It was only another six miles to Snape, but on that brisk winter's night it seemed more like 60. There had been a piercing challenge about that second question and in my heart there was a sense of urgency about answering it; urgency and - well, trepidation. Because in a flash I realised I'd been found out. God had known my heart all along.

I didn't speak another word on that journey. When at last we reached the shadowy chapel in Snape I muttered a speedy 'cheerio' and vanished into the night, charging off down the fields to our farm as though my tail was on fire.

Do you really know me?

Soon the house loomed up in the darkness - no lights on;

everyone in bed - and I raced across the yard and into the kitchen, my heart pounding with the answer I knew I had to give.

Up the stairs, into my room, and down on to my knees . . .

'Lord, if that's you speaking to me - yes, please! I really want to know you.'

Much later, stepping into the hotel where the Full Gospel meeting was to be held that night, that phrase was still buzzing around in my head.

'No hopeless cases.'

Almost certainly that would be a word for someone at the dinner tonight, I mused. And yet at the same time it would be a word for everybody, for in God's eyes we had all been without hope until Christ stepped into our world. And how thankful I was that I'd met Him. After all, it was only because of Him that I had a story to tell at all.

2/Adventures in faith

The Yorkshire Dales lay muffled by snow that sharp winter of 1948, but as I worked away at my chores on Dad's farm - The Hollins at Thorp Perrow - I barely noticed the biting winds and hampering drifts because in my heart a strange and exciting fire was starting to burn. I'd never realised that being a Christian could feel this good and suddenly I wanted everyone else to have what I'd got. At every opportunity I would drop in a word for the Lord, and as for those Mission Band services, hardly a sermon went by (my own sermons now!) without my making an appeal for people to give their lives to God.

But it wasn't until some months later that I realised just how much I'd been blessed. I was now 19 and visiting the optician for one of my periodic eye-tests. Wearing glasses had been necessary since I was six years old and had gone over the handlebars of my bike on my way home from school one summer's afternoon. As usual I'd been rushing to reach the farm in time to join Dad on his evening milk round in Aiskew and Bedale, but on this night Dad would be going alone: my tumble ended with a smashed brow-bone. In time, of course, the bone healed, but I was left with faulty vision in the bruised eye, and on top of that I was to suffer occasional severe migraines. I was told I would always need spectacles. But this time, when I went for the eye-test, something had changed. 'You've 20/20 vision,' the surprised optician informed me. 'Your problem seems to have cleared up naturally.'

Naturally or *super*naturally? In my own mind there was no doubt that the correction of my vision was one of the wonderful bonuses of the work of God in my life. The migraines still bothered me from time to time, but the eyesight was perfect. I was so thankful. I'd never felt at ease with spectacles, anyway, and it gave me a real kick to throw them away.

Released from the self-consciousness those glasses had caused me, I was now bolder than ever in my efforts to win others for the Lord. Sometimes, when there was a special evangelistic outreach planned, I just couldn't wait for the day's work on the farm to end. Whatever the occasion, if it presented an opportunity for people to receive Christ, I was there in the thick of it. Street evangelism, home visitation, Guild rallies, summer barbecues - there was always something going on, always a fresh opening for the Gospel. And as a result many people gave their lives to the Lord.

But the time came when, despite our efforts, it seemed that the church wasn't doing enough. This came home to me when I learned that one of our young people had been converted through an evangelistic campaign down in Topcliffe near Thirsk. In fact it so disturbed me that I mentioned it to one of our church members, a returned missionary by the name of Rev. Ransome.

'It doesn't seem right that one of our own members should have to go down to another church to find the Lord,' I complained. 'Why can't we have our own mission?'

Rev. Ransome, himself a keen soul-winner, laid the matter before the church, asking us to pray about it - and within a year the Bedale Methodist Circuit was holding its own campaign.

It was a tremendous week - a time when the Holy Spirit moved on the villages in conviction and blessing, and a time when I learned a great deal that was to help me in the years ahead. Best of all it confirmed the vision God had given me to see people responding to the message of the cross. More than 70 people committed their lives to the Lord that week.

Yet while that vision was being strengthened there were certain aspects of the work of God's Spirit that I could not bring into focus. And just as the mission had come about largely through the enthusiasm of Rev. Ransome, so too had my confusion concerning the activity of the Holy Ghost.

In the Methodist Church we had always been warned off Pentecostals. They weren't like other Christians, we were told. They spoke in strange, babbling languages and could never worship God without making a lot of noise. They believed in a very dubious doctrine called 'the baptism in the Holy Spirit', which any self-respecting Christian would steer well clear of. In short, they were weak people who needed an 'experience' - something extra to keep them going. We would do well to keep away from them.

Every time I heard this I would nod my head in hearty agreement. I didn't need anything added to my Christianity. I was soundly born again, I had my Bible, I was eager in prayer - and what's more I was a good Wesleyan. I was totally secure and satisfied in my faith. No, the Pentecostals couldn't give me anything.

But . . . then there was Rev. Ransome.

He had returned from missionary service in Nigeria shortly after the war and had come into our circuit as a breath of fresh air. He was a small, slight man with a bubbly, infectious laugh and bright, almost blazing eyes. In some indefinable way he always seemed larger than life. There was an energy about him, a spiritual energy that brought a new and exciting dimension to our Bible studies and a dramatic lift to the preaching of the Gospel. When Rev. Ransome was taking a service there were few empty seats.

It never occurred to me to ask why he was different. I suppose I assumed it was simply a natural gift - that he had been blessed with an effervescent character and manner. But from time to time he would relate his experiences in Africa, and then I began to wonder whether his exuberance had more to do with his encounters as a missionary.

He had some amazing stories to tell: stories of African Christians suddenly bursting forth in unknown languages as they worked away in the bush, planting amongst the trees. Some, he said, would fall flat on their faces and lie there in the dust, weeping non-stop for hours on end in the heat of the day. Then there would be times when these same black Christians would be filled with a great joy, a joy that would come upon them as suddenly as the weeping, sweeping through their community in great waves of laughter.

'And what was the cause of this astonishing behaviour?' Rev. Ransome would ask us from the pulpit. 'Why, it was the movement of the blessed Holy Spirit as He fell upon those people, moving them first to a great intercession as they wept for the work of God to be released upon their people, and then filling them with an overflowing joy as they received the assurance that God was indeed moving sovereignly upon their land in a great outpouring of His love and power.'

Indeed it could have been nothing but a sovereign work of God, Rev. Ransome assured us, because what was happening was way beyond the experience of the missionaries working there, and in an incredible about-turn situation the white Christian workers found themselves learning about the Holy Spirit from their African converts.

'It was revival, of course,' beamed the Reverend, 'and in revival you are very aware of God's sovereignty. Why He chose to move upon our African brothers first only He knows, but it was nine months before He touched us missionaries in the same way; nine months before we too were baptised in the Spirit.'

He talked too about 'the gifts of the Spirit', about 'miracles of healing', and about other 'divine acts'. He even had some little booklets which explained such things, and these I read, partly out of curiosity and partly with disbelief - but mostly in confusion. I would wonder about them as I went about my work on the farm, or as I walked the cattle to Masham market on a Tuesday - a job which swallowed up most of the day if some of the stock was unsold and had to be walked back home again.

On such occasions I would turn these things over in my mind. How was it that Methodists were told to keep away from Pentecostals and yet Rev. Ransome was preaching with great conviction about this strange 'baptism in the Spirit'? Perhaps it was all right for Africans, I told myself. After all, they needed an extra something to brighten up their spartan village life. And perhaps it was hardly surprising if some of that Holy Spirit stuff had rubbed off on the missionaries working with them. No one would blame Rev. Ransome for getting excited. Strange things might happen to anyone who ventured into a strange country, particularly if they stayed out in the sun too long. Besides, everyone knew that missionaries were . . . well, different. Probably it would be all right as long as he didn't start suggesting that we too needed this mystical 'baptism' experience.

But one nagging question remained. What if the baptism was the key to that indefinable yet undeniable quality that somehow set this man apart from everyone else I knew? And as I pondered this I found myself wishing I'd known the Rev. Ransome who had set sail for Africa those many years ago - the green young Methodist missionary who probably hadn't had a good word to say for those crazy Pentecostals.

As the months and years passed, however, I thought less and less of these things. It seemed there were no easy answers to such grey areas of Christian experience and it was best to get on with what I knew and loved best: preaching the Gospel. Yet it was while I was doing just that - out with the Mission Band one Sunday evening - that God began the foundational work of providing me with His own answers to those questions.

One of the grey areas for me was healing. Did God heal today in the same miraculous way as did Jesus in the Gospels? It seemed unlikely for two good reasons. Firstly, we had the enormous benefits of medical science which the people of Jesus' day knew nothing about. If God didn't heal them supernaturally then they remained unhealed. Secondly, divine healing was prominent in the teachings of the Pentecostal Church - they even advertised 'healing meetings' - and if *they* believed it then it was definitely suspect.

Yet at the same time Rev. Ransome's stories of healing miracles in Nigeria refused to go away, and I was also becoming more bold in my own faith, declaring that if God's Word said it, I believed it. At that point I hadn't begun to grapple with any of the Scriptures that spoke specifically about the Lord healing people, but the less prickly ones that promised we could have what we asked for in faith were definitely under my belt. It was one of those promises - 'If you ask anything in my name, I will do it' - that came to mind when for the first time in my life I felt compelled to pray for someone who was sick.

It was shortly before Christmas, 1953. A group of us had been up to the little chapel at Langthorne just beyond Bedale to take the evening service, and at the close of the meeting we were invited home for supper by a local farmer, Mr William Thompson. Still as eager as ever to help clear other people's dining tables, we accepted, unaware of what awaited us.

Propped up in bed in the living room was Mrs Thompson. We learned that she was due to enter hospital for a hysterectomy - in those days a very serious operation - and that she had been told to expect to be in hospital for about three weeks. Following this she would need four to five months' convalescence.

Several of us felt that we should pray with her for a successful operation and speedy recovery and agreed that we would pray a prayer of faith. Exactly how much faith we were able to muster I'm not quite sure because we insisted that Mrs Thompson's husband and two sons also be in on the prayer, probably so that there were plenty of us to share the blame if our faith didn't work.

But it did. To our astonishment Mrs Thompson returned home after only two weeks in hospital, and within another couple of weeks she was up and about, easing herself back into the busy farmhouse routine.

Perhaps secretly some of us were waiting for the backlash of this unusual recovery - would she have a relapse? - but it never came. Her good health continued well into her eighties, having ailed hardly a thing since that memorable Christmas Sunday.

The following spring we were moved to put the prayer of faith into action again, this time in order to save a wedding and hoped-for honeymoon.

On 6 May, 1954, my cousin Lorne was due to be married to Mary Lowes, a girl who'd been evacuated with her mother to our farm at the beginning of the war and whose family had settled in the area once peace had returned. But a few days before the big event Mary began to feel unwell. By the Wednesday, the day before the wedding, she had turned yellow, been consigned to bed, and told by the doctor not to move. The diagnosis was yellow jaundice. She and Lorne would have to postpone the happy day.

But how could they notify all the guests in time? Few people had a telephone in those days. And what about the honeymoon? Two weeks booked and paid for and no refund possible.

At the prayer meeting that evening we laid it before the Lord, asking and believing for a miracle.

Again to my utter surprise, we got it. The following morning, as originally planned, Mary Lowes got out of bed and into her wedding dress and went and married her man. Every trace of the sickness had gone. Her eyes were bright, her smile broad, and her skin the radiant pink of the blushing bride.

The service that day included a special note of thankfulness to God for Mary's miraculous recovery, and I was as grateful as anyone. But I was also intrigued. Yes, I was ready to pray for healing, even able now to believe that it would happen . . . but for God actually to act upon our faith in miracle-working power! Well, it needed some thinking about. And I hid these things in my heart, buried beneath the surface like the grain seeds lying in the soil of Hollins Farm.

Those years of the early 1950s brought enormous changes to my world. With the war behind us - a war whose ravages we'd not escaped, having the strategic Leeming Airfield on our doorstep - the economy of the farm was picking up along with the economy of the country. Dad's careful management through the recessions of the war years had given us a good basis on which to build, and now we were seeing what amounted to revolution in the farmyard. The old shire horses with which we'd ploughed the land since before I could remember were on their way out to graze, and trundling into their place came the enormous mechanical beasts that were to change the face of farming beyond recognition.

I was sad to see the old methods go - there was an earthy magic about tilling with horses that no machine could ever replace - but at the end of the day farming was about productivity and we had to keep up. The brutal business world would not wait for dreamers.

At the same time my other world, the world of evangelism, was also expanding, in its own way becoming more efficient, more productive.

In 1952 I had been involved in forming the Wensleydale Evangelistic Crusade, along with two other men, local farmer Alf Suttill and Mr Kit Calvert, who was the manager of a Wensleydale cheese company. Under the banner of this crusade we had entered into a period of intensive evangelism in the area, holding weekly outreach meetings in the near-redundant Congregational Church in the Wensleydale village of Leyburn. From there we had also launched out to take regular open-air services in many of the little villages up and down the Dales.

This was effective, but in the same way that harvesting had been effective before the combine harvester appeared on the farm. Now, in evangelism too, a more efficient, potentially more productive method had arrived: Billy Graham was coming to London.

I was in with both feet. There were coach trips to Harringay Stadium to be arranged; prayer meetings to attend; homes to visit with invitations to the crusade ... For weeks beforehand we didn't have a moment to spare, and I was in my element, helping to make a way for folk to hear the great evangelist, and hopefully to commit their lives to Christ.

Two years later, in 1955, it happened all over again, only this time the coaches were heading north instead of south, to Kelvin Hall in Glasgow.

One of those trips we made was particularly memorable. Always on these occasions some members of our coach party would become Christians, but on this special trip every one of the people we were praying for received the Lord. Eleven Christians and 22 guests had gone to Glasgow, and 33 Christians came home rejoicing!

But there was to be another reason why I would not forget that night. One of those new converts was a slim blonde girl called Cynthia Biker. I'd met her casually through the Methodist Guild up at Leyburn and I'd got to know that she had a very fine gift for singing. An exceptional gift, in fact. Her talent had first come to light as a ten-year-old in the local Methodist choir. From there her mother had encouraged her into singing lessons and, later, the local operatic society. By the time she was 16 she was singing the soprano part in all the oratorios - *Creation, Elijah, Isaiah* - and the prediction was that she was destined for great things.

But my thoughts had been different; I wasn't too interested in worldly success. I was hoping Cynthia would give her life to the Lord so that she could use that wonderful voice for Him.

Now she had, and she could.

But I could not have known that a storm was about to break.

That trip to Kelvin Hall was in April. In September of that year Cynthia was due to leave the Dales to enrol at the Royal Academy of Music in London - and at no charge. The tutor who had interviewed her was so confident of her potential to be a top-flight operatic star that he had taken her on as his own personal student.

But two weeks after committing her life to Christ, Cynthia backed out of the Academy, gave up her singing lessons, and calmly told her parents that from now on she was going to sing only for the Lord.

The storm broke. Her parents exploded. Her tutor tore up her music and threw it in her face. 'Get out!' he fumed. 'GET OUT!'

When the dust had settled her mother tried to reason with her, but Cynthia was adamant. Not because of any conversion whim, but because God's love had won her heart and she had felt impressed deep in her spirit that this was what He was asking her to do. It wasn't so much a case of giving up her gift, she tried to explain, but of dedicating it to the Lord.

To the delight of so many in the local churches, that is exactly what she did. She committed her singing ability to Christ's service, accepting every opportunity that came her way to sing for His glory.

To me this was wonderful. We were short of good singers in our Mission Bands and now I had someone top-rate I could call upon when I was invited to take a church service; someone through whose music the Lord really spoke. Many times when Cynthia was singing the Holy Spirit would move upon a church and there wouldn't be a dry eye in the house. That sort of singing ministry was a Godsend to anyone who had to follow it with the preaching of the Gospel.

But the one person I had not expected God to speak to while Cynthia was singing was myself. And He did it once again in that unforgettable, audible voice.

It happened at a little church in the village of Warsill, about 20 miles from Snape. Cynthia was up front, her beautiful voice filling that building with praise as I sat in my pew ready to get up and give the Gospel address. It was then that the Lord spoke.

'That's the girl I've got for you.'

For a moment I was stunned. Had I heard right? But really there was no doubt. That voice - the same gentle voice that had brought me into a living relationship with the Lord seven years earlier - had been unmistakable. And the message, even in the midst of Cynthia's singing, had been as clear as the texts hanging on the church wall. God was at work in my life, directing me in terms that I could not fail to understand. There wasn't a shadow of doubt in my mind as to what my heavenly Father was saying: *Jim, my plan is for you and Cynthia to be married.*

Sprung upon me so suddenly this was a bit daunting, and perhaps the natural man would have tended to panic. I could think of several reasons why such a suggestion was not on.

For a start, sitting beside me in the pew was Mary Wilson, my girlfriend of two years and a lass of whom I was very fond. Our parents would have put it in stronger terms than that and already had us married off. Only the announcement of the engagement was preventing them from making plans.

To further complicate matters, Cynthia had a boyfriend. Perhaps he had his own thoughts about whom Cynthia should marry.

And to cap it all, the prospect of calling at Cynthia's house did not exactly excite me. Her mother, having come to the conclusion that Cynthia had been brainwashed, blamed 'that Jim Wilkinson'. If it wasn't for him and his extreme religion her girl would be on her way to the top of the operatic world. In short, Jim had smashed her dreams. There was no way she was going to let me have her daughter's hand as well.

But all that reasoning left God out and I had been a Christian long enough to know that the Lord does not make mistakes.

Furthermore I had learned that His design for my life was born out of His love for me: if He asked me to do anything I could be sure that I'd be blessed in doing it.

And I'd learned to trust Him. He had never yet asked me to do anything without also showing me how to go about it, and I knew that in this situation too - prickly though it might be - He had already worked out the details. My part was simply to obey.

I didn't waste any time in setting things in motion. Something else He had taught me over the years was that His timing is always perfect: He was never early, never late. He always brought His word at the precise moment of His sovereign choosing. So who was I to delay?

Even so, I knew that the first step wouldn't be easy, and as I pulled the car to a halt outside Mary's home later that night I felt a little tremble in the pit of my stomach.

'I've something to tell you,' I said, switching off the engine. Then a voice from somewhere - an alien voice - tried to tell me I was being very foolish. Why throw away two good years of happy relationship? Stick with Mary.

But I'd learned to recognise the enemy's voice too, and I pressed ahead. Taking hold of Mary's hand, as though that would soften the blow, I went on:

'The Lord spoke to me tonight, Mary. I - I believe He wants us to part.'

She glanced at me, a sudden pain in her eyes, then turned away.

'What makes you say that?'

I tried as best I could to explain about Cynthia and the voice.

'It's not that I have any feelings for her, you understand. She's a lovely girl, I know, but I'd not thought of her in the same way as I've thought of you. We've had some good times together, you and I, but . . . well, what can I say? I just know the Lord has spoken.'

I didn't want to hurt Mary, I really didn't - and all at once I knew that God had taken care of that too. There was a touch of moisture in her eyes but her lips were smiling as she said: 'Can we pray about it? I want to be as sure about it as you are, Jim. But - if that's what the Lord wants, that's what He'll have.'

Our parents were less understanding, but of course at first we couldn't divulge exactly why we'd broken up - not until I'd told Cynthia. At that point I realised how much simpler it would have been if the Lord had told her of His plans, too. But He hadn't. Yet the Spirit was at work preparing her, for already she had begun to realise that the relationship with her boyfriend - a non-Christian - was not what God wanted for her. At the same time Jim Wilkinson was asking her for a date. Could this be the Lord? I assured her that it was; that God had spoken very clearly to me about it. But she was not so sure. Anyone could manipulate events to their advantage by claiming that 'God told me . . . ' And for a while she was very cautious of me. Gradually, though, the boyfriend was phased out and Jim was phased in. Another hurdle over.

But then there was Mother. As I'd guessed, the news that I was now dating her daughter did not endear me to Mrs Biker. It was bad enough that this religious maniac had lured her girl into accepting his fanatical beliefs - a scandal roundly condemned by her own minister, no less - but actually to have the man calling at the house was an outrage.

She did her best to discourage me. Often I would call for Cynthia only to be told, 'She's not in. She's gone for a ride up the Dale with friends.' While all the time Cynthia would be in the house, unaware that I was on the doorstep.

But eventually love won through - a love the Lord had given me both for Cynthia and her parents - and when, a year later, we told them that we wanted to get engaged, they grudgingly agreed. Things were eased still further a few weeks later when our parents met for the first time and took a liking to each other.

The timing of the wedding - set for the summer of 1957 - fitted in well with Dad's plans for getting the last of his children off his hands. My brother Alan and his wife Joyce had a farm at Rainton; Derek, married to Vera, was well into his chosen career as a draughtsman with Durham County Council; and now, after a good deal of searching, Dad had found a small farm for his youngest boy at Sandhutton, an old village perched at the northern tip of the beautiful Vale of York.

It was an arable farm of 76 acres known as The Limes, and it had come up for sale under rather sad circumstances. The vendor, a Mrs Fawell, had lost her husband after a long illness shortly before the war and since then she had been trying to keep the farm going with the help of a daughter and hired help. For a long time now it had been an uphill struggle and at last she had decided to sell up.

We heard about the sale before the farm came on to the market thanks to Derek Alsop, one of Dad's friends and an auctioneer in the market town of Northallerton.

'It might be just what you're looking for,' Mr Alsop had told Dad on the phone. 'A nice little place. Needs a bit doing to it, but the potential's good.'

We drove down to Sandhutton after tea that evening and saw the property for ourselves. It was exactly as the auctioneer had said. The Limes was a farm of manageable size for a young man starting out on his own, and considering Mrs Fawell's circumstances it wasn't in too bad a condition. Some of the buildings were derelict and would have to be replaced, and the place was badly in need of some concrete working areas around the barns, but those things were incidental. What mattered was the condition of the soil and Mr Alsop had thought it promising.

After calling at the house Dad and I walked out over the land, feeling the give of the earth beneath our boots. Dad was more expert at this than I, of course, but even with my limited experience I could tell that we were treading on good soil. If your foot barely makes an impression there's too much clay; if it sinks in too far the soil's too light. But the earth here felt right.

Out in the middle of the field Dad bent down and scooped up some soil in his big work-gnarled hands, at first feeling the body in it and then letting it sift through his fingers. His craggy, weather-tanned face, at first thoughtful, cracked into a smile. 'That's good stuff,' he declared. 'That'll serve you well, son.'

I nodded, pleased. 'There's a lot to be done,' I said, pointing to fields beyond that were overrun with couch grass. 'But if the soil's all right . . .'

'Aye. You could really make something of this little place.'

'What about the house?' I asked as we walked back up through the tumbledown farm buildings. 'That'll need some work on it too.'

'A bit of renovation,' Dad agreed. He stopped in the yard, pushed back his cap and stood looking up at the great bulk of the old farmhouse. 'If I were you I'd divide the place in two, then you could let the other half to one of your men. It's much bigger than you'll need, anyway.'

It was a good idea; the rent from sub-letting would help with the overall rent I would be paying Dad for the farm. We went into the house and had a further talk with Mrs Fawell, and then Dad drew me aside.

'You think it would suit you, then?'

'It's ideal,' I replied. 'An answer to prayer. Cynthia's going to love it.'

We took possession of The Limes in April, 1956, and it was then that Dad officially pushed me out of the nest.

'From now on you're on your own, son,' he told me as he handed me the keys to the new farm - which may sound brutal but really was the best thing a father could have done for his son. And there was more to come. One of Dad's insurance policies had recently matured and he said he wanted me to have the money. 'It'll help you get started,' he explained, as though he hadn't done enough for me already.

The cheque was for £599 - in those days a great deal of money; enough to buy the best tractor on the market.

Over the next year or so I spent many long hours over at Sandhutton carrying out the alterations to the farmhouse and decorating right through. By June, 1957, the place was ready for Mr and Mrs Jim Wilkinson.

But before our own happy day Cynthia and I were pleased to

hear of another couple's wedding. The groom was an old pal, Leonard Abel, and walking up the aisle on his arm that glorious July day was someone I was glad to know was so happy - my old flame, Mary Wilson.

They were well suited, I knew that, and I was so thankful for God's leading in this all-important matter of choosing a life partner. For I was aware that when the Lord had spoken to me so clearly that Sunday evening He had not only released me to marry Cynthia, but He'd also released Mary to marry Len. Their marriage was important too, and I was grateful that day for the reminder God gave me that in His sovereign will He has a plan for each of us; that to Him, *everyone* is special.

Our own wedding took place a week later - 25 July, 1957 - but this time the sun was not in attendance. Cynthia walked to the chapel from her nearby home in pouring rain, her father holding the umbrella - and we had to be thankful that the downpour let up long enough for the wedding photos to be taken.

But nothing could dampen the joy of knowing that we had been married in the Lord, and crossing the threshold of The Limes later that day for the first time as man and wife we were very aware that if our marriage was to be blessed it had to be a threesome: the two of us, plus Jesus.

Likewise with the farm. So, during that first week in our new home, we knelt together and asked the Lord to take us into partnership with Him there at The Limes. We also agreed that we wouldn't plan any children for seven years: that those first years of our marriage partnership would be the Lord's.

'Father,' I prayed, 'we dedicate our marriage, our home, our work to your service. Whatever you want for us, that's what we want. We are totally open to everything you wish for our lives.'
I didn't realise it at the time, but it was a dangerous prayer to pray, and one which at a future date I would be tempted to regret. Was I *really* willing to accept everything God wanted me to have?

3/Winds of change

I'd signed up two men to work with me at The Limes: Bill Abbott, a fellow Yorkshireman who moved his family into the labourer's half of the farmhouse, and Erich Wolf, a German P.O.W. who had stayed in England after the war. Between us we had our work cut out.

The priority, of course, was the land. We had to get that right as quickly as possible and so our first weeks there at The Limes were spent in ploughing up acres of couch grass and hand-forking it on to a wagon. Gradually, yard by yard, day by day, we cleared six fields of the wretched weed and burned the lot down in the wood on the edge of the farm.

Then we started again, ploughing up every one of our 76 acres and carting away tons of large and small stones before fertilising in preparation for the sowing.

It was all tough manual work and it didn't stop there. During the war the Air Ministry had commandeered some land from The Limes for the perimeter of Skipton-on-Swale Aerodrome. A rusted wire fence marked the old boundary. That had to be ripped out with tractor and chains, along with much of the broken-down hedging which separated some of the fields.

Then there was the concrete to lay: new floors for the dilapidated buildings and work areas for the yard. By the time we were through we didn't want to see a concrete-mixer ever again.

But even now there was no letting up. Seed-time was upon us and before our last strip of concrete was dry we were plunged into sowing the fields. We wanted a mixed cropping and settled on wheat, barley, oats, potatoes and sugar-beet.

On the livestock side we limited ourselves to a handful of breeding pigs (brought with me from Dad's farm) and a hundred hens. Cynthia fed these each day and took charge of the egg-sales, but apart from that she had little else to do with the farm. I figured that a woman had enough to think about with running a home - and besides, Cynthia's parents had not been overjoyed at the idea of their girl marrying a farmer (any farmer, not just a religious one!) and I was determined that my wife should not end up as an unpaid labourer.

'Your place is in the home, love,' I told her, and that suited her fine. Cynthia had already decided that she would be a home-maker - not just a housewife - and her energies were spent in making the place comfortable and inviting.

'I want it to be a place where people will be happy to come,' she'd told me. 'A place where people can meet the Lord . . . where the Lord Himself will feel at home.'

Well, I agreed with that because what she was describing was just the sort of home Mum and Dad had - the sort of place I was used to. And so it quickly became known in the village that there was 'open house' at Jim and Cynthia's. Word was spread through the folk at the nearby Methodist Chapel which we started attending on our first Sunday in Sandhutton. And very soon The Limes became a meeting point for most of the young people in the village.

The adults were not quite so quick off the mark. Perhaps they'd heard about Jim Wilkinson's fanatical religion and were a bit wary. Probably they were half expecting us to come flying into the quiet little chapel and take over. But our first weeks there should have eased their fears. We too had seen the heavy-handed, over-zealous types who breeze into a situation and expect to take command, and to make sure nobody got the wrong idea about Jim and Cynthia we all but tiptoed our way in, determined not to do anything unless we were asked.

Even so, the members tended to keep their distance, and if it hadn't been for the warm welcome of two older couples - the Allinsons and Allisons - we might have felt quite neglected.

Eventually, however, we were accepted, and when the Minister realised we wouldn't bite he asked us to consider taking on the young people's work, the Wednesday night Guild meeting. That suited me down to the ground. The only bone I had to pick with the Methodist system was that the Guild was strictly for the 14 to 25-year olds. When you'd notched up a quarter century you were out, like it or not. I was 27 so I'd not been to a Guild meeting for two years. But now . . .

Before long I was asked to do some lay preaching, too, and shortly after that came the invitation for us to help out with the Sunday school. In addition we started an informal fellowship meeting in our home on Friday evenings - and that still left us one or two evenings each week for evangelism. Invitations to preach the Gospel at chapels and house meetings continued to come in, as did requests for help with open-air outreach programmes. Sometimes the invitation would come from as far as 40 or 50 miles away, but if we were free we would accept it, simply for the privilege of telling people about the Lord.

At the same time we continued working with Alf Suttill and Kit Calvert under the banner of the Wensleydale Evangelistic Crusade. Our latest project was the biggest so far: a three-week mission with evangelist Eric Hutchings and team. This was to be held in March of the following year at the Methodist Chapel in Masham, the largest public building in the area.

Our plans for the big event went very smoothly from the beginning - so smoothly in fact that we began to wonder if the devil wasn't interested. Here we were, preparing for the biggest crusade in the area for generations, and the enemy was just letting us get on with it. It wasn't natural; you expected a bit of flack when you started planning to win people out of the devil's camp and into the Lord's. So what was going on?

We found out a day or two before the crusade was due to begin. The March winds brought a howling winter storm that left the Dales snow-bound. Nowhere was the crisp white blanket less than a foot deep and in many places it was much more.

Immediately our earth-bound imaginations began to foresee problems. Who would want to come out to a meeting in weather like this? And how would they get through the snow-clogged roads even if they decided to give it a try?

But we should have realised that God had it all under control. In fact the weather conditions turned out to be the very best for a crusade in a farming community. While the roads were soon cleared sufficiently to be passable, the great blanket of snow remained on the farms and fields for the duration of the crusade. No farmer could work in such conditions, save feed his livestock in the barns, and once that chore was complete he had nothing else to think about and was entirely free to attend the meetings.

Every night we were packed out, and by the close of the crusade 110 people had committed their lives to Christ - including, to my delight, my brother Alan and his wife Joyce. Hundreds more had heard the Gospel in unmistakable terms.

This spurred us on to broaden our outreach in our own community. As winter finally relinquished its chilly grip and spring brought in the warmer days we began holding monthly Saturday night rallies in our barn. One month we would invite a local music group to come and present the Gospel through their songs and testimonies; the next we'd book an itinerant evangelist or local lay preacher to come and speak. We really didn't mind who came so long as they lifted up the Lord Jesus, for we knew that when that happened people would be drawn to Him. It was a guaranteed spiritual reflex - God's own pattern for building His kingdom.

On the farm we were engaged in another type of building, and as with the evangelism this was an ongoing thing. Tearing down old buildings and putting up new ones was very much a matter of time and money. Both were in short supply during our first couple of years, but by the summer of 1960 things were beginning to level out and we were able to make some of the necessary improvements. I was particularly keen to put up decent buildings for the livestock - especially pigs - for with market prices riding quite high there was a good return for the investment. So with the help of various government grants for improvement we established a new piggery - a broad, low-ceilinged building divided into pens - and gradually increased the pig stocks from our modest initial dozen to a 1962 figure of 400.

At that point everything was swinging along nicely. The books were balancing, our debts were gradually being paid off, and there was a little money left over for further speculation. But then one morning I caught sight of something that was going to take the spring out of my step. It was a morning when Dad happened to have dropped into The Limes.

'Come and have a look at these pigs,' I called to him. 'Something's not right - they're not eating properly.'

The trouble was with the latest batch of weaners I'd bought in a couple of weeks earlier. They were definitely off their food, and if I wasn't mistaken their stomachs were beginning to look distended. Dad scratched his head then threw me a troubled glance.

'Better isolate 'em for a while,' he said. 'Time'll tell.' They were no better the following morning and positively sick the next. It was time to call the vet and have our fears confirmed. 'It's swine fever, all right,' he told me. 'D'you know the procedure?'

I nodded glumly. 'Aye. Seal off the farm and wait for the man with the gun. But it's such a waste. . .'

He stood in the yard washing his hands and arms in a bowl of disinfectant. 'It'll have to be confirmed by the Ministry vet, of course, but I don't think he'll say different. I'm sorry, Jim.'

'Well, there's nowt to be done about it,' I said. 'I suppose we'd better get a notice up at the gate.'

The man from the Ministry of Agriculture came down the same day and gave the pigs the death sentence - all 400 of them. Not that every pig was affected, but with a disease as virulent as swine fever you daren't take any chances. Before he left he gave me an official notice to replace my hand-painted one. It read: SWINE FEVER. KEEP OUT. THIS FARM IS UNDER QUARANTINE.

The next morning I hired an excavator and we dug a huge hole behind the barn. Then the men from the Ministry came out to destroy the condemned stock.

Farmers have to be philosophical about such things, of course, but it was hard to be objective, standing there watching the marksman shoot one pig after another and then having to drag the blood-spattered carcasses out of the pens, across the yard and into the hole. This was my livelihood I was burying.

When the killing was all done the straw was raked out and burned, then the men in protective suits moved in with their pressure-hoses and washed the place out with powerful disinfectants. It was all over in less than two hours.

Adjusting to it was going to take a bit longer. In fact the tragedy of the situation didn't even sink in until the following morning when in the grey light of the dawn I went down to the piggery and stood looking around at the empty pens with the sickly stench of the disinfectant in my throat. But it was the silence, the stillness which got to me the most. It was so unnatural. Almost uncanny. And then I realised what that awful stillness was. It was death.

I suppose a number of quite natural questions might have presented themselves to me at that moment. How were we going to recover from such a setback? Could I make up the losses on the grain yields? Would the bank extend my loan? Should we take on more pigs? Had we been wrong in dealing in them in the first place? Why had God allowed it to happen?

But, strangely, none of these thoughts even crossed my mind. Somehow, instinctively, I knew that the Lord was still in control and that in His own way He would see us out of trouble.

Which left the way clear for the one thought that did break into my mind - a thought which surely originated outside of myself.

This is like hell, it was saying. This terrible sense of cutting-off, of separation is what awaits everyone who dies outside of Christ. This desolation will be the lot of every unbeliever.

It was a hard way to be spurred on to preach the ever-lasting life of the Gospel, but it was also a reminder I was not likely to forget.

That same year, as though to balance the setback of the pigs, we received a tremendous boost on the land. As usual we had planted a potato crop and were now preparing to harvest. A surveyor from the Potato Marketing Board, to whom we were selling the crop, had visited us earlier in the season to measure up and tell us how many tons of potatoes we could expect. His figure was 45 tons. Out of that he reckoned we would have three tons of 'brock' - tiny potatoes that would be riddled out during the packing process - and so our total expected sale would be 42 tons.

I was happy with that because I had extra bills to pay that month and the money would go a long way towards meeting them. So it was with some satisfaction that we began packing the potatoes the following Monday. The Board had asked us to bag up ten tons per day, which was a reasonable output for three men working together, and so we brought up the sorting machine to the potato heap and set to.

By late afternoon every trace of the morning's smile had been wiped away. We had bagged up ten tons of ware and it looked as though we'd got a good third of the pile.

Despondent, I sent up a silent prayer. 'Oh Lord, there's not going to be 42 tons of potatoes here. There's not even going to be 30!'

I don't know whether the men had realised this but they certainly took notice the following day when, strangely, the situation was reversed.

'I dunno,' said one, as we completed another ten tons, 'this pile don't seem to be gettin' any smaller.'

Which was true because we hadn't moved the sorter any further into the potato heap all day. And we didn't move it for the rest of the day, either. In fact that machine stayed where it was throughout Tuesday and Wednesday.

By the end of that third day, having now bagged 30 tons, we were all amazed. All, that is, except the man from the Potato Marketing Board. He was just puzzled. He'd come down to see how we were getting on and decided there was definitely something very odd going on. This man was dealing with potato mountains all the time and he knew his business.

'You're not bringing in potatoes from somewhere else, are you?' he asked. He'd now taken delivery of 30 tons of potatoes and we hadn't yet got half the pile.

'Certainly not,' I said. 'We've only got the one heap.'

The following day he was back with his chief to measure the field again and when they came into the barn they were both shaking their heads.

'It's not possible,' said the surveyor. 'You're *sure* you're not bringing in potatoes from somewhere else?'

By now I couldn't resist a smile. 'I'm sure, and the men here will bear me out.'

He shook his head again and glanced at the potato heap. 'Doesn't make sense,' he muttered. 'You're getting more potatoes out of the heap than it's *possible* to get.'

There was no answer to that. All we could do was carry on bagging. When at last we'd finished we had a staggering 62 tons of good-sized, saleable potatoes. . . and a story that was going to raise eyebrows for a good while to come.

Coincidentally (or was it?) the extra money was just the right amount to meet those extra bills.

From the very outset at The Limes we had sought God's blessing on our work, praying specifically over every crop we planted, but we had never expected miracles. Yet here we were rejoicing in one. Like those surprising healings, here was something else for me to ponder in my heart. Why had the Lord sovereignly intervened in our lives in this way? Was it simply to bless us? Certainly I believed that God's desire was to bless His people, and I had known many times in my life when He had blessed me apparently for no other reason than that it pleased Him to do so - just as a father delights to give good things to his children, no strings attached.

But I'd also learned that sometimes the Lord's motives would go beyond this; that He would bless me in order to teach me something, or perhaps to prepare me; to increase my vision, or to enlarge my heart so that I might be more ready to receive what He had in store for me.

Somehow I felt this was the case with the potato crop miracle. But what was God saying? I had the feeling that in some way or other He was calling me to go on with Him, and yet at the same time I was not at all sure what He was calling me to. I was aware that the Christian Life was a day-to-day walk with the Lord and that in order to grow in Christ I needed to keep close to Him, but I thought I was doing that. My prayer life was healthy, I was spending time with the open Bible each day, I was totally committed to the Lord's service through the chapel and numerous outreach activities . . . and I'd even come into a place where I was practising the Scriptural principles of tithes and offering. (I knew that until God had your heart he wasn't likely to have your pockets, but once he had your pockets he surely had everything!)

So what was left for me to give or receive? In my own little table of reckoning I figured I was doing all right.

I had a lot to learn. But all in the Lord's time.

Meanwhile the Lord's timing - and blessing - was to be seen in another area of our life. During those first few years of our marriage we'd never given a second thought to the question of raising a family. We'd made that promise that the first seven years of our life together would be the Lord's and that we wouldn't have any children until those years were up. We knew for a fact that the Lord had accepted that promise and endorsed it, for throughout our married life we had enjoyed a happy physical relationship without ever worrying about trying to prevent conception. It wasn't a question of planning or not planning a baby; we simply trusted the Lord.

Now, in our eighth year of marriage, and with our promise fulfilled, God chose to bless us with a little one. We called her Joanna.

Her arrival was a rude awakening for me. I figured I'd had plenty of experience of babies from all my dealings with new-born lambs, piglets and calves, and that probably there wasn't a lot of difference between rearing these and a brand new human being.

How wrong I was! Suddenly we were plunged into the completely unfamiliar world of nappies and bottles and cuddles and more nappies and colic and disturbed nights and still more nappies!

But for all that our little girl was a great delight to us - and to her grandparents too. Though as Dad rocked her in his arms for the first time he said I should have been more practical and had a boy. Girls, he said, were not a lot of good around a farm and goodness knows how he would have managed if he and Mum had produced three daughters!

That was April, 1965 - springtime. And truly our little Joanna had brought with her all the loveliness and freshness of the season itself. But soon we were to be reminded of another, very different season.

The previous September Mum and Dad had retired from

Hollins Farm to a little bungalow in the heart of Bedale. They had been looking forward to the move for some time, eagerly planning their retirement activities as well as anticipating some lazy days. But they hadn't long moved when a cloud came scudding into their lives. Mum was experiencing heart trouble.

It was something of a recurring illness but it had never been so serious as now. Over the months her health gradually deteriorated until in October, 1964, she was admitted to hospital, critically ill.

The doctors told us she had three negative heart-valves and that there was nothing they could do for her. To make matters worse it seemed there was little Mum could do for herself. Even eating became a problem and soon Dad was going in to the hospital at Northallerton each morning, afternoon and evening to feed Mum with a powdered health-mix - about all she could manage. But she wasn't getting the nourishment she needed and before long her weight was down to a worrying six stone.

By the middle of November she was so weak that she could barely talk and it appeared she was just wasting away. It was distressing to see her like that and on the way home from the hospital one Tuesday evening I finally released the problem to God.

'Lord, Mother loves you and knows she'll be coming to be with you one day. If this is the right time, please take her quickly. If not then please heal her. But don't leave her as she is, Lord - *do* something.'

That same night, to the astonishment of the nurses, Mum sat up in bed - the first time she'd been able to do so unattended for more than two weeks. The following Thursday, still frail but smiling, she walked out of the hospital under her own steam and went home with Dad.

It was cause for great rejoicing throughout the family, of course - and for me yet another miracle to ponder - but the smiles had barely faded from our eyes before they were replaced with tears.

It was November 13 - Mum's birthday. Dad had promised to

take her for a spin in the car through the Dales, but in the morning Dad's friend Harold Sanderson had phoned to ask if he was going to the cattle market up at Hexham. Even though Dad was no longer farming he still kept up his lively interest in farming activities and liked to get to the various markets and shows. But perhaps he would give it a miss today, he told Harold. Today was special.

Mum knew how Dad enjoyed those outings. 'You go, George,' she said. 'If you're not too long we can have an early tea and still have time for a bit of a ride out.'

So Dad kissed his wife goodbye, promised not to be late, and went off to look at cows. More than that, for Dad had never been one for just looking - he liked to get in there among the beasts and he was never more happy than when some fellow farmer asked him to look an animal over and give the man the benefit of his experience. Dad didn't need to be asked twice to step into the pen.

And that's where it happened, there in the cattle enclosure. How or why the steer became riled no one ever knew, but it suddenly went berserk, tossing its head around and lashing out with its vicious horns until Dad lay gored and bleeding on the straw-scattered floor.

Cynthia and I were up at Leyburn in the middle of an outreach meeting at the Congregational Church when the news reached us at around 8.30 pm. Dad had been badly injured, we were told, but he was in hospital and his condition was stable. We weren't to rush.

We got away as soon as we could, of course, and drove down to Bedale to see if Mum was all right before going on to the hospital. It was then we learned that the message we'd received had been stale news.

Dad had died just after seven o'clock.

For a few days afterwards I wondered whether we might have to expect a double funeral. Many years ago we'd buried my grandfather and grandmother side by side on the same day. Grandfather had died quite suddenly and within 24 hours his wife had followed him. It was the shock.

Would the strain of Dad's death, coupled with the effects of her recent illness, be too much for Mother?

But no. Mum didn't feel strong enough to attend the funeral - she asked that the hearse be driven past her front door - but she was quite happy to have the traditional funeral tea at home.

Which was yet another evidence of the very real miracle that the Lord had performed for her. Without a doubt she had been miraculously healed, and so strong was Mother's own conviction of this that two weeks later she threw all her tablets on the fire. She wasn't to take another pill or see a doctor for many years.

And so we had another miracle to juggle with. Just one more sign of God's wonderful compassion and grace - or yet another stepping stone? I suspected that it was indeed another pointer, but where were all these pointers leading? I seemed to have no light on the mystery at all.

But there wasn't long to wait now, for the pieces would start to fit together the following year, and the links would come through a man who himself was a walking miracle; a man who was to play a strategic role in the amazing scenario that was yet to unfold. His name was George Breckon.

George was a local man and like myself from Yorkshire farming stock, except that he could trace his farming ancestors back to the sixteenth century. His family had always owned the same rambling little farmhouse, Duck House, which even today sits in the lee of the hill over in Farndale.

It was there that George took over the business from his father in the 1940s and there that God began to move in his life in a dramatic way.

It began in 1951. That year George severely injured his back and was told by the doctors that he was without hope - a physical write-off. They sent him home to bed where he spent much of his time for the following two years. Only occasionally did he feel fit enough to work and even then he had to take care not to damage his back even further. The result was that the farm began to run down, his capital ran out, and his morale lay in pieces. As he put it, he was physically, financially, mentally and spiritually broke.

Until then George had had a fairly lively faith - converted at 17 and lay preaching at 19 - but now he felt totally abandoned by God. And yet his faith somehow managed to hang on. Each week he would listen in to Christian radio programmes in the hope that sooner or later someone would somehow throw him a lifeline. When it came it took him completely by surprise.

One of the programmes that intrigued him was hosted by American evangelist and Bible teacher Oral Roberts. Almost every week Rev. Roberts made some mention of God's power to heal, and occasionally the preacher's wife would read out letters sent in by people testifying that they had experienced that healing for themselves.

Could this be true? George wondered. Could God really heal as dramatically and miraculously today as did Jesus when He walked this earth? Before many weeks had passed George had an opportunity to find out.

Having spoken on 'How to receive faith for healing', Rev. Roberts said he would pray a prayer of faith which the listener could make his own.

'If you desire to be healed,' he went on, 'may I encourage you to reach out in faith and lay your hand upon your radio set while I am praying.'

This wouldn't actually heal anyone, he pointed out, but it would most certainly help to release the listener's faith.

A moment later Rev. Roberts began praying, and more in desperation than faith George reached out his hand . . .

As he connected with the radio he felt a shock-wave flash up his arm and suddenly his whole body began shaking with a tremendous power. Healing power!

Within two weeks George was back at work, lifting the heaviest loads and not even feeling a twinge. He had been completely cured.

More than that, his life had been revolutionized. He returned to lay preaching with a fresh and burning zeal, he committed himself to studying his Bible with an excitement he'd never known, and in his prayer times he hungered after knowing more of the God who had so powerfully touched him. Sometimes his longing would be so great that he would spend days in prayer and fasting, determined to draw closer to the heart of God and to hear more clearly from Him.

But one thing he had not expected to hear was the call that came to him in the summer of 1963 - the call to leave farming and to commit his time to preaching the Gospel. This took him by surprise because only recently had he moved from Duck House to a bigger farm down at Pickering. (God not only healed him but prospered his business, too!) Nevertheless the call was so clear - and his wife, Gladys, agreed this was the way the Lord was leading - that George immediately began making plans to sell up. By March of the following year it was all settled - and centuries of Breckons farming the Yorkshire hills had come to an end. From now on George would be planting a very different type of seed and looking for a very different type of crop.

It wasn't long after this that Cynthia and I first met him. He turned up at one of the Leyburn meetings one evening and we immediately took to him. He was a big man with a booming voice and bright, laughing eyes; a charismatic figure whose fiery preaching and flowing, swept-back hair put me in mind of another Methodist whose burning passion for souls had brought him to thunder out his Gospel message in these same hills hundreds of years before - the great John Wesley himself. Clearly George Breckon would be an asset to our outreach meetings, and I was delighted to learn that his association with us was not simply a preacher's whim. The Lord, George explained, had specifically told him to come and identify himself with the work we were doing.

What an encouragement! But before long a niggling little cloud was to drift into this promisingly bright picture.

It was the summer of 1966. For many weeks George Breckon had been coming to our Friday night meetings and from the start he had been a great help, drawing on his vast Bible knowledge and deep understanding of the Scriptures to teach and build up the many young Christians who were now meeting regularly with us. But now and then he would slip in certain things that I would be unhappy about. Certain things that weren't . . . well, they weren't Wesleyan. At first I thought it best to ignore these little asides in the hope that nothing would come of them, rather than take issue with the man and blow the remarks out of proportion. That would only draw attention to what I saw as dubious doctrines. Best to say nowt and let them pass.

But George wasn't letting anything pass; he was just getting warmed up. It came to a head one Friday tea-time. We'd invited George and Gladys for a meal prior to the evening's meeting and I could tell from the moment I opened the door that George was excited about something. It wasn't the first time I'd seen him like this - bright-eyed and beaming - but I'd never actually got around to asking him about it, perhaps because I was afraid of what the answer might be. But this time the words just slipped out - and I could have kicked myself.

'Jim! Cynthia! I've just got to tell you - there's something more!'

It was too late to back out now. 'More than what?'

'More than what you've got. It's the Spirit. You need to be baptised in the Spirit. There's just so much more!'

My hackles spiked up. I'd known it was coming - for months I'd known it was coming - but still it grated. Maybe I could laugh it off.

'You've got the wrong man, George. I don't need any new experience; I'm quite happy as I am, thank you. The only experience

I'm interested in right now is Cynthia's chicken casserole. Come on in, it's all ready.'

But George wouldn't be stopped. 'You can be filled with the Spirit, Jim! You can know power in your life and in your preaching - enter into a new dimension of faith. And all you have to do is ask. Do it, Jim, do it - you'll get blessed more than you ever thought possible.'

Instinctively I reached out for the stock answers. 'I don't believe in all that stuff,' I countered as we settled round the table. 'The baptism in the Spirit isn't for today; it was a once-and-for-all experience at Pentecost - to get the Christian Church off the ground.'

'But look at me,' beamed George. 'It happened to me and it changed my life.' 'I received the Holy Spirit when I was born again,' I protested. 'It was part of the package. There isn't anything more - you're just fooling yourself, George.'

He gulped a mouthful of casserole. 'I know we receive the Spirit when we're born again, but that's just the beginning. There's a glorious infilling, too, and you need that before the gifts of the Spirit can be released in your life.'

'But we've seen miracles,' Cynthia piped up. 'We know all about the work of the Holy Ghost.'

'Aye, we've prayed for people and they've been healed,' I said. 'That's power.'

'But that power came direct from God,' argued George. 'He wants you to receive power for yourself, so that you can use it in your own life, too. The Scripture promises it: "Ye shall receive power!" Acts 2.'

'And I've preached on it. But that was just for the Early Church, George. The gifts petered out with Peter.'

The casserole disappeared and in came the strawberry shortcake. But it wasn't about to sweeten me up. In fact as the discussion bounced back and forth across the table I found myself becoming more and more irritated. Whatever I said George seemed to have an answer for it and in the end I began clawing for an escape in the muck of personal remarks.

First: 'You're more emotional than I am, George. Maybe you needed some sort of experience to keep you going. Me, I've got my feet firmly on the ground.'

Then: 'Let's face it, George, you were in a bad way when God picked you up. He had to do something pretty dramatic else you were a gonner.'

And inevitably: 'I don't need your Pentecostal ideas. I'm a Methodist and always have been. My father's faith has always been good enough for me before and I don't see any reason to add to it now.'

The meeting that evening did not go well - at least, not for me. Our confrontation - for it seemed that was what it was - had left a bad taste in my mouth, not least because I'd been driven to realise I had no real answers to George's enthusiasm - only prejudices. And though I wouldn't have admitted it then, he had stirred up an ugly part of me that nearly 20 years of walking with the Lord had failed to touch. Pride. It was an old enemy and perhaps my biggest, but because of its very nature I would never own up to its presence in my life. And by denying it I allowed it free rein.

That night as Cynthia and I climbed into bed I was still smarting from George's blundering approach. Why had he brought this up now? From a comment in one of the meetings I knew that it had been three years since he'd received his so-called 'baptism in the Spirit', so why try foisting it upon us now? I'd known his views for months, just as he must have known mine. I'd thought, foolishly, that we had an understanding. Certainly I was happy to work with George in evangelism so long as he kept his peculiar ideas about the Holy Spirit to himself. But now . . . well, now he'd rocked the boat.

To add insult to injury that night Cynthia would not agree with me when I complained that George had ruined our meal together. To my horror I discovered that she was not at all convinced that George had got this business of the Holy Spirit quite wrong.

'Maybe there is something in what he says,' she suggested, snuggling down between the sheets.

'I doubt it,' I snorted as I fumbled in my bedside cabinet for the indigestion tablets. 'Take it from me, Cynthia, he's on a loser there. You wait and see.'

She turned towards me, her eyes wide open again, and her words were like a spear to my heart. 'But what about Reverend Ransome up at Snape? You remember you once told me about him and how he'd got this baptism thing when he was out in Africa. They can't both be wrong, him and George - can they?'

She'd hit a tender spot and I had to cover it fast. 'It was spending all that time in the sun did that to him,' I spluttered. 'There's nothing in it, not really. Shall I turn this light out?'

But Cynthia did not look ready for sleep. Suddenly fully awake, she propped herself up on her elbows and looked squarely at me.

'But if it is of the Lord - if there is something more . . .'

'Then the Lord'll give it to us,' I said, irritably. 'We won't have to go asking and fussing about it; He'll just give it to us.'

She fell back against the pillow and lay staring up at the ceiling, lost in her thoughts. I switched out the light and settled down to sleep, certain I'd escaped. But then Cynthia spoke again.

'D'you remember that prayer we prayed when we first came here, love?'

'What about it?'

'I've never forgotten it,' she murmured. 'We said that we wanted whatever the Lord had in store for us - that we'd welcome everything He wanted to give us.'

In the darkness she couldn't see my anger.

4/Last stand

Summer mellowed into autumn, autumn shivered into winter . . . but George Breckon would not go away. As regularly and irritatingly as the migraines which continued to plague me, the man persisted in turning up for our Friday evening meetings and barely a week passed without him hounding us with talk about 'the baptism'. It was annoying. I liked George, but he was making life difficult for me. His persistence was irking me, robbing me of my joy, pushing my normally endless patience to the limit. Why wouldn't he give up? Take 'no' for an answer? Go and peddle his Pentecostal ideas elsewhere?

It would have been easier, of course, if others in the Friday group had found him overbearing - but no one did. They all loved him and apparently couldn't hear enough about his Spirit-baptised experiences. It was just me - and as host of the house meetings, as well as one of the longest-standing Christians in the group, I had to love him too. It was not easy.

Eventually I developed a defensive mechanism. When George came to tea (Cynthia would insist on inviting him) I brushed aside every reference to Pentecost or the gifts of the Spirit with either a little joke or a cutting wise-crack, depending on the degree of threat it posed. I was sure that if I laughed it off long enough George would lose heart and give me up as an impossible case.

He didn't.

I tried another tack. Monopolise the conversation. Talk about anything and everything - the new family at church, the price of breeding pigs, Joanna's latest antics - any subject to keep George off his hobby-horse. But occasionally I'd have to stop for a mouthful of food and before I could swallow George would leap in with, 'Well, have you thought any more about . . .'

Where would it all end? I think from the very beginning George had never doubted where it would end . . . and Cynthia was giving him every encouragement to believe he was going to see his goal achieved. It was very unsettling. While I was pulling further and further away from the likelihood of ever pursuing the things George spoke of, Cynthia was clearly edging nearer.

From her early 'If there *is* something more . . .' she had now moved on to 'If God's in it, I want it.'

But how could it be of God, I reasoned, if it was driving us apart? (I didn't realise it then, but that's one of the devil's favourite lines.)

On the surface of our relationship everything was fine - well, more or less, as long as I could pretend not to be rattled by George - but underneath I was seething. I was the spiritual head of our home - Cynthia ought to be taking her lead from *me*. (All my arguments were sound - until they were examined closely. Then they were identified for what they were: cleverly disguised pride.)

Occasionally these mental volcanoes would erupt and I would try to convince Cynthia that she was wrong; that she should close her mind to George's crazy ideas. But I should have known better. From the moment Cynthia had welcomed Christ into her life 12 years earlier she had pursued the things of God with a zeal that put even my enthusiasm in the shade. She had always meant business with the Lord - and there was no stopping her now. If the baptism in the Spirit was for real and it would enable her to receive more of God then Cynthia was going for it with arms wide open. Hers was an uncomplicated faith - and perhaps even naive, I thought - but it always seemed to bring results. It was no different this time.

It happened the following spring at Valley Road Baptist Church, Northallerton. George was holding a week's mission there, taking a different theme each night. One evening it would be 'The Blood of Jesus', another 'The Christian Life', and so on. The last night, I discovered, he was to preach on 'The Baptism in the Holy Spirit'.

'You'll not get me along to that,' I told Cynthia. 'I have enough of that man trying to indoctrinate me here in my own home without hearing it from the pulpit.'

'But you don't mind if I go, Jim?'

'For all the good it'll do you . . .'

Cynthia said no more about it and that night I stayed home to baby-sit while a friend drove her into town.

Three hours later she was driven back again . . . though she might just as easily have flown. She was still walking on air when she came into the lounge. Never in my life had I seen someone so elated.

'I got it, Jim!' she said unnecessarily. 'I got it!'

I'd been dreading this all evening and was ready with my reply. 'Never mind, Cynthia, it'll soon wear off.'

It was hurtful, I know, but in fact she never even heard me. Or if she did the words just bounced off. With a sudden laugh she did a little twirl there on the carpet, then turned and floated out of the room.

When at last she came down to earth a few days later I learned that at the close of the meeting George had invited all who wished to receive the baptism of the Spirit to go forward for prayer. Cynthia had almost leapt out of her chair and had been one of the first to the front of the church. There, two or three Christians had laid hands on her and prayed over her, some in 'tongues' - those strange babbling sounds the Pentecostals called a prayer language - and before she knew what had happened she felt power flowing through her whole body, along with an overwhelming joy. Moments later she too was 'speaking in tongues'.

I was not pleased. George's persistence, with Cynthia at least, had paid off and she had now experienced the phenomenon I had been fighting to save her from. The chances were he would now step up his pressure on me and so I would need a new line of defence. It was the one I'd been saving for just such an eventuality.

'Of course I don't doubt that something's happened to Cynthia,' I told George the following Friday, 'but that doesn't mean to say it's of the Lord. The devil can counterfeit the works of God, y'know. And as for this speaking in tongues lark, that's just a lot of mumbo-jumbo. It's all of the devil, the lot of it.'

Evidently George had heard that argument before. Unruffled, he smiled and said, 'Well, let's wait and see.'

At first I wondered what he had meant, but as the days and weeks passed by I began to understand. Cynthia was changing, but in no way that I could attribute to the enemy. She seemed to be getting so much more out of her Bible reading each day . . . she was spending far longer in prayer every morning and thoroughly enjoying it . . . she was more joyful in herself and more loving toward other people (including me!) . . . and she seemed to have so much more faith to exercise each day in matters both large and small.

That didn't sound like the work of the devil to me. In fact it sounded very much like the type of Christian life I had been exhorting people to live in numerous sermons down the years. And, ironically, I now realised I hadn't been living that kind of power-packed life, either.

But wait a minute . . . what was I saying? The thought had come so fast I'd been unable to check myself. Power-packed? Was that really how I had summed up Cynthia's new lifestyle? I hated to admit it, but yes, there was a new dynamic in her life.

And then, to my annoyance, I remembered that verse from the book of Acts: 'Ye shall receive power.' That was the promise

George had made so much of over the months. And now I saw that promise fulfilled in my own wife. It was maddening. I wanted so much to be able to dismiss this baptism business as heresy - or at the least a bubble that would soon burst - but my years of experience as a Christian wouldn't let me. When I allowed myself to be totally honest I had to admit that Cynthia had been blessed, and tremendously at that. Regardless of my own opinion of how she had come into this blessing, the truth was that she was going on with God.

But worse than that for me was the equal truth that I was being left behind. This was what hurt the most. This was what left me smarting. And this was what began to eat away at me as I tried to get to sleep at night. I would lie there, tossing and turning and thinking how unfair it was. Why should she get blessed? Look at her lying there, sleeping like a baby. Even in her sleep she's getting blessed. It's all wrong.

At the same time I had no intention of following her into that blessing. George could coax and push and even pray all he wanted - he wouldn't find me chasing after his Pentecostal experiences. As the months dragged by it seemed to me this was my best line of defence. Denominationalism. I knew I couldn't prove a case against the baptism from Scripture (I'd tried that one but every anti argument had gaping holes in it), and it was no use trying to dismiss it as a now-you-see-it-now-you-don't illusion; Cynthia's deepening experience of Christ knocked that one for six.

No, I would have to take my stand on the time-tested argument of tradition. I was a good Wesleyan. Why, I was now Superintendent of the Sunday school (with 100% attendance from the village children, no less). I was a respected Methodist lay preacher. Youth leader. Church steward. Circuit steward. A member of half a dozen Methodist committees. In fact I'd been a Methodist longer than I'd been a Christian. It was inconceivable that I should change now, and a good Methodist would never embrace the doctrines of another denomination.

That was it, I would stand on the rock of my Methodism. A sound rock it was too, for it had given me everything I'd ever needed. My Bible, a belief in prayer, and ultimately an introduction to Jesus Christ Himself.

But then a strange thing happened. One afternoon I was out in the yard tinkering with a misbehaving tractor and thinking through my argument for the nth time when I remembered the question that had come to me all those years ago - the question that had brought the challenge to my heart: *Do you really know me?*

Yes, thank God, I could truly say that I now knew the Lord well. Jesus was real to me. The Father was a friend. But there was a niggle at the back of my mind. What about the Spirit? Did I know the Holy Ghost?

I twitched at the thought and tried to wriggle out of it. Of course I knew the Spirit. It was the Spirit that made God real to me in my own experience. Without the Spirit there would be no communication with the Father, no awareness of Jesus. It was God's link between Himself and His people; the supernatural presence of God in the world. It was what the Father had sent into the world after Jesus had ascended into heaven.

But the thought persisted. *Do you really know me?*

The truth came to me as clearly as if a light had been switched on in a darkened room. Did I know *Him*?

I'd always thought of the Spirit as an 'it'. A force, a power, a presence. Never a person - a 'he'.

I put down my tools and wiped my hands on a grease-rag, leaning back against the tractor wheel. All these years and I'd missed such a lovely truth. The Holy Spirit was a person! Different from the Father, without a body like Jesus, but just as much a person. Of course! There was that phrase I'd often used from the pulpit: 'the Holy Spirit, the third person of the Trinity'. He was just as much God, just as much one who possessed all the attributes of a person. True, His work was to reveal Jesus, but that made Him no less a person in His own right.

The thought intrigued me - and at the same time disturbed me. For I could not escape the fact that now closed in on me. I did not know Him.

Who was He, this mysterious and wonderful Third Person? What was He like? How could I get acquainted with Him?

It's odd, but as I began to think of the Holy Spirit in these fresh, new, personal terms I no longer felt afraid of Him. I could feel my defences slipping away, at first with much apprehension but then with more and more relief. And I felt a great weight breaking free of my shoulders.

The 'baptism in the Spirit'? The phrase still left me cold, uncomfortable. But the person Himself . . .

Over the next few days I searched for Him in the Scriptures, and a whole new adventure began to open up for me. There He was, right at the beginning of my Bible, in the first few words of Genesis. Present at the very creation of the universe: 'And the Spirit of God moved upon the face of the waters. . .'

Throughout the Old Testament He was there, brooding over Israel's history and occasionally stepping into events, coming and going like the wind, just as Jesus had described Him.

On into the New Testament, bearing the holy seed to Mary, sealing the Saviour's identity with the visible manifestation of a dove, leading Jesus into and out of the wilderness temptations, clearly present throughout His years of ministry and His final great triumph on the cross, in the wings at the resurrection and ascension, coming in great power upon the first Christians at Pentecost, moving upon the Early Church and distributing His many supernatural gifts to individual believers . . .

And all this time I'd not known Him. Worse, I'd *resisted* knowing Him. I saw this clearly now. It wasn't just George and Cynthia I'd been fighting - it was the Lord Himself. What a fool I'd been. And what pathetic arguments I'd put up against Him. My Methodism didn't seem to count for a great deal now. And, to my surprise, nor did it matter.

By the summer of 1967 I was half-way there. 'All right, Lord,' I said, 'I'm willing to be baptised in your Spirit, but I don't want to go babbling about in other tongues.'

I had a hang-up about the gift of tongues. I knew from George that it was often regarded as the first outward sign that someone had been filled with the Holy Spirit, but I didn't want that happening to me. It was one thing to lay aside my Methodism, but quite another to be considered Pentecostal.

Yes, I still had my pride. But God graciously dealt with this last remaining reservation in a wonderful way. For if I had sat down to think about what would help me over this final hurdle I would have said that I should like to talk to a man of God outside my own set of circumstances; a man I already had a high regard for; a man who knew his Bible and who had thought through these issues; and a man who shared my Methodism.

The person God sent along was all of these things. It was Dr Skevington Wood.

The Lord's choice, of course, was perfect. As a Bible teacher Dr Wood's ministry had been appreciated at conferences all over the world, and he was also a man I was pleased to call my friend.

He came to us one Sunday afternoon in September, 1967, travelling down by train from his home in Sunderland to take our Harvest Festival service.

Over tea we began talking about the work of the Holy Spirit, but our time was short and we'd barely got into the subject when we had to leave for the meeting. With so many questions yet unasked I decided to offer Dr Wood a lift home in the car that evening (a round trip of 110 miles) and to hope for some answers on the way.

We set off at about nine o'clock and in the course of the journey I opened up my heart, sharing with my friend the events of the past year, my personal battle, my discoveries, and of course my remaining reservations.

'I want to believe,' I said. 'I want to be filled with the Spirit, and have whatever the Lord's got for me. But . . . well, I'm just not sure about some of it, like this tongues business.'

His answer took me by surprise. Dr Wood, I learned, had recently returned from a ministry tour of the Far East where he had witnessed churches in revival, moving 'in the Spirit'. Their meetings, he told me, sometimes lasted all day, beginning as early as 5.00 am and developing from one hour to the next under a powerful anointing, right through till evening. People were being saved, healed, filled with the Spirit, delivered of demons ... 'It was like the Acts of the Apostles all over again,' he said 'And, yes, there was speaking in tongues. Interpretations. Prophecies. Words of Knowledge. All the gifts. Gifts and miracles happening all the time. The power of God demonstrated through His people. It was incredible. Incredible but wonderfully real.' Then he turned to me. 'Yes, it's of the Lord, Jim. And he can do it right here. Here in England, in Yorkshire, in Sandhutton. Seek the Lord, brother. Seek the Lord. Be open to Him. Let Him give you everything it pleases Him to give you, and then ask for more!'

I arrived back at The Limes just after three o'clock next morning, tired but excited. Dr Wood's answer had been the spur I'd needed. There were no doubts now. No reservations. No conditions. 'All right, Lord - your will, your way.' I wanted whatever He would give me and I couldn't get it soon enough.

It happened a couple of mornings later. I was alone in the house and down on my knees before the Lord when it seemed as though somewhere far above me a dam suddenly burst and a great torrent of love poured down upon me, washing over me in waves until I was floating in the most wonderful sense of the Lord's presence. No wonder they called it the *baptism* in the Spirit!

Yet somehow that now seemed too clinical, too limited, for as the wonderful waves swirled around me I found myself laughing and rejoicing, as uninhibited as a little child frolicking in the sea. It was refreshing, invigorating, and deeply, deeply satisfying, as though I had been lifted into heaven itself and was experiencing all the peace and love and joy that are the very heart of the Father.

'Thank you, Lord! Praise you, Jesus! Glory to God!' I struggled in my spirit for the right words, *adequate* words, and realised I possessed none. How limited was my natural vocabulary! Yet even as I was thinking this my tongue began to move around unfamiliar sounds . . . words I had never learned nor understood.

I knew what was happening. I was 'speaking in tongues' - the 'tongues' of which I'd been so wary. But it wasn't the mumbo-jumbo I had once feared it to be; it was a proper language with syntax, expression, inflection. A language that emanated from the Spirit Himself and that reached way beyond the limits of my intellect to enable me to worship God on a new and deeper level.

It wasn't a language that was forced upon me - I'd been so afraid of 'babbling about' in a tongue that was beyond my control - but a form of expression which was mine to use at will. Clearly I could decide when to start speaking in this tongue and when to stop, how fast or slow to speak, how loud or soft to talk . . .

All this plus the sure knowledge that I had received a new and deeply satisfying form of communication with God.

I don't know how long this initial encounter in the Spirit lasted. Five minutes? An hour? But of one thing I was sure when finally I got to my feet that September morning: this was the most wonderful thing to happen to me in 20 years of Christian experience. Why had I resisted so long?

But I knew the answer to that. Neither George nor Cynthia had ever been able fully to explain the tremendous blessing that was to be enjoyed through the baptism in the Spirit . . . and even if they had I wouldn't have believed them.

Cynthia, of course, was ecstatic. It had been six months since she'd been filled with the Spirit and throughout that time my stubbornness had sustained an unhappy friction in the home. Now that was all over. But best of all, we were one in a new dimension of the Spirit.

The relationship with George was healed, too. Every resentment was gone, every irritation forgotten. In their place was a deep thankfulness that the man had not given up on me. For the best part of a year he had refused to take 'no' for an answer and his perseverance had finally paid off. But what had made him so determined, I wondered, when for month after month I'd snubbed him or laughed him off?

'It was the Lord, of course,' he explained through that familiar grin the following Friday. 'Once He'd told me He needed you to be filled with the Spirit I knew I had to tell you and to keep on telling you. It was just a matter of staying true to the vision.'

I was intrigued. 'What do you mean, that he needed me to be filled with the Spirit?'

He laughed out loud. 'Well, you don't think He's blessed you just for your own benefit? No, Jim, I believe the Lord is going to do a mighty work through you and Cynthia, and He's going to do it right here on your farm. You wait and see.'

Things began to move that very evening. It was nothing dramatic, but pervading our meeting was a new sense of expectancy, a new excitement. And no wonder, now that the host had received his inheritance! Naturally I couldn't help but share with everyone what had happened to me, and seeing as I was the one who'd been preventing the group from moving forward there was now no stopping us. From that point on we never looked back. Friday evenings now had a new purpose, a new power, and for the first time the Holy Spirit had real liberty to move upon us. It was beautiful just to watch people getting blessed.

Many of our folk wanted to know more. 'How do I receive the infilling of the Spirit?' 'What about the gifts?' 'Does God still heal today?'

We asked George Breckon if he would lead a series of Bible studies on these subjects - something he'd been bursting to do for months - and inevitably, week after week, the Bible sessions led into ministry sessions with people receiving the baptism, rejoicing in their new prayer language, getting healed . . . it was like our own mini-revival.

But these Friday meetings were not just glory sessions. The work of the Spirit, we discovered, was essentially practical and as well as wanting to bless us and build our faith He was concerned with our Christian walk - with the holiness of our lives. Sometimes this meant there had to be repentance, often with tears, before the Spirit could be released in our midst. Or, more often, he would use the meetings to challenge us in areas of our lives where we needed to be changed or made whole. For some it would be the need to repair a broken relationship; for others it might be a long-standing grudge that had to be dealt with; or a habit that needed to be smashed.

The way in which the Spirit tackled these issues differed too. With addictions, particularly, He would often choose to act in sovereign grace to bring immediate release. This would sometimes come as a wonderful bonus to someone being baptised in the Spirit, or simply in response to a believer's prayer.

Such was the experience of Ernest Hutchinson, one of our regulars from Northallerton. One evening he heard George preach about our body being the temple of the Holy Spirit and went home asking the Lord to break his addiction to cigarettes.

The compulsion to smoke was still there when he awoke the following morning, however, and as usual Ernest went out and bought a fresh packet of cigarettes.

It was then the Lord stepped in.

Pausing outside the shop to light up, Ernest found the taste of the tobacco so awful he had to throw the cigarette away. Half way home he tried another, which tasted even more foul, and back at the house he tossed the packet in the dustbin. God had touched him! His desire for cigarettes had been totally removed.

More often, though, when shaping His people the Spirit would choose to bring about changes over a period of time, and He would do it through various means, not least ministering Christians.

And this is where we made a wonderful discovery: that the Lord's plan is to minister to His people not only through those Christians appointed to the role of pastor, evangelist, teacher, but also through ordinary Christians - housewives, mechanics, shop assistants, farmers (!) - *anyone* who will receive a spiritual gift by faith.

This is what we saw beginning to happen on Friday evenings. Ordinary Christians - some who normally would not so much as open their mouths in a meeting - ministering to the whole group through the gifts of the Spirit.

Most often it would happen after a time of praise. From over here would come a prophecy (not a prediction, but the speaking forth of words given by God for a specific situation or persons) . . . from over there a message in tongues spoken audibly for all to hear . . . and from across the room, moments later, the interpretation of that message, again revealing the mind of God . . .

Other gifts, we discovered, like a word of wisdom or knowledge, would be exercised at a crucial moment when counselling someone . . . while the gifts of faith and healing often went hand-in-hand when praying for a member of the group with physical or emotional needs.

Some gifts were less easy to define but equally vital in a given situation, such as when we were praying for George and Gladys during one of their preaching trips to Denmark. While we were lifting them up before the Lord I suddenly saw before me a living picture - like a video - of a meeting in progress. George was in the pulpit, apparently preaching with great liberty to a packed auditorium, when all at once the mood of the meeting changed. Before my eyes, as though projected on to the opposite wall of our lounge, I saw a man leap from his seat, jump on to the platform and try to push George aside so that he could commandeer the microphone. A scuffle began as members of the platform party - possibly local pastors - rushed to George's aid. At that point, as abruptly as it had appeared, the picture faded.

Instantly I began to share what I had seen, believing it to have been given for a specific purpose, and then we began praying against any attack of the enemy upon George's mission, particularly the disruption of the meeting which we knew would be taking place at that same time.

When George returned to us the following week we learned that what I had seen on the 'video' had been exactly what had taken place that evening in Denmark, and that we had been alerted to pray at the very time the incident had occurred.

Exactly which gift the Spirit used that night was unclear - perhaps the gift of revelation; a visual word of knowledge. Or maybe it was a straightforward vision. It didn't really matter; the Spirit was at work and that was exciting.

Again, on other evenings, we would witness the hand of the Lord upon our gathering as the Spirit touched one here, another there in ways that the Scriptures did not define as gifts but which were no less clear manifestations of His presence. Some of these put me in mind of Rev. Ransome's experiences in Nigeria. Just as he had witnessed men weeping uncontrollably in prayer, so we too now saw the Spirit stir members of the group to intercede with tears and emotion for a particular person or problem. Likewise, as our missionary friend had seen black Christians moved to riotous laughter - 'laughing in the Spirit' - so, from time to time, the Lord would touch first one and then another in our meetings with this wonderfully joyful expression of the rejoicing that is part of His own heart.

But not everyone was smiling. From the moment our meetings had taken this upward turn there had been those who disapproved. This was to be expected, I suppose, yet it was strange to hear all the arguments I'd once put up against the baptism myself now coming from the lips of others. 'Those things aren't for today.' 'That's for Pentecostals, not Methodists.' 'Tongues are of the devil.'

And so we lost a number of folk, some of whom we'd regarded as good friends, and that hurt. It hurt too when other Christians, some from our own church, avoided us in the town as though we'd caught some terrible disease. And worst of all when some of our own relatives turned against us. (They thought we'd got some sort of religious mania. Praise God, we'd never been more sane.)

But for every one we lost, the Lord seemed to send along another two. Word of what the Spirit was doing at The Limes was spreading fast and each week it seemed we were welcoming new faces.

'If they keep coming at this rate,' I quipped to Cynthia, 'we'll need to pray for elastic walls in the lounge!' The room was 18 x 20 and more than 40 people were now squeezing in each week.

They came from near and far - the curious, the hungry, the burdened and the beaming. From every denomination and walk of life. Those who had been following the Lord for many years, and those who had only just begun.

Of course, some of these new Christians were our own contacts. Evangelism, after all, was still our priority. Nothing had changed in that respect, except that the power we had received through the baptism had enabled us to witness more effectively. And that was how it should have been; indeed, there would have been something very wrong if after being filled with the Spirit we had become more inward looking than outward reaching. That would have been to deny the very reason we'd been given the power. What was it Jesus had told his disciples? 'Ye shall be my witnesses, once the Holy Ghost has come upon you.'

Witnesses. That was really what the work of the Spirit at The Limes was all about. The baptism, the gifts, the healings . . . all these benefits were for the ultimate purpose of equipping God's people so that in the *power of the Spirit* they could tell others about the Lord.

And now we had a message for Christians, too. For George had been right - there *was* something more. Life in the Spirit. What a wonderful discovery!

But if I thought I'd arrived I had another think coming.

5/Under new management

Looking back over the struggle I'd had with the baptism in the Spirit I realised that my stubbornness had stemmed from misconceptions about what was right and proper; that I'd been conditioned to believing *accepted* truth rather than *actual* truth. In other words, I'd believed a traditional view instead of the Bible's view. But that was behind me now. Or was it?

Without even realising it I had begun to use the same yardstick of accepted truth against another important area of Bible doctrine.

After Cynthia had been filled with the Spirit she had begun to dig into her Bible with the abandoned joy of a prospector who'd just struck gold. One of the shining seams she uncovered led her to the conclusion that she should be baptised in water, by immersion. Wisely, she had kept this to herself until I had experienced my own Pentecost, fearing I would explode at the thought of her getting tangled up with yet another 'dubious doctrine'. Yet even *after* I'd been filled with the Spirit my reaction was not exactly enthusiastic.

'Baptised?' I said, making it sound a dirty word. 'Whatever for? You know we don't do that in the Methodist Church. That's for the Baptists.'

'But it's here in the Bible,' she replied. 'Jesus was baptised, wasn't He - and He's our example. If it was important for Him then it's important for me.'

'But there's no need, Cynthia. Why make a fuss? You'll only stir it up over at the chapel, and things are bad enough as it is. It isn't necessary, believe me.'

'Well, I want to do it Jim. I want to follow the Lord.'

She'd done it again - got me backed up against a wall and scratching around for an adequate answer. But at least I'd learned something from my battle with the baptism in the Spirit. While I continued to hold my position on water baptism being unMethodist, I also took a look to see what the Bible had to say about it. And this time my search was quizzical instead of critical. When I'd first hunted through the Scriptures on the subject of the baptism in the Spirit I had longed to be able to prove George and Cynthia wrong. But now, on another contentious subject, and to my surprise, I found myself quite willing for Cynthia to be proved right.

It was the work of the Spirit, of course. Gradually, brick by brick, He was dismantling the old wall of pride. But there was another lesson to learn here, too: the traditions of men, which had influenced my thinking for so long, had to go out of the window.

This was an enormous wrench for me because it meant abandoning ideas I'd grown up with, ideas that had come down to me through generations of faithful chapelgoers. Yet here, the Lord showed me, was the very crux of the problem, for the traditions of men are nothing more than that: man's ideas which are given credence because of their endurance rather than their truth.

What was important now was to learn to differentiate between the two because, as I was beginning to see, the teachings of men will always bring us into bondage, whereas the truth of the Scriptures will never fail to set us free.

Freedom was what I needed - the freedom to release Cynthia into following the Lord in her own way, and the freedom to choose that way myself if the Spirit so called. Not surprisingly, it was the Bible that unlocked my prison door.

'You go ahead and be baptised, love,' I told Cynthia a couple of weeks later. 'I'll be there to shout "Praise the Lord"!'

My release had come quite simply when I'd taken the Scriptures at face value and not tried to argue my way round them. If the Word said 'Repent and be baptised,' that's what it meant, and when the Spirit applied that word to your heart you'd better get on and do it.

Cynthia 'did it' about a week later. We held an open-air outreach in Northallerton High Street on the Saturday afternoon and then marched down to the public baths to continue the witness in a baptismal service (the first of many). It was a blessing none of us would have missed.

My own baptism was to come a few weeks later. We were attending an evening service at the Assembly of God Church in Water Skellgate, Ripon, where a farmer friend, Marcus Dawson, was being baptised. Marcus and his wife May were soon to leave farming and enter full-time Christian work with the Wycliffe Bible Translators in New Guinea, and Marcus had wanted to be baptised before setting out.

With great rejoicing we watched as he and several other believers witnessed to their faith in Christ as they were plunged beneath the waters, and then the pastor turned to the congregation with an open invitation for anyone else who wished to follow our Lord's example to step forward.

Well, I'd already reached the point where I'd said, 'Yes, Lord, I'm willing,' and I'd made Him a promise that I would be baptised at the next opportunity. This happened to be it.

Of course, the pastor had forgotten to mention that they hadn't any spare baptismal robes, but I wouldn't have been put off. What was the discomfort of climbing into a wringing-wet robe when compared to the agonies suffered by my Lord upon the cross? Besides, it was all part of the Spirit's work of knocking down the old Jim and building up the new.

On the farm we were doing a similar work of renewal. The process of improving the farm buildings had continued right through our years at The Limes because a farmer's first priority for investment must be his land and livestock. There's no point in putting up big, expensive buildings if you've nothing with which to fill them. So even now, ten years after we'd moved in, there were still areas of the outbuildings that needed renovating or replacing. And some would have to wait a while longer still, for we'd just spent a great deal of money on starting a haulage service.

Always keen to expand the business, and with good profits to be made from transporting feedstuffs, we had invested in a 16-ton diesel wagon. I drove this myself. We still had two men working for us (though Bill and Erich had long since moved on) and with them looking after the farm I was free to operate this new side of the business on three days each week.

But we'd not been hauling long when near-disaster struck. It happened one evening that autumn of 1967. I'd driven the wagon into the yard after delivering a load of haystuffs and as I jumped down from the cab my right foot twisted over and a bolt of pain shot up my leg.

Moments later I lay on the ground looking at what was surely a broken ankle - at least, the angle of the foot and the throbbing pain said so - and lying there in the dust I called out for help. But nobody came running, nobody even answered. I was quite alone.

What now? I couldn't walk on a busted foot, and - the truth hit me - I couldn't drive, either. Oh no! Who would drive the wagon? What would happen to our new business?

But then I checked myself. Hadn't I been speaking to the group about faith and power only the other evening?

Instantly a prayer went up. 'Lord, I need a healing.' And to my foot: 'Be healed - in Jesus' name!'

To my astonishment - and relief - the foot began to move, twisting round of its own accord until it was back in its normal position. At the same time the blinding pain just faded away. Without a moment's hesitation I got to my feet and walked around for a moment, testing the foot. Normal. I jumped up and down a couple of times for good measure. Perfect.

'Hallelujah! Thank you, Lord!' It was another wonderful miracle. Another marvellous healing.

But what I didn't realise just then was that the Lord was also showing me a parable. For what needed healing as much as my foot was my attitude to what I'd been doing when I'd injured it: making money.

Right from our first year at The Limes I had always been on the lookout for ways of making an additional few pounds - any way that fitted in with our farming lifestyle and that would bring in an extra bit of cash. In fact, originally I'd even set myself a target: enough money to cover Cynthia's weekly housekeeping bill. The most obvious answer, and one that I'd relied on down the years, was cattle-dealing.

There was a group of us - a syndicate - who were into this. Each market day we'd go along to the auctionmart at Northallerton and cast our eye over the cattle to be sold. When we'd found a promising lot we would approach the owner and offer to get him a better price for his animals than he could normally expect. If he agreed we would fix a minimum price with him - say, £40 per head - on the understanding that he would go 50-50 with us on any figure realised over that price.

It worked like this. Once the cattle were in the ring we'd look for the man whose bidding showed he was keen to buy the stock. Each time he made a bid one of the syndicate would outbid him, forcing him to bid higher still. The object, of course, was to force the price as high as possible above the agreed figure. The trick was to know when the bidding farmer had reached his limit; if you became greedy and outbid him once too often you could get stuck with the cattle yourself.

This system would regularly pull in an extra six or eight pounds per head over the minimum agreed price, so for every animal in the lot (there might be 12 or 15) the members of the syndicate would share three or four pounds. Then we would approach a second farmer with livestock to sell. A lucrative business.

That was Wednesday. On Thursday I was into a little money-spinning on my own. In the morning I would rush around getting my jobs done so that by lunch-time I was free to hitch up the cattle-trailer and drive over to the market at Gisburn, on the lookout for calves. I'd buy up a dozen or so, load them into the trailer, then motor to various farms in the area where I would hope to off-load one here, a couple there, making a few pounds on every sale.

This was not without its problems. I rarely bought more than two calves from one lot and rarely paid the same price for any two batches, which meant having to keep several sets of figures in my head when bargaining with a potential customer so as to make sure I sold every calf at a profit.

And after all that chasing around and haggling over prices, I was sure to wake up the next morning with a migraine coming on.

Still, I was making money and that was what mattered. With the income from these ventures taking care of many of our domestic bills, the profits from the farm could literally be ploughed back in. That was important to me. Farming was a competitive business and I wasn't going to be left behind in the rat-race. In fact I was determined to be right up front.

It had never occurred to me that God might be anything other than happy with all this. Wasn't the fact that the business had prospered a sign of His blessing? But now, after I'd been filled with the Spirit, I'd begun to feel uneasy about things and I didn't know why.

The picture became clearer when someone loaned me some tape recordings of Christian meetings in America sponsored by the Full Gospel Business Men's Fellowship International. I'd heard about the Fellowship, started by Californian dairyman Demos Shakarian to reach other businessmen with the Gospel, and I was keen to hear what went on at their meetings. The words 'full Gospel' in their name-tag guaranteed they would be seeking to move in the Spirit and I was looking forward to getting blessed. It would be good, too, through the medium of the tape, to rejoice with other Christians who had come into the blessings of the baptism, for at that time this move of the Spirit had only recently begun to touch Britain and it seemed we were almost alone in our experience.

But I got more than I expected from those tapes. Yes, I was thrilled by the anointed preaching, encouraged through hearing gifts of tongues and prophecy being used, and blessed by the lively singing of short, easy-to-learn songs (our first introduction to choruses). But there was more.

These meetings, by the very nature of the Fellowship, centred round the personal experiences of businessmen - ordinary, everyday businessmen, except for the fact that they had entirely handed their business dealings over to Jesus Christ.

At first I thought I was hearing merely an echo of my own testimony - hadn't I asked the Lord to take us into partnership with Him that first week at The Limes? - but as the tapes wound on I realised that the men I was listening to were experiencing Christ in their businesses in a dimension completely unknown to me. It wasn't that their companies or farms were prospering any more than my own. Nor that these men were any more committed to the Lord than I was myself.

It was simply that these businessmen had given up striving. They had stopped chasing after money for money's sake. They had ceased fretting about expansion. Quit worrying about cashflows. And in so doing they had seen God bless their work in ways far beyond anything their scheming and striving could ever have achieved.

The message couldn't have been plainer if the Lord had written the words ten feet high on the side of the barn: *What about you, Jim?*

When the question wouldn't go away I knew I'd have to answer it.

'What exactly do you want of me, Lord?'

His answer was not audible, but unmistakable just the same.

I want you to clean up your business affairs. Get rid of everything that does not honour me.

'But where do I start?' As if I didn't know.

Your cattle-dealing is offensive to me. It's devious, Jim. It has to go.

'But I need the money.'

Am I not able to provide for all your needs?

'Well, yes - but . . .

Trust me.

There followed a few days of intense wrestling as my old nature threw up all the arguments against making what I knew would be a radical change in my life-style. Was the cattle-dealing so wrong? Hadn't I been doing business this way for years? If I gave this up, what else might He ask me to drop? How much money would I lose each week, and over the year? (I worked it out to the last pound.) *That* much! It didn't make sense to just throw away useful, regular cash. In fact the whole idea was illogical.

But God, I came to realise, does not operate on logic. His criteria are so very different from our own. A Bible verse came to me, surfacing from somewhere at the back of my mind.

'As the heavens are higher than the earth, so are my ways higher than your ways, and my thoughts higher than your thoughts.'

That seemed to take care of any argument that what He was asking was unreasonable. But what about our daily bread? For almost ten years I'd counted on the proceeds from the syndicate to meet Cynthia's weekly housekeeping bill. How would I make up the money?

Once again a text presented itself - one I'd quoted often enough to the children in the Sunday school. Now it stood staring me in the face, slightly amused, slightly reproachful of my own lack of faith.

'Do not be anxious about your life, what you shall eat . . . look at the birds of the air. . . . they neither sow nor reap nor gather into barns, and yet your heavenly Father feeds them. Are you not of more value than they?'

But deep down I knew that money wasn't really the issue. No one had ever lost out by yielding to God's leading. The businessmen on those tapes had testified to that. No, the real issue was holiness. Not head-in-the-clouds, sanctimonious piety, but, as we'd been learning in the Friday group, practical, down-to-earth Christlikeness.

That was it. God wanted me to run the farm the way Jesus would run it. No shady deals. No devious activities. No even slightly grey areas.

And no striving, either. No chasing around for that extra few pounds. No sweating over whether I'd remembered the correct price for those calves. And no haggling like a man down to his last crust. None of that was glorifying to God.

Neither was my attitude to money generally. Once I'd given up wrestling with Him and had begun to catch the vision of what the Lord wanted to do in my life these things became clear to me. God wanted people who would keep a light hand on the purse-strings, who weren't for ever fretting about profit-margins or higher yields, and who weren't taken up with the rat-race.

In short, he wanted people who would say, 'Yes, Lord, you're the boss,' and then let Him get on and run the business His way. That was where I'd fallen down. I'd said, 'Take us into partnership with you, Lord,' and then made up my mind how He was going to run His firm.

But that was all going to change now. First to go was the cattle-dealing.

'You can count me out from now on, lads,' I told the other members of the syndicate. 'The Lord wants me out of it.'

'Ee, y'must be mad,' they said. 'Thee's taking this religion stuff too far, Jim. Giving up all that extra money? Yer'll be sorry, lad, wait and see.'

Inevitably, the calf business had to go, too. Not that there was anything immoral about it, but it was part of the old order - something I'd been doing 'in the flesh'. Now the Lord was showing me a better way - *His* way - and that meant doing things in the Spirit. It didn't mean I'd be putting in fewer hours - in fact I'd now be spending more time on the farm instead of chasing around to the markets - but it meant a new outlook, a more relaxed attitude, and a greater freedom to enjoy my work. It also meant that more of my mental energies would be available for channelling into the Lord's work, rather than being wasted on draining anxieties over the high price of pigfeed or the low return on wheat. I would no longer have to carry that burden. I'd handed all the books over to the Lord. They were His problem now, not mine; I was just the book-keeper!

But will this new spiritual approach to the business pay? That was the niggling little worry the devil handed to me. *It's all very well giving up that extra money in the name of God, but who's going to pay the bills?*

Foolishly, I failed to resist the thought - perhaps because it was putting into words my own nagging apprehension - and I allowed the seed to take root. What if the Lord *didn't* make up the money right away? What if He wanted to teach me something by allowing my income to drop? What if. . . One by one the doubts trundled through my mind.

But the following month, when for the first time under this new business arrangement I sat down to do the books, the devil's suggestion was shown up for what it was: a lie.

'Hey, Cynthia, come and check these figures, love.' I leaned back in my chair, scratching a puzzled brow. 'Either I've totalled these columns wrong, or . . .'

'Or what?'

I handed her my pencil. 'Or we've more in hand than we've had for months.'

'She ran a steady finger down the columns, then scribbled some figures on a pad. A few more calculations - then: 'No, those totals are correct.'

I grinned at her. 'Hey, that's great. Thank you, Lord!' I wondered why we hadn't tried it the Lord's way before. Our expenses that month were only marginally lower than normal, our income was down, and yet the books showed that our profit was slightly up. And all without running around to the markets and working myself into a frazzle. What an encouragement!

The benefits didn't end with the bank balance, either. I discovered that in doing things God's way there was physical blessing, too. Those migraines which had plagued me since the day I'd gone over my handlebars as a boy of six, and which in more recent years had regularly followed my hectic afternoon of calf-trading, now completely disappeared. It wasn't that they gradually became less intense as I grew more relaxed; it was that the Lord sovereignly healed me. One week the migraine was there, the next it was not. That, to me, was one of the wonderful bonuses that the Lord drops into our lives from time to time - unexpected gifts from a loving Father.

Another miracle? Without doubt. And in quiet moments it stirred within me those memories of other healings, other miracles which I had somehow felt were stepping stones, each one leading us closer to something special that God was preparing for us. Had those miracles been signposts pointing the way into the baptism in the Spirit? Perhaps. But as I looked back over the years even that wonderful Pentecost experience now seemed a stepping stone in itself. Where *was* God leading us? Exactly what was He calling us into? And what was the significance of all those miracles?

If only I could have seen round the next corner I would have realised that within a few months we would be given the answer to all those questions. But before the vision could be revealed we had one more lesson to learn.

'Boots!' cried Cynthia as I stamped into the kitchen with mud and straw flying from my wellingtons. She couldn't believe that I was ignoring her. 'Jim, I've just washed that floor!'

But I had other things on my mind. Reaching for the phone I glanced at her and said: 'I think we've got sick pigs on our hands.'

The floor didn't matter then. 'Serious?'

I finished dialling the vet's number. 'Could be - but I hope it's not the fever, not with a thousand pigs out there.'

A voice came on the line and I said: 'Mr Wittrick? Jim Wilkinson here . . .'

I suppose I'd never been in any doubt, having seen it all before, but it still came as a shock when the vet confirmed my worst fears. It had been bad enough losing 400 pigs in a morning, but to think we were going to be dragging a thousand carcasses out of the pens . . .

There was a sickening familiarity about the whole nasty procedure of the sign on the gate, the hole in the ground, the crack of the marksman's rifle, the powerful disinfectant sprays. But more sickening still was the loss of our profits. Our pigs were now bringing in more money than the crops and the haulage business together, and in anybody's language - Christian or otherwise - this was an enormous blow.

A couple of days later, as the Ministry men cleared up and left me bulldozing earth over the mass of lifeless pigs, I allowed the questions that had been queuing up to run free in my mind.

Where did this terrible waste fit into God's plan for our lives? How were we to relate it to God's love for us? Had we thought that giving the Lord total control of the farm would be a sort of guarantee against disaster striking The Limes? What would the Spirit want to say to us in this situation?

I talked it over with Cynthia after tea while she did some sewing and I amused Joanna, now a toddling two-year-old. It was one of my few evenings at home and I wasn't going to let the miserable events of the day ruin an all-too-rare time with the family. Besides, to my surprise, I didn't feel particularly depressed about the loss of a thousand pigs. Maybe the Lord had been doing more in my heart than I'd realised.

'Well, it doesn't alter the fact that God loves us,' said Cynthia, matter-of-factly. 'But, yes, maybe we'd begun to think that if we walked in the Spirit nothing could touch us.'

I thought about it for a moment, then nodded. 'I suppose you're right. Naive, weren't we? How many times have we read Scriptures warning us to expect trials and tribulation?'

'The fiery trials,' Cynthia muttered absently, engrossed in a delicate piece of needlework.

We fell silent and I sat guiding Joanna through her favourite picture-book while I thought about that phrase. The fiery trials. Sure enough, the Bible promised those to all who were serious about following the Lord - and it wasn't for dramatic effect that the trials were described as fiery. Fire was a cleansing agent, a purifying force - a powerful element that was used to bring change.

What sort of change, I wondered, was the Spirit looking to produce in us through this present trial?

I didn't find an answer to the question that evening. That was to come a few days later when I came across some startlingly apt verses in the Old Testament, in the book of Habakkuk.

'Though the fig tree do not blossom, nor fruit be on the vines, the produce of the olive fail and the fields yield no food, the flock be cut off from the fold and there be no herd in the stalls, yet I will rejoice in the Lord, I will joy in the God of my salvation.'

It was remarkable. This almost forgotten book of the Bible was speaking right into our situation. *Though there be no herd in the stalls.* That was us, all right. *Yet I will rejoice in the Lord.* Could *we* do that? Could we still say, 'Lord, we love and trust you,' when the mainstay of our income had just been wiped out?

There was no doubt in my mind that this was what the Lord

was saying to us - that He wanted us to be able to praise Him at all times and in all circumstances. Not only when things were going well or when His hand of blessing was evident in our lives, but when the bills were mounting up and the pigs were being killed off outside our back door.

Not that we could ever praise him *because* of those circumstances, but certainly we needed to learn to praise Him *in spite* of them.

I shared this little gem of a discovery with Cynthia in the kitchen later that morning. 'Do you see it, love? The Lord wants us to give Him thanks for who He is, not for what He does for us. He wants us to praise Him, no strings attached. Praise Him whether He prospers us or whether we lose every penny. And when we . . .'

I jumped aside as a doll's pram came hurtling by with a giggling Joanna charging behind it. A moment later she came to an abrupt halt as the pram crashed into a leg of the kitchen table, knocking over a bottle of milk and sending our labrador, Mally, scooting for the door. Cynthia rescued the milk bottle as Joanna bent to pick up her ejected doll.

'Joanna!' I scolded. 'Be more careful, crashing about like that . . . '

Cynthia mopped up spilt milk, then turned to me with a reproachful smile. 'Praise the Lord in all things,' she said, 'even when your daughter's knocking the house down around your ears.'

I burst out laughing, and then we laughed together.

We were learning a vital lesson. When things appeared to be going wrong our God wanted us not only to continue trusting Him, but to praise Him, too. Difficult though it might be, we were continually to rejoice in Him, refusing to allow adverse circumstances to shake our confidence in His abiding care.

That's what came through that unhappy episode with the pigs

- a sense of His permanent, surrounding care. And in a strange way, rather than throwing doubt upon His commitment to us and to the farm, the whole incident somehow served to confirm that He was Lord of our lives and of the business; that He was in control.

The following weeks proved it. The insurance on the pigs covered our losses, a new contract for the haulage business came in, and we were offered a much higher price than we'd expected for our winter hay. By Christmas things were ticking over nicely again.

But the Lord wasn't about to let me become complacent. Once again it was through George Breckon that the episode of events began.

It was mid-January of 1968 when George stepped into the lobby with a question that was to throw me for a moment or two. Stamping the latest fall of winter snow from his boots, he asked: 'Are you thinking of buying more land, Jim?'

I stared at him. 'Who, me? Not a chance,' I said. 'Whatever gave you that idea? We've only just got straightened out after that pigs business. In fact I've only just finished paying off the loans we've had these past ten years. There's no way I'm taking on more land, not for a good while yet. Do you want a cup of tea? You look as if you need thawing out.'

Inside he sat with his back to the range while Cynthia brewed up. 'What makes you ask about me buying land?' I enquired.

He smiled uncertainly. 'Well, I had this vision, see - a vision of you, Jim, looking out over a vast area of land.'

I laughed shortly. I'd had 'visions' myself that had turned out to be my own imaginings. 'Sorry, George, but I think you've got the wrong man. If God wants to increase me He'll have to make two blades of grass grow where now there's one. Want a slab of cake?'

Later, when he'd left, and I was over in the barn putting out the feed for the cattle, I had a chuckle over George's suggestion. Buy more land, indeed! Not when I'd just got myself straight.

And then I put it out of my mind.

It was two months later, in early March, when the subject came up again. Cynthia and I were driving up to Northallerton for a meeting early one evening. It was only a short drive of eight miles or so and I knew the road so well I could have driven into town blindfold. We knew every feature of the landscape, too; every paddock, every copse, every gateway, every farm. Over there was Mr Scaling's place - a compact holding of 120 or so acres. And there, that was Eric Bell's land, with the rising hill and woods forming the boundary. Just ahead, around the bend, was a place that was up for auction. Hollybush Farm. Quite a spread, that. Two hundred acres, divided by the road, and a big, imposing house. At one time, many years since, it must have been quite a grand sort of place, I mused. Fifteen rooms, maid's quarters, delightful gardens . . . Yes, that was quite a place. It needed a touch of paint here and there (I knew that the owner, Mr Sowerby, had been unwell), but someone with the right sort of money would have a handsome property in Hollybush Farm. Idly, I wondered how much it would go for. The auction was next week.

Not in a million years could I have guessed who was going to buy it. But as we sped by the gateway with its sale board swinging in a bitter March wind I suddenly knew.

'I want that place for my glory.'

It was that voice again. Clear as a peal of bells on a frosty night.

I swallowed hard. Oh, Lord! Where was I going to get *that* sort of money?

6/Miracle Valley

I gave myself a few seconds to let the idea sink in, then turned to Cynthia. 'Guess what? I think we're moving.'

After ten years of marriage she was used to some of my mad-cap ways, but this announcement caught her out.

'We're *what*?'

I jerked a thumb over my shoulder, back toward the shadowy house. 'Moving - to Hollybush Farm, if I heard right.'

'What d'you mean?' Then the penny dropped. 'You mean you heard from the Lord?'

I nodded through the winter darkness. 'No mistaking it. It was the Lord's voice, all right.'

Her eyes danced with a sudden excitement. 'Well? What did He *say*?'

I glanced at her, smiling tentatively. 'He said, "I want that place for my glory." It happened just as we went by the gate, by the auction notice.'

She turned quickly in her seat, peering back to catch a glimpse of the house, but it was lost in the night. Swinging round again, she gripped my arm. 'Why, Jim, that's fantastic!'

'Aye.' But I couldn't stop wondering what the mortgage repayments might be.

I don't know what the speaker's topic was at the meeting that night for I spent the duration of the message contemplating the staggering implications of those seven loaded words. There was no doubt in my mind that God intended us to buy Hollybush Farm, for each time the Lord had spoken directly to me in my life His message had demanded personal action and it was no different this time. Our involvement had been implicit by the very revelation.

But where was the money coming from? I didn't own a bean. Even the farm we'd worked the past ten years didn't belong to me. With Dad's death the property had transferred into Mother's hands; it wouldn't become mine until she too passed on, and right now she was in the best of health. In fact she hadn't ailed a thing since the day the Lord had healed her in the hospital three years ago. We were thankful for that, of course . . . but where else could we find the money to buy a 200-acre farm?

One thing was certain: we were going to buy it. The Lord wonderfully confirmed this on our journey home that evening, and this time the revelation was Cynthia's. Once again it happened as we passed the entrance. As we motored by, something caught Cynthia's eye and as she looked back over her shoulder she suddenly caught her breath.

'What is it?' I asked.

Her eyes were wide with excitement, her head still turned toward the big five-bar gate. 'Oh my!' she breathed. 'The glory, Jim I saw the glory!'

Apparently as she had glanced back she'd seen an arc of softly glowing light over the gateway - an unmistakable phosphorescent presence.

'The glory . . .' she murmured again. 'The glory of the Lord!' It could have been nothing else. There were no street lamps, of course, and in all the years we had driven past that farm we'd never yet seen an outside light shining from the house. Besides, the farmhouse stood a good 60 feet from the road. Cynthia's light had hovered directly over the entrance gate. Now we both knew without a doubt.

Back home we said goodnight to our baby-sitter and took mugs of steaming cocoa through to the lounge, talking and wondering about the tiny piece of God's plan that He had revealed and confirmed to us so suddenly. And as we talked I felt all apprehension slipping away - removed, I'm sure, as the Spirit quickened the vision of a new work of God to our hearts. Now, instead, I knew an excitement, an expectancy . . . as though we were poised on the edge of some great adventure. But if God wanted Hollybush Farm for His glory, what were we supposed to do about it?

'Lord, we believe you're telling us to buy that farm, but we haven't a clue how to go about it. Please show us what to do.'

His answer, as so often, took me by surprise. This time the voice was a silent impression in my spirit.

Go and see Eric Bell.

My mind baulked at the idea. I knew Eric Bell by sight - he owned the farm across the way from Hollybush - but I'd never spoken to him in my life. What should I say?

Just tell him I sent you.

All at once I knew how Moses must have felt when God told him to speak to Pharaoh. To me, Eric Bell *was* Pharaoh. He was a rich and successful farmer, and I was . . . I was just a chicken.

Nevertheless, the impression persisted . . . and I knew I just had to trust the Lord.

I glanced at the mantelpiece clock. Just after ten. It wasn't too late to ring.

'Cynthia?'

She looked up as I got to my feet.

'Keep praying, love. I've got to make a call.'

'Who to?'

I was heading for the kitchen. 'Eric Bell.'

'Eric Bell? Whatever for?'

I turned in the doorway, forcing a smile. 'I don't know. You'd better ask the Lord.'

I made the appointment for nine the next morning and put down the receiver, my heart racing with trepidation. Or was it anticipation? Deep in my spirit I knew God was at work, and as I climbed into bed an hour or so later I was aware of a gathering excitement.

Next morning I rose to find encouraging confirmation in my *Daily Bread* Bible reading notes. The Scripture passage for the day was from Luke 12: the story of the rich farmer! Yes, God was in it - and as I left the house and headed across the yard toward the car there was a spring in my step. Yet I knew how much I was going to need the Lord's help and as I turned on the ignition I called out to Cynthia, standing in the doorway, 'Don't stop praying.'

Five minutes later, as the car crunched up the driveway into Leachfield Farm, I saw Mr Bell crossing the yard, a new-born lamb under each arm. He stopped and waited for me to leave the car, and as I got out I remembered Moses again - how he'd told the Lord he wasn't up to speaking to Pharaoh because of a speech impediment. I knew how he felt.

'G-good morning, Mr Bell.'

He offered his hand as best he could with the lamb tucked under his arm, and gave me a quizzical look. I'd not given anything away on the phone. 'Why have you come?'

I looked him in the eye. 'God sent me.'

I don't think anyone had ever said that to him before. Having almost dropped the lambs, he now clutched them with such a grip that I thought any minute they'd need a healing.

'What's it about?'

By this time I'd begun to see the plan. 'It's about Hollybush, across the way. Are you interested in buying it?'

He nodded. 'As a matter of fact, I am - but not all of it. Why? Are you interested?'

I smiled. Everything was going like clockwork.

'Aye. But, like you, only in part. The Lord's told me I'm to buy the house and the ninety acres on that side of the road, and you're to buy the acreage on this side here, adjoining your own land.'

He shook his head. 'I'm afraid that isn't possible. I've already made an arrangement with my neighbour along the road, Mr Scaling.'

My heart sank. I'd been so sure.

'I can't go into details,' he went on, 'but Mr Scaling's going to have the house plus a few acres, and I'm having the rest.'

'Oh, I see.' Where did I go wrong? 'Well, sorry to have troubled you . . .'

Dejected and confused, I drove back home and shared the bleak news with Cynthia. 'I must have misheard the Lord,' I told her. Or had I heard Him at all?

I went out to work with my head spinning. 'What's going on, Lord? Did I get it all wrong?'

But when I returned to the house at lunchtime there was a message. Cynthia couldn't hide her excitement. 'Eric Bell telephoned. He wants to meet you at one o'clock.'

Back I went, my heart racing. It must have been a simple misunderstanding.

'I've had a word with Mr Scaling,' Eric Bell told me, 'and he says if someone else is interested, he's really not bothered about the house. He was only going to speculate with it, anyway. And the bit of land he wants is on the boundary, where his farm meets mine. I can let him have that, all right.'

I nodded. 'And my proposal?'

'I've been thinking about that - in fact it would suit me very well. Come on inside and we can talk.'

We agreed that each of us would come up with a price for our own half of the property and that the total would be the maximum we would go to in the auction. But as I drove back to The Limes I swallowed hard. I had just committed myself to a substantial business deal - talking big figures as if they were pennies not pounds - and yet I didn't own much more than the shirt on my back. It just had to be the Lord, or I was in trouble.

'And, just as a matter of interest, Lord,' I said out loud as I turned the car into The Limes, 'how much *am* I supposed to pay?'

The answer came back with alarming swiftness. £34,000.

I swallowed again. In 1968 that was a small fortune.

Later that afternoon, with Cynthia and Joanna in the back seat, we drove up to Hollybush to see what we were buying. But not for a minute did we view the place with the critical eye of ordinary homebuyers. This was to be the Lord's house, and if He'd chosen us to live here we knew beyond a doubt we'd be happy. What better than to dwell in a house that God Himself had singled out. And so as we were shown around by Mrs Sowerby we barely took anything in. The one impression we did receive was the size of the place. All that space! What would we do with 15 rooms? Come to that, what had Mr and Mrs Sowerby done with them? Like us, they had only one child, a daughter, and she was now away at college. So few people in such a big house. Evidently it was something Mrs Sowerby was aware of.

'If you buy this place,' she said, 'it needs to be filled with people.'

She couldn't have known - and nor could we, at the time - but her words could almost have been prophecy.

Outside, as we wandered round the extensive gardens, pausing to let Joanna romp on the vast lawn, Cynthia looked up at the house - a once-proud house of red brick and white-painted Georgian windows - and she almost sighed.

'It's funny,' she said, 'but I've always thought this looked a sad sort of house. Now we know why - it just needs people.'

I laughed. 'Well, we've plenty of those. We'll soon brighten the place up with a weekly fellowship. Did you see that big room upstairs? I reckon we could get 60 or 70 people in there.'

Before we left I had a walk out over the land to test the soil, just as Dad and I had done down at The Limes. But this time I was assessing the land merely out of interest. There was no decision to be made, no wondering whether this soil was a good investment, for the decision and the investment were the Lord's. And even as I came back across the fields to where Cynthia was waiting in the car with Joanna, I seemed to hear that silent voice within.

You just be here, Jim, and I'll prosper you.

'Thank you, Lord. Just lead us on. Show us the next step.'

The next step seemed to be to line up the money. Where were we to get £34,000? This was Friday and the auction was the following Wednesday. Not much time.

That evening, at the Friday fellowship meeting, we shared with the group what the Lord had revealed to us and what we'd done about it so far. This caused quite an excited stir among our regulars and, encouragingly, some told us they'd felt a witness in their spirit as I'd been sharing the revelation with them. 'Yes,' they agreed, 'this is of the Lord.'

'But we need to pray about the money,' I reminded them. 'Right now we don't have a bean to bid with. I hope to see the bank manager on Monday morning, but it may be the Lord has other plans.'

He had. At least, the bank was to be only part of the provision. On Saturday morning I had a telephone call from our good friend Ernest Hutchinson.

'We've been praying about what you were sharing last night, Jim, and the Lord has spoken a clear word to us. "Lend what thou hast to thy brother." We've £8,000 invested. It's yours to borrow for as long as you need.'

'Why, Mr Hutchinson, I . . .'

'We don't want any thanks, Jim. We can see that the Lord's at work in this and we believe much blessing will come out of it. That'll be thanks enough.'

After I'd put the phone down I made a call of my own. I'd woken that morning with a name in my head. Kit Calvert. I knew

Mr Calvert well, of course, from our long and mutual association with the Wensleydale Evangelistic Crusade, but I somehow knew that on this occasion his name had come to mind not in connection with outreach but because of his wide experience as a businessman. Would he have some advice to give me? I finished dialling the number and then heard his familiar voice on the line . . .

An hour later I was sitting in Mr Calvert's lounge up at Hawes sharing with him the vision of a new work of God at Hollybush Farm, and asking him about borrowing money from one of the agricultural mortgage companies. This was a possibility that had already occurred to me, and Mr Calvert seemed the right man to comment on the wisdom of such a move.

He was not impressed with the idea. 'I'd steer well clear of that sort of involvement,' he told me. 'Stick to your bank and whatever you can borrow from your friends.'

Before I left Mr Calvert had proved his own friendship. He loaned me £6,000.

So, Monday morning found me sitting opposite my bank manager in Thirsk, outlining the Hollybush project and explaining that I had only £14,000. I'd be needing a loan of £20,000 - and that in a time of credit squeeze.

'That's all right,' came the unruffled reply. 'In fact I expect you'll be wanting a little more than twenty thousand, with legal fees and so on. I'll get the paperwork drawn up today.'

I walked out into the biting March winds, mentally reeling at how easy it had all been. But of course it had. When would I realise that when God is at work His children just sail through.

But borrowing money is relatively easy. It's paying it back that's the problem! Back home I told Cynthia that the first year's interest on the loan would be around £3,500. 'And then we've our own tax to pay, our tithes and offerings to give, our living expenses - and only then can we start paying back the actual capital.'

She set a mug of tea down beside me. 'Well, the Lord'll provide. He's never failed us yet. Look at George - sold up his farm, gave most of his money away, and been living by faith from that day to . . .'

'Hey, that's a thought,' I cut in. 'I'd forgotten all about that.'

'About what?'

'George's vision - remember?' I got up and went to the phone. George hadn't been at the meeting on Friday evening so as yet he would know nothing about Hollybush. I dialled his number up at Northallerton, where he'd moved to from Pickering the previous year. A moment or two later he came on the line.

'George, it's Jim. Do you still have that vision of me looking out over land?'

'Aye, I do. It's as clear as ever it was. Why?'

'Well, if I took you to a certain place do you think you'd be able to tell me if it fits what you saw?'

'Of course. Do you have a place in mind?'

'Most certainly. Do you know Hollybush Farm?'

I met George at the gateway just after three o'clock. Before we went in I quickly told him all that had happened in the past few days and then I called at the house to ask Mrs Sowerby if I could show a friend round outside. I thought I knew what George must have seen, and when I led him round to the rose garden at the back of the house I knew I was right.

'Hold it right there, Jim,' George called out as I walked the last few feet to the low wall that separated the gardens from the farmland. 'That's it! That's exactly the vision. Glory to God!'

I turned and gripped his shoulder. 'Bless you, George. I believe great things are going to happen here.'

'Amen to that!' Then he laughed suddenly. 'And to think you told me that if God wanted to prosper you he'd have to cause two blades of grass to grow where now there's one.'

I too had to laugh, but for no special reason. It was the joy of the Spirit welling up inside me. George was right - great things were afoot!

The morning of the auction arrived and there was much excitement in the house. It hardly seemed possible that within a few hours we'd be clinching the deal that would bring Hollybush into our possession. We'd had word that there would be other interested parties making a bid for the farm, including a brewery that wanted the house for one of its directors and an entertainments company that had designs on turning the property into a sophisticated night-club, but none of these worried me. God had said He wanted Hollybush for His glory, and He was going to have it.

Even so, a telephone call around noon came close to hitting the panic button.

'It's Mr Scaling,' Cynthia called to me from the back door.

Mr Scaling! Whatever could he want? I hurried from the barn, a sudden worry gnawing at my mind. What he had to say did nothing to dispel it.

'I want to meet you outside the hotel, half an hour before the auction. Is that all right?'

'Er - yes. Two-thirty, outside the Golden Lion. I'll be there, sir.'

I put down the receiver and felt a knotting in my stomach. 'He's changed his mind - I'll bet he's changed his mind. He wants to buy the house after all.'

At 2.15 I dropped Cynthia off at Mr and Mrs Hutchinson's home in Northallerton - the three of them to pray while I bid - and I drove on to the Golden Lion Hotel. All the way there the worry about Mr Scaling was snapping at my mind like a terrier at my heels. Why did he want to see me? What would he say to me? Come to that, what would he think of me? The previous day I'd had most of my teeth out and now had a thick scarf wrapped around my face to keep out the bitter cold. With that and my cap pulled down against the wind I looked more like a gangster than a businessman-farmer. He'd probably think I looked a right slippery customer and be more determined than ever to have that house.

But how wrong I was. Mr Scaling, I discovered, had been sent by the Lord. No, he wasn't interested in Hollybush, but he did want to see that Eric Bell and I got the place. He was older than both of us, more experienced in salesroom techniques, and determined to steer the auction of Hollybush Farm to a satisfactory conclusion.

In short, he was there to father us, and for that I was so thankful. If Dad had still been alive he would have been here with me today, but as that wasn't possible the Lord had sent along Mr Scaling with all the fatherly advice we could use.

Confidently, he ushered us into the inner sanctuary of the hotel ballroom - suitably transformed for the occasion - and marched us down toward the front. 'Buyers always sit in the second row,' he directed. Then: 'Jim, you sit there, then me, then Eric, and Nigel on the end.' Nigel was Mr Bell's son who presumably had come along for the fun.

Obediently, we did as we were told, and then in the pre-sale din Mr Scaling turned to me and said, 'Jim, you're bidding. But don't start till I tell you.'

My scarf was hanging round my neck now and I gave my mentor a toothless grin.

It was 3.15 before they got round to Hollybush. Together we listened to the auctioneer's glowing description of the house and land - the place God wanted for His glory - and then the bidding began.

Forty thousand. Forty-five. Fifty. Fifty-five thousand.

Shouldn't I be bidding? But the look on Mr Scaling's face told me he knew exactly what he was doing.

Sixty thousand. Sixty-one thousand.

A nudge in the ribs - and my hand shot up. Sixty-two thousand.

From over there - sixty-three.

Me – sixty-four.

Up went the bids, a thousand at a time, until I was bidding on the edge of my seat. Seventy thousand. Seventy-one.

I swallowed hard. The joint limit I'd agreed with Mr Bell was £72,000.

'Sold-over here for seventy-two thousand pounds.'

That was at 3.21. At exactly the same moment, in the front room of the Hutchinsons' home not a quarter of a mile away, Cynthia was leaping to her feet, rejoicing as a conviction suddenly sprang up within her spirit. 'He's bought it!' she cried. 'I saw the hammer go down and I heard Jim's name! He's bought it!'

And I had. Hollybush was the Lord's!

But why did He want it? For His glory, yes - but what was going to happen at Hollybush Farm to cause Him to be glorified? This remained a mystery to us throughout the spring and summer of that year, for while we had access to the house from the beginning of May we chose not to move in until we'd carried out various preparations. Floors had to be scrubbed, walls washed and papered, woodwork painted . . . And while we were at it we decided to have the old fireplaces removed from the bedrooms. It seemed sensible to get all this done before we actually settled in, but we'd never realised what a job we'd taken on. But for the willing help of so many good friends, plus the expert assistance of Cynthia's builder brother, Tony Biker, with the fireplaces, we would have been slogging away till Christmas. Even so, the house wasn't ready until late November.

We couldn't wait to get all this finished, of course, but perhaps even the waiting period was in the Lord's plan. Perhaps he was teaching us patience. Certainly that had been one of the themes in our so-helpful Daily Bread notes around the time of the sale. But we wouldn't have to wait until we'd moved in before we knew something of what was in the Lord's mind . . . and on the evening when the prophecy was given in our lounge at The Limes we'd never been so thankful for the gifts of the Spirit. Brian Smitherman was the Lord's mouthpiece that night.

' . . . and it shall be, saith the Lord, that this place shall be called a place of miracles - Miracle Valley - for here will I perform great and wondrous things, the likes of which you have never seen before. A place of miracles it shall be, for even as the sick and suf-

fering come and step upon its holy ground they shall receive healing from the Lord. Yes, this place shall be known as Miracle Valley - a place where the Lord God of heaven and earth abides, and where His glory shines for all to see.'

Miracle Valley! What a prospect! What a promise! And what rejoicing that word from the Lord caused that evening. Now we were more impatient than ever to get into Hollybush. And who could blame us? God was going to do mighty things in our midst and they couldn't begin soon enough.

But we didn't have to wait before dedicating the place to the Lord. In fact we did so on the very first Friday that the property became ours. About 20 rejoicing Christians met with us at Hollybush that night, and together we marched around the outside of the house, singing praises and confirming the territory as the Lord's. Then we moved inside, claiming each room for God as we passed through the house, and finally ending with a session of prayer and praise in the kitchen.

We prayed again in that kitchen, just Cynthia and myself, the evening of the day we finally brought our furniture in. Cynthia sat with three-year-old Joanna on her knee while I perched on one of the many tea-chests, committing our new home to the Lord, commending our little family to His keeping, and thanking Him for all the good things we could look forward to here at Hollybush. My, what blessing there was to come.

The thought was still with me later that night as I pulled on my pyjamas up in our room. Cynthia was already asleep, having come up earlier, and so I changed in the dark - or rather, by the moonlight flooding in through the big sash-cord window. I hadn't noticed till then just how bright the moon was that night, and peering outside I realised I could see way into the distance.

So this was Miracle Valley, this land now silver beneath the lantern-moon. It felt good. And standing there, scanning the Hollybush horizon, I was somehow aware of a sense of destiny, as though we'd been moving toward this place not merely since the night when God had spoken earlier in the year, but since long, long before that, as though so many things in our lives had been but stepping stones.

The phrase stuck in my mind. Stepping stones . . . All at once, springing from somewhere in the back of my mind, came half-forgotten ponderings about miracles. Miracles of healing we'd seen down the years . . . The miracle of the potato crop . . . Of course! I'd been so sure there was a deeper purpose behind those wonderful acts of God; so sure they wouldn't remain isolated miracles, but in some strange way prove to be an investment for the future; that through them the Lord was telling us something, preparing us . . .

And now I knew. All these years we'd been on our way to Hollybush Farm . . . to Miracle Valley. I could barely wait for next Friday!

7/Naturally supernatural

The solid old house was almost vibrating with expectancy that first fellowship night. God Himself, through prophecy, had promised to do mighty things here at Hollybush and over the years we'd learned that the one thing He cannot do is fail. As the people arrived and we ushered them through the kitchen and up the stairs we saw excitement on almost every face. What wonders would the Lord perform in our midst this night?

The way into God's miracle-working presence that first evening was as it had always been, through the doorway of thanksgiving and praise. No one in our group of 30-odd needed coaxing to rejoice in the Lord's goodness and we sang ourselves hoarse. But as we settled to prayer we found our thankfulness gradually giving way to a much deeper emotion - our unworthiness. And as the Holy Spirit moved upon us we realised afresh something of the holiness of the God we loved. Tears were quick to flow, and before we knew it a sobbing brokenness had totally transformed the spirit of our gathering. We had cried together before, of course, but this was something new, and something that was to characterise many of the meetings in coming weeks. It was as though God was laying a foundation for the work He had planned for Hollybush, and that foundation was to be bedded in the tears of a broken spirit and contrite heart.

But if weeping was necessary before God would manifest Himself, then weep we would. It was worth every tear when, all at once, we became aware that the Spirit was among us. And when George stood up to teach us from the Word - we'd asked him to come and pastor the Friday meetings - it was as though the Lord Himself was speaking, such was the anointing of God in the room.

When it came to sharing personal needs no one hesitated. God was there with us and we each one knew that if we asked for His touch He would not pass us by. Besides, He Himself had called this place Miracle Valley . . .

'I'd like prayer for my knee,' said Mrs Hutchinson. 'It's been playing me up no end this week.' She reminded us that years ago she'd fallen and broken her knee-cap and had suffered discomfort ever since. The pain had worsened recently because of the many hours she had spent scrubbing floors here in Hollybush House.

'Right, let's gather round sister Hutchinson,' George directed, but we needed no encouragement to pray with this dear lady; even before we laid hands on her and asked the Lord to touch her knee we knew she would be healed. What we didn't expect was the bonus healing that was to come with it.

For some years Mrs Hutchinson had been deaf in her left ear - so deaf in fact that even in the dead of night, if she was lying on her right side, she couldn't hear the ticking of the alarm clock. But that night God had breathed healing into her whole body . . . and she couldn't get to sleep. After an hour of tossing and turning she nudged her husband.

'It's no good, Ern, I can't get a wink of sleep with that clock ticking away.'

And then she realised - God had healed her hearing, too. Mr Hutchinson put the clock outside the room and then they went to sleep, rejoicing together.

A couple of weeks later Mrs Hutchinson brought Janie Dixon, her elderly cousin, to the meeting. Janie had been suffering with phlebitis in her leg and Mrs Hutchinson had told her how the Lord had healed her knee and ear. 'He'll heal that leg of yours, too, if you'll ask Him.'

Janie didn't need any prompting. She was a retired missionary who had seen the power of God displayed in the lives of countless people during her years in India and she knew only too well that God was still in the healing business. But through Janie we were to be reminded that someone else was still active, too.

'In the name of Jesus, receive your healing,' we told Janie as we prayed with her that evening, and though the pain persisted we encouraged her to believe that God had touched her.

Next morning the pain seemed worse and Janie told Mrs Hutchinson: 'I'm sorry, dear, but my leg hurts more than ever today. Would you mind ringing your doctor for me?'

But after Mrs Hutchinson had phoned her GP she also phoned me. No sooner had she begun describing the persistent pain than I was aware of the real cause of the problem. I felt anger rising within me - anger that Satan was robbing God of His glory.

'Now look, sister, get back in that bedroom and lay hands on that leg and rebuke the sickness in the name of Jesus. That phlebitis has already gone - it's just a trick of the enemy.'

The doctor called at eleven o'clock and confirmed what we already knew. As he unwound the bandage Janie's eyes grew wider by the second. Her leg - her so-painfully inflamed leg - was normal.

'You may have had phlebitis there at some time, Miss Dixon,' the doctor informed her, 'but there's certainly no sign of such a thing now. That's a perfectly healthy leg.'

A few weeks later the miracle we'd all been waiting for happened. That 'Miracle Valley' prophecy had assured us that such would be the presence of God here at Hollybush that as the sick stepped on to the ground surrounding the house they would be healed. And if God had said it, it would come to pass.

'There's a lady downstairs in a wheelchair,' we were told as the Friday meeting got underway, and a group of us went down to pray with her. Our faith to see miracles was growing week by week and we no longer waited for someone to request prayer before asking God to heal them. They were going to get healed, ready or not!

We found her outside the back door, being helped from a car into her wheelchair. Already her feet had touched holy ground.

'In the name of Jesus . . .'

At first she couldn't believe that it had really happened and looked around, half smiling, half wary of believing that God had actually touched her. Could it be true, after all these years of severe arthritis?

'You can get out of that wheelchair, sister - you won't be needing that again!'

She almost leapt into the meeting room upstairs, her eyes dancing, her voice trembling with excitement. 'He - He healed me!' she gasped. 'Out there, just now - He healed me!'

We nearly lifted the roof with our rejoicing that night. In fact we had the tiles jumping just about every week from then on because by now we'd realised that the miracles we'd seen were not merely isolated demonstrations of God's love and power but evidence of a growing, ongoing work of the Holy Spirit. The prophecy, had anyone ever doubted, was for real and its fulfilment was being gloriously enacted before us week after week. Barely a Friday passed without some miracle of healing thrilling us all. One week it would be a woman healed of breast cancer, the next a partially paralysed boy being liberated to full mobility. The following Friday, a man healed of circulation problems or a woman of migraines; the next, God would deal with varicose veins, club feet, kidney disorders . . . Hollybush Farm had indeed become Miracle Valley.

Not that there was anything special about the place. It was only the Lord Himself who was special and it was important that we never lost sight of that fact because Cynthia and I were continuing to visit churches and fellowships outside the immediate area and we needed to know that the God of Hollybush was the God of everywhere: that He could touch lives in any location, any situation. Thus, when opportunities to take meetings came our way, we were able with confidence to tell the congregation that our God was a God of miracles. Sometimes this resulted in us laying hands on folk and praying with them; at other times we wouldn't know whom God was healing. That's how it was when we were up at Exelby, taking the Sunday school anniversary services at the local Methodist Chapel.

'There's someone here with a bad back,' I told my hearers, speaking out a word of knowledge God had dropped into my spirit just a moment earlier. 'If you'll reach out to Him in faith He'll heal your weakness right now.'

That word, it turned out, had been for Arthur Bennison, a young man who had been meeting with us almost since our Friday meetings had begun back at The Limes. He had come along to the service to support me, never dreaming that it would be here, rather than at Hollybush, that God would speak directly to him and heal him.

Apparently Arthur's back had been bad for several years. A farming man like myself, he'd damaged his spine while lifting milk-churns. For a while he had been left bent almost double, but though that initial damage seemed to clear up he continued to experience great pain. But no longer.

That evening Arthur reached out in faith . . . and God did a miracle for him. From that moment on his back was totally healed.

Arthur was delighted, of course, but he wasn't unaccustomed to his God performing miracles for him. He had often quipped that, being in a constant state of financial embarrassment, it was always a miracle that he ever had the petrol to drive the 50-odd miles to and from the fellowship each week. It was only later that I realised he wasn't joking. (You could never tell with Arthur for he always had a smile on his face!)

'It were no joke,' he told me. 'I was working for my dad up at Bilsdale and he wasn't able to pay any wages, only a bit of pocket money now and then. Rarely did I have any cash to put petrol in the van.'

It was a real dilemma for Arthur and his equally penniless pal, John Mattison, who worked on a neighbouring farm.

'But we were determined to get to the meetings and so we told the Lord about it. That was when he sent the rabbits.'

When I heard this I thought I was in for some of Arthur's leg-pulling, but apparently he'd never been more serious. Rabbits were fetching five shillings a pair, and in 1968 five shillings' worth of petrol would take you a long way.

'We first saw them on our way home from the meeting one Friday night,' Arthur told me. 'They were sitting there in the road, waiting for us, picked out in the beam of the headlights. If they started to move off all I had to do was flash the lights on and off a few times and they'd freeze right where they were, sitting up on their hind legs, their heads at just the right level to take a clout from the front axle. It was quick and it was clean - the butcher didn't want them if the skin was broken - and one night we bagged seven. Almost every week we got one or two - always enough for our petrol the following week.'

But perhaps the real miracle was that these rabbits appeared each Friday night during a time when mixamatosis had all but wiped out the rabbit population in this part of Yorkshire. Maybe they were a Godsend in more ways than one.

Arthur and John's determination to be there at those Friday meetings reflected the excitement each one of us felt. In fact come Friday lunchtime and we just couldn't wait. Whatever would the Lord do tonight?

But it wasn't just the miracles that had gripped us, for miracles on their own, however wonderful, quickly fade in significance. No, the real draw of those meetings was the one who was causing the miracles to happen - the Lord Himself. And, as we discovered, there was always a freshness about being in His company. Never would two meetings be exactly alike, and quite often the manner in which the Lord chose to manifest Himself would vary from week to week too.

Some called it 'the power of God', some called it 'the glory', but almost every week we were aware of its presence. To some it appeared as a fine mist descending upon us, while others saw it as a bright light, much like the glow Cynthia had seen over the farm gateway that night the Lord had told us He wanted the place for His glory. This time, though, the brightness came not as an arc of light but as an enveloping cloud. One of our regulars found this so dazzling she could barely open her eyes in the meetings; another said he couldn't begin to pray until he felt this anointing fall upon us.

Perhaps it was only natural to expect the Spirit to *descend* - after all, that's how the first Christians experienced their baptism with fire - but now and then the Lord would take us by surprise and move from another direction. Once it happened when I wasn't even aware of it. I was standing in front of the fireplace sharing a few thoughts from the Word when I noticed Mrs Lamb shifting in her seat, moving from side to side as though trying to see past me. The fire wasn't alight so she couldn't have been worried about that.

'What caught your eye?' I asked her later on that evening.

'Well, at first I thought you were on fire,' she laughed. 'I could see something like flames rising up from behind you and wondered what on earth was happening. Then I realised - it was the fire of the Spirit!'

'Glory!' I said, beaming at her. 'No wonder I felt so good preaching that word.'

At other times the Lord's presence had quite the opposite effect and someone praying or ministering would have to abandon their words. In fact many times an invited speaker would come to share testimony or teaching with us, only to find himself so humbled by the Lord's presence that he couldn't get through his message. Sometimes he wouldn't even be able to begin. Walter Gash was one such man. He'd come up from York to share some Bible teaching with us but could barely open his mouth.

'I'm sorry, folks,' he told us, 'but I'm not worthy to minister here.' And he sat down again.

We had a great deal to learn about the presence of the Spirit. In no way was He predictable and we had to be prepared for Him to move upon us in the way that pleased Him at any moment. Quite often He fell upon us in such overwhelming power that some would pass out, 'slain in the Spirit'. We had seen this happen in earlier meetings down at The Limes, but never had we experienced it happening so often and to so many. One evening when we had a group from Scarborough visiting us the Spirit came upon about a dozen of our number, many from the Scarborough group, and they remained laid out for so long that we were still carrying them to their cars at midnight.

Some people were uneasy about this strange phenomenon. What was going on? They'd never been in a meeting where people started fainting. But we were able to put their minds at rest; everything was in order - it always is when the Spirit's in control - and there was no harm done. We couldn't explain exactly what was happening, and we couldn't point to any examples of the same thing taking place in the Scriptures, but two things we did know for sure. When the Spirit fell upon someone in this way they never got hurt, however awkwardly they fell; and being slain in the Spirit always did a person good: they got up feeling really blessed. Another discovery we made was that when people were slain in the Spirit it was best to leave them where they lay. If it became necessary to move them, for the sake of getting them home, we had to be very careful how we handled them; to be gentle was essential. Any manhandling seemed to grieve the Spirit within them.

Another expression of the Spirit which caused some consternation was the laughter. This too fell upon us suddenly. We would be sitting having a time of prayer when some would feel a great joy welling up inside them. At first they would chuckle, then laugh, and eventually hoot with joy as they collapsed to the floor. Frequently they would rock from side to side or roll about on the carpet, helpless. A stranger might have thought them drunk - and indeed that's what they were: drunk in the Spirit.

It had to be in the Spirit, of course, for when someone was moved in this way they would laugh so hard and so long that to do so in the natural would strain the heart. We were aware of this the first time Mrs Hutchinson laughed in the Spirit. She was not a young person and when she rolled off her chair and lay rocking with hearty laughter at our feet we felt certain she would burst something; in fact to laugh like that and to keep it up would almost certainly be fatal outside of the Spirit. But, once again, when it's the Lord there's no harm done; on the contrary, anyone who laughs in the Spirit feels great afterwards - and so does everyone else in the room: it's a real spiritual tonic.

There can be a price to pay, however, as Tommy Spence found out the first time this wonderful laughter fell upon him in our kitchen. One Friday, shortly before the meeting was due to begin, a few of us were gathered round the big pine table in prayer when in walked Tommy and Jean. Immediately, the Spirit fell upon Tommy and within seconds he had tears of joy streaming down his face. Roaring with laughter he fell back into the corner of the room by the door and stood there rocking on his heels until, overwhelmed, he slid down the wall and ended up sitting in our coal bucket! Apparently on his way to Hollybush that evening he'd been asking the Lord for a new touch of the Spirit. 'But I got more than I bargained for,' he said afterwards, grinning. That was the first of many times that Tommy was to laugh in the Spirit, but ever after he was careful where he sat down!

We were to learn about another emotion of the Spirit, too. For years I'd puzzled over what the Bible described as the 'groaning of the Spirit', but not until the Hollybush meetings got underway did I discover what that meant. The first time we experienced it was when Ian Brown came to us. I met Ian when he called at the house one afternoon with a car full of farming supplies and a sheaf of papers under his arm.

'I'd like to introduce you to our range of oils,' he told me, pressing a leaflet into my hand.

'That's fine,' I said, 'before you try to sell me any of your goods I'd like to tell you about something you can have for free.' And I told him about the Lord - how He loved Ian and had died for him on the cross. I didn't make a practice of buttonholing everyone who came to the door, but on this day I felt the Spirit stirring me to be direct with this young man. I sensed that God had His hand on him, and this was confirmed to me when we moved on to talk about where Ian was living.

'My wife and I have a house up at Sunderland, but at present I'm in digs down here because of the job. We're hoping to move soon, but at present we're having difficulty selling the other house.'

'You go home at weekends?' I enquired - and as he nodded his reply I felt a word of knowledge being quickened in my spirit. 'Well, you'll be moving soon.'

'I hope so.'

'You will. In fact when you go home this weekend you'll find that your house is sold.'

He stared at me for a moment. 'Can I interest you in any of these oils?'

We did a bit of business and then I told him about the Friday meetings. 'We'd love to see you - you and your wife. Any time.'

As he drove away I felt certain we'd be seeing Ian Brown again, and not just to talk farming. He knew it too, come the weekend, for the word of knowledge I'd spoken to him was fulfilled on the Friday evening: by the time he got home his house was sold. That set him thinking. But it was his wife, Margaret, who turned up for the next meeting and when we discovered that she was a Christian and had been praying for Ian's salvation for years we began to see how the Lord's plan was being worked out.

Yet there was a hitch. Margaret's experience as a Christian was much as my own had been before I was filled with the Spirit. She wasn't used to seeing Christians really enjoying their worship. And then there were tongues, prophecy, people passing out in the Spirit . . . Half way through the evening she walked out.

'You're all crackers,' she told Cynthia, who caught up with her at the back door.

'Well, it may not be what you're used to . . . '

Eventually Cynthia managed to pacify her but Margaret wasn't going to come back into the meeting. And it was doubtful that we'd ever see her again.

But we prayed, and within a few weeks Margaret and Ian turned up together. They came to us on and off over the next few weeks and then one evening after they'd moved down to Northallerton Ian came on his own. This was an encouraging sign and during the meeting, which included a challenging appeal to accept Christ as Saviour and Lord, many of us were quietly praying that Ian would respond. At the same time some of the group were experiencing what they later described as a groaning within their spirit; a longing of the Holy Spirit that those to whom the Lord was speaking that night should welcome Christ in. So intense was this groaning that those who felt it were sure that someone - probably Ian - would commit their life to the Lord before the meeting was over. But it didn't happen, and when the meeting broke up we were left wondering why so many had experienced such powerful groanings within them. But then, at one o'clock in the morning, the telephone jarred us out of our sleep and I went downstairs to hear Margaret's voice on the other end of the line.

'I'm sorry to ring you, Jim, but it's Ian - he's sitting here in a cold sweat and can hardly get his breath. I've had the doctor in but he says there's nothing wrong with him.'

'You mean there's nothing wrong with him *physically*.'

She agreed. 'I think it's because he's fighting the Lord.'

'All right. I'll come straight over.'

Twenty minutes later I was standing in their lounge up at Northallerton, agreeing with Margaret's diagnosis. Ian was afflicted with a dose of good old fashioned conviction. No wonder the Spirit had been groaning that night - Ian must have been putting up a terrific battle against the Lord to have got into this state. And clearly the Spirit wasn't going to give up. I had no choice but to tell the young salesman straight.

'The Lord's seeking entry into your heart and life, Ian, and you're resisting. You know the choice you should make but you won't give in.'

He looked up at me with desperate, haunted eyes as he struggled for air.

'You've nothing to fear,' I went on. 'The Lord loves you and wants only the best for you. If you'll say yes to Jesus you'll be shot of all this discomfort, and you'll get blessed into the bargain. Why fight Him?'

Happily, Ian surrendered all to the Lord that night and I left him and Margaret with their arms around each other. But best of all they both now embraced the Lord.

Many young people were to come to Christ during those first months at Hollybush, and always by the same method: word of mouth. It was when Christians began to 'gossip the Gospel' that their friends and relatives began to sit up and take notice. And regardless of their motive for coming to the meetings - curiosity; to please the one who had asked them; or plain, downright need - almost every person who came to the meetings ended up entering into the joy of a relationship with the living God.

But it wasn't all rejoicing. The Friday meetings had not been going long before we began to learn about another, more ugly aspect of life in the Spirit.

I had known for a good many years that Christians, by definition, are engaged in a spiritual battle, but that had always been a rather vague term to me. I realised that Satan was my enemy and that I was to fight against him, but not until Christine arrived on our doorstep did I appreciate that from time to time the battle has to be fought at close quarters.

It began at about five o'clock one Saturday evening when two friends, Terry and Shirley Heslop, called at the house along with this young girl. Terry and Shirley had a guest house up at Ilkley and Christine had been working for them. She'd recently left school and was helping out at the guest house to earn a bit of cash before going on to study at university.

Three weeks earlier the girl had become a Christian, but rather than experiencing greater peace of mind she had become tormented, suffering from terrifying nightmares. She certainly looked in bad shape; cowed and tense. Terry had no doubts about the cause.

'She's possessed, Jim,' he told me privately while the women set to preparing some tea. 'She needs deliverance.'

'What, from evil spirits?' I replied. 'I don't know much about that sort of thing. What do you suggest we do?'

'I don't know, but we've got to help her - the poor kid can't sleep at night, and it's getting worse.'

One good thing about being green is that you have to trust the Master, and that's what we did. We spoke with Christine for a little while and assured her that we wanted to help and that the Lord was going to set her free. Exactly how we didn't know, but that didn't seem to matter. All we knew for sure was that Satan had no right to trespass on God's property, and that if we asked in faith God would show us what to do.

'Lord, we need your help,' I began as we gathered round the kitchen table.

Read the Scriptures, came the unspoken reply.

Well, where should we begin? For no special reason I turned to John's Gospel and began reading about Jesus. Barely three verses had passed my lips when suddenly Christine shot up out of her seat, threw her arms straight up in the air, then crashed face-down on the table, trembling.

Oh, Lord! What now?

Lay hands on her and pray.

So we did. 'Lord, set her free! Set her free!'

Within two minutes it was all over. Confronted by the name of Jesus - the name at which every knee shall bow - the demons fled. The trembling ceased, a smile replaced the torment, and Christine became relaxed and at ease. Her eyes, too, were different - as though a child of God rather than a foul spirit was looking out at us. And of course that was exactly the change that had taken place.

But how had the spirit entered in the first place? What had opened the door? We had no trouble pinning down the answer to that one; Christine had known all along.

'We used to play with a ouija board at school,' she confessed. 'It seemed like a bit of fun at the time. But now . . .'

It had never occurred to me that for Spirit-filled Christians spiritual warfare would occasionally entail confronting evil spirits, but as Cynthia and I talked about it we began to realise that such a thing was inevitable.

'I suppose it stands to reason,' I said. 'If you get filled with the Spirit you enter a new dimension of spiritual living. I guess just as we're bound to be more aware of what the Spirit's doing, so we'll be more conscious of what the devil's up to.'

Cynthia agreed. 'But it's not the sort of thing I'd want to do very often, casting out demons and such.'

'Aye. But I'll tell you one thing: I'll never be intimidated by the devil again. I used to be a bit nervous of the powers of darkness and all that stuff, but after witnessing those demons fleeing at the name of Jesus I'll never give 'em an inch from now on. We've got the victory over Satan and he knows it.'

This was a useful tool, this ministry of deliverance. As Cynthia had said, it wasn't something anyone would want to rush into, but its value seemed enormous. If Terry hadn't been aware that demons were the cause of Christine's problem it might have been months or even years before she'd been set free. Who knows, she might even have ended up in a mental hospital. Come to that, how many people were in institutions right now because of evil spirits? People who weren't mentally ill at all, but simply afflicted by the enemy of our souls.

This raised another question. How many people had we counselled over the years whose deep-seated problems could have been dealt with swiftly and decisively by deliverance? Obviously it would be quite wrong to start blaming every person's problem on demon possession or oppression, but at the same time we had to admit that there had been those whom we'd never really been able to help. Hours of counselling and prayer had failed to ease the situation. Could those people have been helped by simple deliverance? I began to look into what the Bible had to say about the subject and came up with some positive conclusions.

'Funny how I'd not noticed these things before,' I told Cynthia as we tackled the washing up after dinner one evening. 'The Lord Himself told us to cast out demons in the same breath as He told us to preach the Gospel and heal the sick. It's there in Mark 16 - among the last instructions He gave to the disciples before He ascended to heaven. Beats me why the church has ignored it for so long.'

She nodded. 'Jesus didn't hesitate.' Aye, that's another thing. The Lord always distinguished according to the need. If someone needed healing he healed them; if they had a demon he cast it out. For too long we've thought that every affliction can be dealt with by prayer. But you can't pray out a demon; you have to *cast* it out and no messing. It isn't a question of faith but of authority.'

'But we can't always be sure what's needed,' Cynthia reasoned.

'The devil's very crafty; I'm sure he's quite capable of fooling us. How can we know when deliverance is necessary?'

It was a good question and one that sent me back to my Bible. Surely God wouldn't leave us in the dark about such a thing? How *could* we know when evil spirits were about?

I found the answer in a passage that I'd read many times since being filled with the Spirit - 1 Corinthians 12. It was a passage that listed the gifts of the Spirit - a list we'd referred to many times in our meetings - and yet somehow I'd always overlooked the gift that was now jumping off the page at me. There it was in verse 10: 'the working of miracles . . . prophecy . . . discerning of spirits . . . ' Of course! I'd never understood that phrase before - hence I'd ignored it - but now it made so much sense. Through a particular spiritual gift God had made provision for his Spirit-filled people to discern when evil spirits were operating.

But how to get that discernment? I believed and taught that the distributing of the gifts was at the Spirit's discretion; that He gave them as He saw fit. Did that mean we could only *hope* that He would bestow upon us the gifts we felt we could profitably use? It was then another verse came to my rescue, a verse from the same chapter: 'Covet earnestly the best gifts.' Maybe we did have a choice. There was certainly one way to find out. So I asked.

Perhaps if I'd known what it would entail I might have thought again. I certainly wanted to be able to help anyone who needed to be freed from demonic bondage, but I wasn't ready for the way in which the gift would function within me. I made the discovery in the most unlikely of places - a fish and chip shop in nearby Thirsk. I was travelling home from a meeting late one evening and stopped off in the town for a take-away supper. As always the place was crowded and as I took my position in the queue I suddenly became aware of what felt like invisible arrows bombarding me. This, I discovered, was the way in which the discerning of spirits was to operate within me: whenever I came within a few yards of someone or something to which demons clung, I would feel the vibrations.

A little surprised, I looked across to where the queue swung round towards the counter and where the arrows seemed to be coming from. Within seconds I had identified the problem. Opposite me was a middle-aged woman in a thick woollen overcoat and with a brown paper package under her arm. I could not have approached her without the boldness the Spirit had given me.

'Excuse me,' I said, stepping across to face the woman, 'but you've got a ouija board in that packet, haven't you?'

She glared at me. 'How do you know that?'

'Because I'm a Christian and the Lord has revealed to me that you've something evil there.'

She laughed shortly. 'Evil, indeed! I've just been down my daughter's and we've been playing all evening. There's nothing evil about ouija.'

'I'm sorry, but that game's of the devil and you'd do well to burn it. Otherwise you'll be inviting trouble.'

She glared at me again and turned away. I suppose she thought me some sort of crank, but there was no use my denying the gift God had given me at my own request. Whatever the circumstances, if the gift was activated I would have to act upon it. In the coming months and years I would have much cause to.

Discerning of spirits was one thing, of course; seeing them was something else. I had no desire to come eyeball to eyeball with a demon, which apparently some people had done, and I hoped that God would keep all my encounters with the enemy in the spiritual realm.

Angels, though, were another matter. There would certainly be nothing unnerving about the appearance of a being who dwelt in the presence of the Father, and knowing how powerfully the Spirit had manifested that presence in our meetings it wouldn't have surprised any one of us to find angels in our midst. But when the first one came only Cynthia was permitted to see it.

It was almost 10.30. George had brought his message to a close and we were just enjoying the Lord together, everyone worshipping in his own way. For some, like Cynthia, this meant tears, but when eventually the meeting was over Cynthia's tears just would not stop. She was excited about something; something that apparently only she had experienced.

'Didn't you see it?' she gasped, when at last she'd found her voice.

'See what?'

Her eyes were dancing like those of a delighted child. 'The angel! Oh my, what a sight!'

She told us it had come from behind George where he stood in the recess of the bay window and slowly walked across the room, straight towards her. It had been very tall, around seven or eight feet, stood firmly on the floor, and appeared to be solid, just like a human being.

'And beautiful? Why, I never saw such a beautiful thing. And the wings! Spread out they were, fully extended, right across the room.'

We listened in amazement. 'But - but what did it *do*?'

'Well, it just walked towards me,' she said, 'looking right at me, and then stopped and brought its wings round, folding them across its chest. Then it closed its eyes and inclined its head as though bowing; a sort of greeting or salute.'

By now we were almost as excited as Cynthia. But why had she alone seen this wonderful being? We agreed that the purpose of its appearance must have been a personal visitation - and that had staggering implications. But had she actually seen it? Did an angel really enter our meeting room or had Cynthia merely seen a vision in the Spirit?

'Oh, it were here, all right,' Mr Hutchinson confirmed. 'I heard the rustling of its garment, clear as anything.' Others testified to the same experience.

'And its fragrance!' added Mrs Hutchinson. 'Did anyone else

smell it? Like the loveliest flowers.' And even as she was speaking the truth dawned on her. 'Why, of course! The Rose of Sharon! The Lily of the Valley!'

These were among the names the Bible attributed to Jesus. We stared at one another, wide-eyed.

'Do you mean we had the angel of the Lord here in this room?' someone asked.

We had a job getting to sleep that night. Whatever would God do next? It was just too exciting for words. What a place God had brought us into. The place of healings, of power, of authority over demons, of visiting angels . . . and there was so much more to come. A week or two later the Lord spoke to us through another startling word of prophecy:

'I will bring people here from the north, south, east and west to minister to you and to be ministered to. You will be a lighthouse set on a hill, and people shall come and be blessed of me, and return to their respective places of abode and worship to share what they have received.'

No one could contain their excitement that night. How powerfully and wonderfully God was at work, and what a promising future lay ahead of us. People coming from every direction to minister to us and to be ministered to. And who knew what else? It seemed absolutely anything was possible here in this place; there was just no end to what the Lord might do. Glory! We were really flowing in the Spirit and nothing could stop us or hold us back.

But if only we'd known.

8/Mountains and valleys

With so much happening on Friday nights and through the week as people dropped into the house for prayer or fellowship it would have been quite easy to forget that we had two farms to run. And at times, when George came down to join Cynthia in praying over prayer requests that had arrived in the morning's post, I had a struggle to tear myself away from the kitchen table and to get on with the chores. But unlike some businesses farms have to be worked on a steady rota. It's no use allowing jobs to pile up because the seasons won't wait for us; we have to keep pace or lose out. That was doubly true now that we had the Hollybush acreage to tend. But if ever I needed extra incentive I only had to remember the loans which had made it possible for us to buy the place. My reckoning was that it would take 25 years to clear the debts, and that was provided we worked the farm to its full potential.

I'd decided that we would have a mixed crop more or less the same as at The Limes, and having had access to the land since March we had already harvested our first crop of spring barley and sugar-beet and were now busy lifting potatoes and sowing winter wheat. In addition there was a good deal of clearing up to do and long stretches of old hedging to rip out and replace with wire fencing. Many of the farm buildings were in poor condition and would need renovating or replacing, but as with The Limes this would have to wait. Besides, at present I didn't need to concern myself with the buildings; many of them I'd rented out to Eric Bell. He said he could make use of them as an overflow facility to his own buildings and so we agreed that he should have them for a period of ten years.

There was one building we were to make use of, however, come the spring. The old granary building, though run-down and of little use even to Eric Bell, had potential as a meeting place for the occasional barn rally.

'We could have a rally on a Saturday night, once a month,' I suggested to the group one Friday. 'All we need do is give it a good sweep out and bring in a few chairs. It'd be ideal.' We didn't advertise. All we did was pray and put a hand-painted notice out at the gate: 'Barn Rally here tonight.' Come eight o'clock the place was packed with young people, and as our guest speaker, evangelist Roger Teele, got into his message we prayed for the Spirit to apply the Gospel to those young hearts, believing that, once again, the Lord would not disappoint us.

Among those the Spirit touched was a soldier over from Catterick army camp. After Roger had given the appeal, George and I went with this lad to one of the wagon-sheds where we counselled him and led him through to a personal commitment to Christ. He was one of several who gave their lives to the Lord that night.

But the Spirit's work was not finished. As we climbed the last of the stone steps to the granary and headed through the door George came to a halt and raised a hand, signalling for silence. The rally was over and people were up out of their seats, 50 voices going all at once.

But even before George had everyone's attention his powerful voice was booming out above all others in prophecy. *'Stand still and behold the power of the Lord your God . . .'*

He spoke for less than a minute, but when he opened his eyes barely three out of the 50 young people remained standing. None of us had seen anything like it. Almost simultaneously more than 40 young people had been slain in the Spirit.

That was around 10.30. At midnight we were still carrying them out to their cars, their clothes dusty from the granary floor and their spirits blessed in the Lord.

The following month, in our second barn rally, the power of God was manifested again, but this time it was confined to nine youngsters sitting in the first two rows. No sooner had the speaker finished and sat down than the Spirit fell . . . and these young people toppled like cards.

We learned afterwards that they were from Lancaster and had been returning home after spending the week at the Filey Christian Holiday Centre. Passing by, they saw our sign and decided to stop off for the meeting. They had no idea they'd get so blessed.

Unfortunately their parents took a slightly different view. Not because they were so late home or because their clothes carried our granary dust, but because those same young people were slain in the Spirit again the very next evening as they met after church for a house fellowship. On Monday morning I had a very irate father roaring down the phone at me. What was going on? What was this strange religious trick we'd taught these young people? Who were we, anyway? Didn't we know better than to encourage young Christians to go falling about all over the place?

I tried to explain that we had no control over what the Holy Spirit chose to do in the lives of His own people, but that didn't seem to satisfy my fire-breathing caller. He thought it impertinent to blame the Spirit for something which, quite clearly, we had engineered.

I told him the best I could do was to meet with the concerned parents and try to put their minds at rest. 'Would Thursday evening be any good?'

It was with some trepidation that I made the 80-mile journey that evening. Explaining the ways of the Spirit was sometimes difficult enough to a group of *reserved* Christians, but when those who wanted answers were openly hostile . . .

We met in the home of Mr David Gardiner, in the same room in which those nine young people had passed out in the Spirit the previous Sunday. Two other fathers were there, Mr Bill France and Mr Tom Parker, along with their sons and one or two of the other youngsters. Mr Gardiner, the man who had given me the telephonic blasting, acted as spokesman.

'This whole business is most disturbing,' he told me. 'It completely ruined our Sunday evening meeting. One minute these young people were being handed cups of coffee, the next they began slithering off their chairs on to the floor.'

'Well, I'm sorry if . . .'

'I called our minister immediately and he raced round here and we spent the next two hours trying to snap the lads out of this faint.

Well, you must appreciate . . .'

'It's all most upsetting. Now exactly what did you do to these young people to make them behave like this?'

'And just who are you people?' asked Mr Parker. 'What denomination are you?'

I had a sneaking suspicion they weren't about to jump with joy at the answers I was going to give them, and I was right. In fact the whole business was very unpleasant, as though I was on trial and the verdict was a foregone conclusion. But what were we guilty of? Doing God's will and allowing the Spirit freedom of movement? Yet whatever I said seemed to make no impression on these three Christian men. It appeared we had violated their traditions and that was not far short of the unforgivable sin.

Throughout the evening, despite offering many a prayer under my breath, I failed to see how God was going to work it out. But I should have realised He had it all under control, and when it happened I had to stifle a smile.

Without having reached any conclusions, and with our time gone, I suggested we might have a time of prayer before we broke up, committing everything to the Lord. Two or three of us prayed, including Mr Parker's son John. Or rather, John *tried* to pray. Getting to his feet and beginning to address the Father, he was suddenly cut short as the Holy Spirit fell upon him and he slumped to the floor once more, falling directly across his father's feet.

Thankfully, I hadn't been sitting anywhere near him. 'You see?' I said, quite relieved. 'It's nothing to do with me or anyone else. It's the Lord.'

But for that simple act of the Holy Spirit things might have turned out differently. As it was, those three men gradually did an about-turn. In years to come they were to enter into the blessings of the Spirit for themselves and to become some of our best friends.

Meanwhile the power continued to flow, and through the monthly barn rallies and Friday meetings we saw many people give their lives to Christ - sometimes individuals, occasionally married couples, and from time to time brothers and sisters. One evening up in the granary we rejoiced as Tommy and Jen Spence's four children committed their lives to the Lord. Unfortunately, Tommy wasn't around to see it happen. It seemed that more often than not the Spirit didn't fall on the barn rallies until the meeting was over, and that meant Tommy usually missed the excitement because he was ferrying borrowed chairs back to the Baptist Church in Northallerton. But what a surprise when he returned - his whole family now trusting Christ as Saviour . . . and all baptised in the Spirit, too.

In the granary, as in the house, the Spirit would often take us by surprise. Perhaps inevitably, we expected certain things to happen before the Spirit would move, as though various conditions had to be met before He could be released into our midst. Gradually, however, we were learning that the Holy Spirit acts upon His own initiative, moving as He chooses. We were so thankful the night He moved upon our barn rally after the shortest Gospel message we'd ever heard. It was given by the Rev. Bill Kennedy, a former professional footballer from Ireland who was now minister of a Congregational church up in Scotland. Cynthia and I had met him during our holiday in Jersey and had invited him down to speak.

We didn't know what the Lord would do that night, of course, but as always we were expectant. That is, until our speaker came to the end of his message . . . just six minutes after he'd begun. He'd woven his talk around the story of Noah's ark, which was fine, but I thought it was just the children's message - now for the main sermon.

But instead our guest speaker sat down. He was through. Finished. I blinked in disbelief. Had he come all the way from Glasgow just to tell us a children's story?

But how much we had to learn. That same night, through the anointed preaching of the Gospel in simple, child-like terms, the Holy Spirit swept in upon our gathering. . .and 20 young people gave their lives to Christ.

Not surprisingly, word of what was happening at Hollybush was spreading fast, and though this prompted strange looks from some of the locals it also resulted in more and more new faces appearing at the meetings and more and more lives getting blessed. And the more the Lord blessed, the more people wanted to be in the place of blessing. Before long a number of folk were gathering with us for a prayer meeting each Tuesday evening, and soon those who had no regular place of worship were asking, 'Why can't we meet on Sunday evenings, too?' Others, with children, wanted to know if we could start a Sunday school in the house.

It sounded to me as though they were suggesting we start a church of our own, which didn't interest me. How could it? We were still heavily involved with the Methodist Church at Sandhutton. Coming to Hollybush had made no difference to our

Sundays. Cynthia continued to play the organ for the morning service and we were both as committed as ever to the Sunday school. My Sunday evenings were committed, too, as a lay preacher on the Methodist circuit. Almost every week I was at a different chapel, leading the worship and preaching the Gospel. And I loved every minute of it. There was no way I wanted anything to change.

On the other hand, I couldn't deny the Hollybush folks the use of the house, and if they wanted to organise something for the children and to meet for worship on a Sunday evening, I would be the last person to stand in their way. Besides, I was totally open to what the Lord wanted. This was His house and He must be free to use it for His glory in whatever way He wanted. Above all, I wanted to see the blessing continue to flow.

It looked as if nothing could stop that happening. The more miracles we saw the greater our faith became, and the greater our faith the greater the miracles. There wasn't a doubt in our minds that God could do anything, and probably would.

'Even if there was a dead man laid out on this floor,' Cynthia told me, 'I just know we could lay hands on him and pray in the name of Jesus and watch that man get up and walk away.'

It was a sentiment shared by just about everyone who met with us regularly. But so far we'd never been confronted with the challenge of raising the dead. Or had we? Didn't praying for the terminally ill require just as much faith? To see someone healed of a fatal disease was surely no less a miracle than to see them brought back to life.

The person who needed such a miracle at that time was June Fletcher, a woman in her forties who had been sentenced to death by cancer. The growth, a huge swelling that hung from her neck like a marrow, was grotesque. For some weeks now Cynthia had been going with George and Gladys to her home in York to pray for her healing, and as they did so they were acutely aware of being engaged in a spiritual battle. Even so, they never doubted that the victory would be snatched from Satan and this woman would be set free.

But as they prayed, week after week, month after month, they saw little sign of change. In fact the growth sometimes seemed bigger not smaller. Why?

'I can see we're going to have to fight this one out,' George told us when Cynthia and I called in to his house on our way back from Northallerton one evening. 'It calls for fasting. We're going to have to show the devil we mean business.'

A few days later George and Gladys moved into Hollybush to look after the place while we went away for a short holiday. By that time George had started fasting and when we set off for a week or so in Jersey we left him sitting in a deck-chair on the lawn, praying.

Ten days later we returned to find him in exactly the same place, still praying, still fasting. And clinging to the promises of God. As we all were. Didn't the Word of God promise that 'What things so ever you desire, when you pray, believe that you receive them, and you shall have them'? Then that settled it. It was only a matter of time. Sooner or later Mrs Fletcher would be healed. Just like everyone else we'd prayed for.

But still there was no change. In fact to the human eye she seemed worse. George would not give in. He fasted on and on. For 40 days.

On the fortieth day Mrs Fletcher died.

Perhaps if we had not seen so many miracles it would have been easier to take. But we had not known failure before - not on this scale, anyway - so what had gone wrong? Cynthia was confused.

'Didn't we have enough faith? Didn't we pray enough? Why wasn't she healed?'

George, to our utter amazement, was unperturbed. 'Cynthia, there will always be things we don't understand. It doesn't mean we've failed, because our faith was in God and He *never* fails. It doesn't mean the devil's won, either, because he's been a loser ever since Calvary. No, we just have to accept that in this situation, as in all others, God is sovereign.'

'But - but what do we do now?'

'Pick ourselves up and carry on,' George replied. 'What else?'

It appeared we had something to learn about disappointments. Even when walking in the Spirit we were not immune from life's let-downs. But wasn't that a contradiction? Didn't the Scripture promise, "In all your ways acknowledge Him, and He shall direct your paths"? Did disappointment mean that we had failed to involve the Lord in our everyday plans and had therefore missed the path He wanted us to walk? Or did it simply mean that we were still measuring life's eventualities by our own values instead of God's?

I'd once heard someone remark that 'Our disappointments are His-appointments'. Was that a twee platitude or profound truth? One thing was for sure: God always knows what's best for us. And when we have our feet on that firm foundation we can afford to be 'disappointed' over even our most cherished plans.

Arthur Bennison discovered this for himself that same summer. His father had reached retiring age and was hoping that, like his father before him, he would be able to hand the farm he had worked all his life to his son. Arthur hoped so, too. When the time was right he approached the land agent to whom the family paid the rent and asked if he might take over the property from his dad.

'I'll have a word with the landlord,' said the agent. 'I don't see why not. Your family's been farming that land for generations, hasn't it?'

While he was waiting for the reply Arthur shared his vision for the future with the Lord. 'I'd rather like to take on the old place. You know I've applied for it.'

Yet even as he was praying he knew that his future lay elsewhere, for the Lord spoke to him very clearly.

You'll not get the farm.

That was all God told him. Yet it was enough. And when the agent brought the landlord's reply Arthur was ready for the disappointment.

'I've some bad news for you,' he said. 'You can't have the farm - the landlord wants it for himself.'

'Oh, that's quite all right,' Arthur replied. 'The Lord's already told me.'

The man stared. Had he heard right?

Arthur laughed. 'I knew I wouldn't be getting the farm,' he said again. 'God's got something better for me.'

He had no idea exactly what that plan was, he told us shortly before the farm's stock went up for sale that autumn, 'But at least I'm free to do what the Lord wants.'

By this time his father had retired and Arthur needed to find work to tide him over until the farm changed hands the following spring at the end of the year's lease. Only then would he be completely free to take on a new job; in the remaining months he had to spend a day or two each week cutting hedges and clearing ditches, so that the farm was in good shape when he finally moved out.

'What will you do for cash?' I asked him.

'Well, I suppose I could catch rabbits,' he said, grinning. 'John and I have got that down to a fine art.'

'Or you could come and pick potatoes for us here at Hollybush,' I ventured. 'We could use an extra pair of hands.'

And that's what Arthur did. He drove down from Bilsdale three or four days each week to help us lift our first potato crop.

He wasn't our only extra help that winter, but our other potato picker hadn't been invited - she just turned up. Or rather, one of our regulars turned up *with* her.

Bert Laverick was an itinerant evangelist and former missionary who often made trips into Europe where he ministered to groups of local believers. On this trip he did not return alone. With him came Mary Feldy, a 16-year-old from Yugoslavia whose family had been suffering hardship because of their faith. Bert had felt the Lord prompting him to smuggle Mary across the border and back to England in order to give her a break from these circumstances. He hoped she would be able to spend a few weeks with us at Hollybush until he returned to the Communist-bloc a few weeks later. She arrived on our doorstep with nothing but what she stood up in - a dress she'd been given in West Germany to replace the rags and tatters she'd left home in - and with only five words of English on her tongue: 'Yes, please,' and 'No, thank you.'

'Will you have her?' asked Bert, who knew we'd never turn the girl away.

'Of course. Besides, the Lord said He would send people to us from other parts, north, south, east and west. East is as good a start as any. But I wonder why she's here? What are we supposed to do for her?'

It didn't occur to me that the Lord might have sent her to do something for *us*! But as the days passed, and the 'few weeks' Bert had spoken of grew into months, we began to learn a thing or two from young Mary. To begin with we were humbled by her reaction to our standard of living; the comfort of our home, the fact that we were never short of food, and the general ease of our life came as something of a shock to this normally deprived girl. We had read of the austerity of life for the working people of Communist lands, of course, but not until we had one of those people in our own home did we begin to appreciate how well off we were.

And then we were impressed by Mary's commitment to her faith. Fridays, we learned, were special to Mary because they were days of fasting. From the moment the sun went down on Thursday evening till sunset on Friday this girl would not allow anything past her lips, food or drink, not so much as a sip of water. Nothing could tempt her to alter this long established pattern, no matter how hard the work she shared with us. Even when helping us harvest a late wheat crop - the thirstiest job on the farm because of the dust that gets in your throat - she refused a drink of water and wouldn't even consider munching a few wheat-grains while we worked, something we always do to keep the saliva glands working. No, Mary had set Fridays apart for God and nothing would sway her rock-firm dedication. Did *we* love the Lord that much? Mary set us thinking. And as she learned more of our language - she was a bright and eager student - so we were able to talk with her about the Lord . . . and to learn lessons we had thought *we* would be teaching *her*.

But there was another reason why Mary had been sent to us - a reason that wasn't to be realised until she had returned to Yugoslavia the following spring. Before that farewell, however, there was to be another, more painful parting of the ways.

Perhaps we were not taken completely by surprise for we had been aware that trouble was brewing down at Sandhutton for some time. But still it came as a shock when a member of the church drew us aside after the service one morning and asked if we could give him a few tips about running the Sunday school. 'I understand you won't be with us much longer,' he said.

I stared at him. 'Oh, is that right?'

'Well, I thought you knew. They've asked me to take over when you leave.'

It had been coming for a long time. I suppose it had begun after we'd been baptised in the Spirit, though it wasn't the baptism itself that had sparked things off because we'd been careful not to say too much about it in the church circle. But certainly the new zeal and boldness we'd received as a result of the baptism had stirred things up. As we motored home we could think of only two reasons why they should be planning to get rid of us: jealousy and fear. Jealousy because they had watched us throw ourselves into the children's work and had seen the way we had got results: 100% village attendance, with some youngsters committing their lives to Christ. And fear because the bogeyman that had haunted them ever since we'd joined the church had finally got the better of them: they were simply afraid that Jim and Cynthia would take over.

'I think there's another reason, too,' I said as we turned into Hollybush. 'I reckon there's been protests from some of the kids' parents because they don't like what their youngsters have been bringing home.'

'Very likely,' Cynthia agreed. 'But we know we've done nothing wrong.'

If we *had* done anything wrong it was to teach the children the Gospel - God's life-changing message of salvation - and that had meant repercussions in the home. Children who had accepted Christ had asked their parents why they didn't say grace at mealtimes. Others wanted to know from mum and dad why they used bad language in the home, or why they were always rowing. It wasn't that we'd taught the kids these values; they just came alive to them as the Holy Spirit worked in their hearts.

Another big issue was Sunday itself. We'd always taught 'Remember the Lord's day to keep it holy.' But mum and dad did not always respect the Sabbath and their children began to ask why. This didn't go down too well in a farming community, especially when the child's parents were also members of the church.

'Do you remember last harvest,' I said to Cynthia as the car rolled to a halt, 'when we'd been teaching the kids about the Sabbath?'

'When we came out of the church to see that combine harvester and trailers go by?'

'Aye. I'll never forget those kids' faces as they stood and watched members of the church riding by on their way to work. They just couldn't fathom it.' One minute we'd been teaching them how important it is for Christians to keep the Lord's day, and the next they were watching a group of men - church members - doing the opposite to what the Bible said.

There was no doubt about it, our total commitment to God and His day had been a thorn in the side of our fellow church members, and with complaints from non-churchgoing parents to back them up they had finally decided it was time to get rid of us. I don't think I had ever sat down to Sunday lunch with such a heavy heart.

The crunch was due to come the following month at the annual church leaders' meeting, and in the intervening weeks I became more and more uncomfortable about any sort of showdown. It seemed the only thing for it was to resign.

'But think of the children,' Cynthia protested. 'We've taught those kids and loved them for the Lord all these years . . .'

She was right, of course. It would be terribly hard to make the break. Cynthia said she would find it far harder to give up the Sunday school than it had been to give up the promise of an operatic career. On that occasion she had not hesitated - she had known just what the Lord wanted her to do and there was not a moment's regret. But this was different. This was a corner we were being forced into, and it was almost unbearable to think that we would be leaving the children in the hands of a man who, as far as we knew, wasn't even a committed Christian.

But there was nothing for it but to commit the situation to God and bow out gracefully.

Even so it was with swirling bewilderment that we entered that downstairs room at the church that November night. The prayers of our friends back at Hollybush were with us, we knew, but nothing could remove the awfulness of walking into a room full of people whose hearts were set against us. In fact seeing the room packed was confirmation of what was going to happen. For the past nine years the most we'd ever had at a church leaders' meeting was six; on those occasions nobody had been much bothered to take an interest in the work. But tonight was different. Tonight there were 25 people present - just about everybody who had a vote in the church's affairs. It was like walking into a courtroom where judge and jury had already decided that the accused was guilty.

Chairing the meeting was the new junior minister, a man for whom we had a high regard, and we were sorry to see that he too had been dragged into this mockery. Ah well, let's get on with it.

When the future of the Sunday school came up on the agenda I didn't waste a second. 'Mr Chairman, ladies and gentlemen, Cynthia and I have something to say before you go any further. Knowing the feelings of the church towards us, and unable to continue in our present roles in such unhappy circumstances, I regret that we have no choice but to tender our resignation from the Sunday school. In fact we shall be leaving the church altogether.'

It had been the shortest and most difficult speech I had ever made, and as we drove back home we shared a wrenching of the heart, almost as though there'd been a death in the family. But we couldn't put the matter behind us yet. Having accepted our resignation the committee had asked if we would stay on until the end of the year to give the new Sunday school superintendent time to settle in. We'd said yes. In our hearts, though, we knew that our work for the Lord at Sandhutton had already come to an end. Even our resignation had been a formality. The end for us had come when the unthinking church member had let slip the church's plans.

We went up to bed that night with great sadness of heart. It was, we knew, the end of an era. The sense of loss did not hit us, though, until that first Sunday in January, 1970, when for the first time in our lives we rose on the Lord's day with no church to go to. It was a desolate feeling, a sense of being abandoned, of being out in the cold. 'What now, Lord?' we cried. 'You gave us the call to preach your Word and the Methodist church gave us the opportunity. What now?'

By this time the Sunday school had started at Hollybush, the various classes each occupying one of our six bedrooms, and so we knew we wouldn't be idle. But it wasn't the same. The children's work at Sandhutton, along with the Sunday night preaching engagements on the Methodist circuit, represented a lifetime's investment. We had loved the work and the people too. Could we let it go just like that?

'We have to,' we told each other. 'It's over and done with. The Lord has something better for us.'

Yet despite this assurance in our hearts, those first weeks of the new year were difficult. It was our first real valley experience. We could not even lift our eyes to see the potential of the Lord's work at Hollybush. After all, our Friday meetings, barn rallies and prayer meetings were just informal happenings - they weren't a church.

But therein lay the key to the future, as we learned one evening when the Lord spoke directly to us through prophecy.

'Men have closed doors and I have closed doors, says the Lord, but as doors have been shut into one church I will make a way for you to go into every church. And as I have brought you out of one denomination I want you to be willing to participate with every denomination and to be friends with them. But do not affiliate yourselves to any one group, for I the Lord have brought you out of denominationalism.'

So the Lord had been in it all the time. But of course! Why hadn't we seen it before? He wanted us to be free - free of traditions, free of the structures that hinder the working of the Spirit, free to do and go and be what He wanted, and no ties.

It would take a bit of getting used to, of course, but if that's what God wanted that's what He would have. Above all, we desired to be in the centre of His will.

It soon became clear that from then on we were to throw all our energies into building up the work of God at Hollybush, and when we began to do that our eyes were opened to the full potential of an independent fellowship that was totally available to God.

As we thought on this we realised how good it was to be free. No rules and regulations save the Scriptures. No historical ties bar the Lord Himself. No one to tell us what we should be thinking and doing except the Holy Spirit.

Perhaps it was because I'd been so engrossed in the work at Sandhutton that I'd failed to appreciate just how much the Spirit had already brought into being. Now, for the first time, I saw a unity and ongoing purpose behind the various meetings that had been started, realising that the prayer meeting, Sunday school and Sunday evening gathering had not come into being simply because they'd seemed a good idea or met a need, but because they had been ordained of God. Now there was another meeting, too.

Since the Sunday school had begun, those parents who had travelled long distances to bring their children to the house had either sat about in the kitchen or waited outside in their cars. Now someone had suggested the obvious: 'How about a little Bible study and prayer time while we're waiting?' That was okay by us, and so yet another meeting began in the big room upstairs.

At last I had caught the vision. These meetings that had started as a spin-off from the Friday fellowships were not just 'added extras' but an integral part of the work God was doing. Each had its role to play and each complemented the others. Looking at it in this light it was exciting to see how the work had grown, and thrilling to contemplate the future. In George Breckon we had a gifted and anointed pastor; in the people who came - now more than 60 to the Friday meetings - we saw a real hungering after God; and in our own lives we now knew a total commitment to what the Lord would do here at Hollybush. There was only one way we could go and that was up.

But just a few weeks later, at Easter, 1970, we came crashing down to earth. It came suddenly, at the close of the Friday fellowship - an announcement from George that was to shake us to the foundations.

'As from next week, brothers and sisters, I won't be with you.

Some of you may have heard, I've accepted the pastorate down at Valley Road Baptist Church. So maybe I'll see some of you there.'

That was all. And it was totally devastating. Why hadn't George told us? He might at least have shared the move with us before announcing it to the world, so that we'd have been prepared. But to come out with it cold . . .

I couldn't understand it. Gladys had vaguely mentioned that George had been approached by the deacons at Valley Road, but we'd thought he was committed to the people who met with us at Hollybush. Whatever was going on? Didn't George realise what damage would be done if he walked out on us now, just as things were getting going? It was unbelievable that he could be with us one week and down in Northallerton the next. Like a bad dream. But at least with dreams you wake up and know it's all over. This dream simply became a nightmare. The following Friday confirmed it.

As usual we'd set out the books and arranged the chairs, and by 6.45 we were ready for the first arrivals. Everyone knew that if you wanted a seat in the same room as the speaker you needed to be at Hollybush by 6.50. Otherwise you had to sit on the landing or on the stairs. But there would be no need for that tonight. By 7.30 just six people had turned up and in that big room we were lost.

'What's going on, Lord?' I cried. 'Where are all the people? If they're down at Valley Road instead of here - *why*?'

Some could not even pray, such was the gloom and rejection that enveloped us. At last we looked up at one another, bewildered. Cynthia put it into words for each one of us.

'Well, what now? Is that it? Is it all over? Is Miracle Valley finished?'

9/Battle stations

Some people called it sheep-stealing. We knew better. In our eyes we had simply lost a lot of good friends. As it turned out our numbers had not been reduced quite as drastically as we'd first thought. Several people had been unable to come that first week without George and, in fact, we'd been left with about 20 regulars. But, even so, to lose nearly 50 people all at once was an enormous blow. Coming to terms with it was going to take time. This would be easier for some than for others. Jean Allison, for example, was not over concerned about our loss. Jean had been meeting with us from the earliest days down at Sandhutton where she had seen a vision of a packed meeting in a large room. She could describe the room in detail but had no idea where it was . . . until she walked into Hollybush. Now that the meetings were less than packed she clung to the vision, believing we were but passing through a period of pruning and that in God's time the numbers would build up again until we were overflowing down the stairs once more.

Was Jean right? Were we being pruned? As we met together over the following weeks, moving downstairs to the kitchen while our numbers were reduced, the Lord seemed to confirm this to our hearts. Two men were instrumental in encouraging us to hold fast while God pared us back for further service. One was

Edgar Parkins, a Bible teacher and missionary who had spent many years in Nigeria, and the other was our old friend Bert Laverick. Bert had recently driven Mary Feldy back home to Yugoslavia and returned rejoicing because our visitor had become so fluent in English after six months on the farm that she would make an excellent translator when Christians from the fellowship visited Eastern Europe. This was something the Lord had impressed upon us over the years we'd been meeting together - to pray for and visit our brothers and sisters in Communist lands. Several members had expressed interest in making such a trip, but we had often wondered about the language barrier. Now, thanks to the little girl God had sent to pick potatoes with us, that need not be a problem. And that, we guessed, was the other reason why she'd come.

But right now we didn't feel much like rejoicing with Bert over God's provision of a translator, so Bert did what the Scriptures exhort us to do with those who weep: he wept. He was a man of great compassion and fully entered into the sadness we all felt. Yet at the same time he encouraged us to look up, believing that God had allowed this whittling down of our numbers for a reason.

'Yes, it's a pruning back,' he assured us, 'and it's of the Lord.'

That same evening the Lord explained to me what He was doing. As we prayed I saw a picture. Before me was a rose bush with the flowers in bloom. It was a beautiful sight but instinctively I knew that it was figurative; it represented the work God had been doing at Hollybush. Then things began to change: the rose bush was being pruned, at first lightly, but then almost brutally. The bush was being cut right back, and along with the stems and thorns went the roses. It seemed terribly harsh, even unnecessary, but as the pruning came to an end I was aware that the harder you prune a rose bush the better the roses will be. Presumably the same was true of the fellowship. And then, deep in my spirit, I seemed to hear the Lord speak. It was a small, distant voice, yet unmistakably clear.

Stand still and see what kind of a rose I make of you now.

From that moment on I knew it would be all right. But if we'd needed any confirmation that God was with us it came a couple of weeks later when just a handful of us were gathered for prayer. This time we were meeting in the study. As usual we'd begun with praise and gone on to lay our requests and petitions before the Lord, and now we were looking to one another to see if anyone needed prayer.

'I do,' said Cynthia. 'I've had this terrible pain in my side all day and I just can't shift it.'

As she spoke she moved her chair into the centre of the room so that we could gather round and lay hands on her. Mrs Hutchinson was the first to her feet and moved in behind Cynthia, placing her hands on her shoulders. But our friend had barely started to pray when the Spirit fell upon her and she sank to her knees, then keeled over on to the floor. As she did so the hat she'd been wearing fell off and I stooped to pick it up and put it out of the way on a chair. Immediately it fell off, back on to the carpet. I bent down and picked it up again, but it was no sooner on the chair than it was back on the floor. Whatever was going on? It was a perfectly flat chair and a perfectly flat hat. I retrieved it a third time, but that hat would not stay on the chair. After the fourth attempt I gave up. 'Blow it,' I muttered. 'It can stay there.'

I might have realised something was going to happen. The others already knew. Mr Hutchinson, I noticed, was shielding his eyes as though from a bright light, and the others were seated again, staring towards the far corner by the desk.

I turned . . . and caught my breath. It was the first time I'd seen an angel. It was just as Cynthia had described, though this angelic visitor did not move. It remained in the corner of the room, seemingly hovering a foot or so from the floor, with its wings folded and head bowed. It was, of course, a stunning sight, in no way alarming but wonderfully reassuring. The longer I stared at it the more I seemed to enter into the atmosphere that surrounded it - an enveloping sense of God's presence. Surely this was the purpose of its visit, to bring down to us the glorious peace that prevailed around the throne of God. Or was it that we were being lifted up into that presence? For in the ever increasing brightness the walls of our room seemed to fade away as we were lifted out of ourselves into a different dimension of time and space.

How long this lasted no one knew, for when the angel eventually withdrew - or when we were returned to our own environment - we were all too excited to think of anything so trivial as time. Even Mrs Hutchinson was unconcerned about how long she'd been laid out on the floor. When she came round she was just thrilled to have been blessed in her spirit. She was disappointed at not seeing the angel, though, and to cheer her up I told her about her hat. Nobody knew the significance of a hat that kept falling on the floor, of course - or even if the incident had meant anything at all - but it raised a few laughs.

'From now on I'll call it my glory hat,' she chuckled. 'Who knows what the Lord might do when I've got it on!'

That evening was a turning point for the fellowship, for after such a positive confirmation that God was with us we were able to put the crisis of George's departure firmly behind us and press on with whatever the Lord had for us in the future. Growth would come, we knew that, and so too would change. Our part was to be ready, so that as the Spirit led we could follow.

The same applied to the farm. When changes came we wanted to be sure the Lord was in them. Above all we were aware of the importance of having the right men working with us, and in the coming years the Lord was to leave us in no doubt as to the men of His choice.

One morning that spring I came down to breakfast with one thought in my mind: offer Arthur Bennison a job. The timing was right; a man who'd been with us for the past year was leaving at the end of the month.

'What d'you think, Cynthia? He's a good lad is Arthur; a good worker and a strong Christian. I think he'd be good to have around the place.'

Cynthia agreed. 'But where would he live? He'd need digs, wouldn't he? Unless . . . '

'Unless he came here, to live with us?'

She came to the table and spooned boiled eggs into our egg-cups. Six-year-old Joanna was all ready to dip her bread-and-butter 'soldiers' into the yolk.

'It's a thought,' she said. 'I mean, Arthur's easy-going.'

'And Joanna gets on well with him.' I turned to her. 'You like Uncle Arthur, don't you, Joanna? Would you like it if he came and lived with us?'

She giggled shyly and dunked her first soldier. That seemed to settle it.

Our offer came as no surprise to Arthur. As the end of the financial year had approached and the lease on his father's farm ran out Arthur had been seeking the Lord as to his future. In reply had come the distinct impression that he was to identify himself more closely with me. God had shown him this in quite a dramatic way.

'I wouldn't say it were a vision,' he explained, 'but I got this picture of Moses being supported by Aaron and Hur during the Israelites' battle with the Amalekites.'

I knew the story well. It was a tough battle fought in the valley of Rephidim while Moses looked on from the hillside. God told Moses that his people would prevail so long as he kept his arms raised to heaven. When he lowered his arms the battle would swing in favour of the enemy. In order to achieve victory, Aaron and Hur had to help by supporting Moses' arms.

'I believe that's the job God's got for me,' Arthur went on. 'To support you in the battle.'

I couldn't argue with that. 'When can you move in?' I asked.

He joined us the following week and plunged straight into the busy spring routine. There was sugar-beet and spring barley to sow, potatoes to plant, fertiliser to spread on the grazing pastures ... plus the numerous other little jobs that had to be done at that time of year. In all of these, Arthur quickly fitted in as a member of the team, working some days at Hollybush, others at The Limes. His experience and capacity for hard work were a real Godsend.

Yet we both knew that the contribution he would make to the farm was only part of the reason for his being here. The vision he had received had impressed upon him the fact that he was to support me 'in the battle', and from that I knew that Arthur would be a source of strength to me in the fellowship. But his support for me was not to be limited to what the Lord was doing at Hollybush. As we soon discovered, the Lord had other plans.

It had begun with the 'Miracle Valley' prophecy received at The Limes two years earlier. That prophecy had informed us that '... *from this place, saith the Lord, there shall be a coming in and a going forth, for it shall be as a wheel within a wheel, the blessing which I shall pour upon you flowing out from your own circle to a wider circle beyond. This shall be the Lord's work, reaching far and wide to touch the lives of countless men and women, and bringing glory through it all to His name.*'

At the time, this revelation of what the Lord planned to do at Hollybush had excited us, but we had no idea as to how this reaching out to other areas would work. Gradually, though, we began to see how the prophecy might be fulfilled. From the earliest days of our Friday night meetings at Hollybush we had welcomed Christians from other areas. Some came from as far as Southport, almost 100 miles away, and they came frequently, if not regularly. Evidently they felt that the type of teaching and fellowship they received in our meetings was meeting their needs, but obviously the geographical arrangement was not ideal. If only a fellowship like Hollybush could be started in each of their own areas ...

Arthur had not been with us long before he received a vision that was to confirm what we should be doing about it.

'I saw this sort of roundabout,' he told me, 'with roads going out from it like the spokes of a wheel. The roundabout, or hub, was Hollybush, and the roads led to other fellowships.'

The vision had come to him, he said, while he'd been in prayer in his room one evening. Obviously it was time to act. The first step was to ask those who travelled so many miles to us each week whether they would like our help in starting a fellowship in their own area. The response from three directions was a very positive 'yes'.

So began a very hectic phase of outreach from Hollybush that was to involve Arthur and me travelling many hundreds of miles almost every week for the next two or three years. On Monday evenings we drove to Dolphinholm, near Lancaster, a round trip of 150 miles. Wednesday evenings saw us heading out to Hesketh Bank, Southport, a journey of 96 miles each way. And on Thursdays we travelled the 104 miles to Silksworth in Sunderland and back.

In each case the journey and active support given to these new fellowships occurred after a full day's manual labour. The routine rarely varied: knock off at five o'clock, gulp down a quick meal, change out of our farming clothes, and be on the road by 5.30. We never arrived back home before midnight and frequently crept in at gone two o'clock in the morning.

The pace of all this activity was gruelling and very quickly we realised that we couldn't keep it up in our own strength. But, of course, there was no need to. We finally did something about it as I swung the car into Hollybush at two o'clock one morning, feeling totally exhausted. We had to be up again at six.

'Well, Lord,' I prayed aloud, 'this is Miracle Valley and we're looking to you for another miracle. You know we've been out on your business, and so we want you to make up to us the hours of sleep we've already missed.' I glanced at the car clock. 'We'll get only four hours' sleep again tonight, Lord - but grant us eight hours' rest.'

We woke with the dawn, totally refreshed. And from that day on, for as long as we continued to support those distant new fellowships, God performed that same wonderful miracle for us time after time. In fact the day never dawned when we rose yawning and sluggish, if the previous night we'd been out on the King's business.'

But the best miracle of all was that, in time, we no longer needed to make those journeys. And we were just thrilled to know that we'd helped to play a part in establishing what are now thriving Christian fellowships in these other, once needy areas.

How thankful we were, too, for the gifts of the Spirit which had been instrumental in prompting us to embark on that course. More and more we were proving the importance and value of prophecy, visions and other works of the Spirit. Indeed, not even Hollybush, let alone these other fellowships, would have got off the ground without them.

Yet at the same time it remained vital to test every supernatural revelation to make sure that it was of the Lord. And sometimes we would find ourselves disagreeing as to what was of God and what was not.

It happened one Sunday in January, 1971. Arthur was on his way down to tea when I met him on the stairs.

'Hey, Jim, the Lord's just shown me we're going to be having a camp meeting out in that field beyond the barns.'

'Oh yes?' The idea didn't ring true with me.

'Aye. It were a vision with all tents and cars, and a big marquee over in that far corner beside the road. We're going to have a camp meeting before long, I just know it.'

I asked Arthur if he hadn't imagined it - sometimes our 'visions' can be nothing more than wishful thinking - but he was adamant: this was a God-given revelation.

'Well, we'd best pray about it,' I told him. I didn't want to discourage him but, at the same time, I didn't receive a witness in my spirit that this was of the Lord. In fact, privately, I thought the prospect of having a camp meeting at Hollybush highly unlikely. Besides, I had enough to think about without getting involved in another big project. Tent meetings, I knew, took an awful lot of organising.

Yes, there was plenty happening at Hollybush to keep me occupied. The Sunday school was growing; more people were meeting upstairs on Sunday morning, even those without children in the Sunday school; our Sunday evening meetings were beginning to get crowded; our Tuesday prayer meetings were swelling and of course the Friday evening numbers were growing, too.

Alongside this growth was the continuing fulfilment of the Lord's promise to us that he would 'bring people here from the north, south, east and west to minister to you and to be ministered to'. It was quite amazing. The phone would ring and a friend would tell us they were bringing so-and-so, a well known Bible teacher, along to the meeting. Could we give him the opportunity to minister?

On another occasion I'd be at a meeting somewhere and be introduced to an itinerant evangelist and feel the Spirit prompting me to invite him to speak at Hollybush.

Sometimes someone would simply turn up. We didn't mind, providing they were sent by the Lord, in which case we were eager to hear what they had to say to us.

Usually these visiting speakers would be with us for just one evening or sometimes the weekend, but now and then the Lord would send someone to stay a few weeks. Ladin Popov, from Bulgaria, was one such man.

We'd already heard of Ladin and his brother Haralan through reports published in the west following their imprisonment and torture in Bulgarian prisons. Anyone who had undergone such persecution for his faith had our highest respect, and when the opportunity arose for us to accommodate Ladin for three weeks we jumped at the chance. We sensed that this man, a Pentecostal pastor until he was exiled from Bulgaria, had much to teach us.

But we hadn't expected him to be so big! His six foot, 16-stone frame just about filled the doorway into our kitchen and his larger-than-life personality filled the room.

Yet Ladin Popov turned out to be a gentle giant, and as we listened to him recounting how he had been beaten and tortured because he refused to deny his Lord our hearts went out to him with tears. But perhaps his most challenging testimony to us was the one for which he needed no words. Removing his shirt one evening he turned around for us to see his back - what was left of it. There were burn marks, weal marks, and great chunks of flesh that looked more like a ploughed field. How many of us, we wondered, would be willing to suffer as much if the circumstances ever arose?

But Ladin was with us 'to preach Jesus,' he told us, 'not to glory in my infirmities,' and whenever he was given the opportunity he was quick to speak up for his Lord. One such occasion occurred when I took Ladin with me to a harvest festival service at Brough Sowerby Methodist chapel up near Kirkby Stephen. (Though I'd resigned from the Methodist Church I was still invited to take services at some of the chapels from time to time.) Arthur was with us, too, as was Liz, a young girl who'd been coming to the fellowship for several months.

I asked Ladin to say a few words during the service and there in his slightly broken English he simply shared the love of God. At the close of the service I turned round to see him counselling someone - our own Liz. Many of us had been praying for her, and at last she had decided to commit her life to the Lord. The love of Christ, preached in the power of the Holy Spirit, had won her heart.

But that night we were also to be reminded of that other power that contends for our souls. The service had been over only a few minutes and the church still packed when Ladin motioned to me and drew me aside.

'This girl has evil spirits,' he told me. 'They should be dealt with straightaway.'

I nodded, for I'd already felt the 'arrows' coming at me, but I wondered whether the gentle folk of Brough Sowerby had ever encountered demons before and what their reaction was likely to be. But we weren't going to back off just because of that. Perhaps the Lord wanted them to learn a thing or two about spiritual warfare.

'Could I have your attention, please, everyone,' I called out. 'There is someone here at the front who needs special help tonight - that is, deliverance from evil spirits. Ladin and I are going to minister to her in a moment and we'd like those of you who will believe with us to stay and pray. But if you can't do that, could I ask you to leave the building.'

To my surprise a good number stayed - some probably out of curiosity - and then we got down to business. Liz, we discovered, had been dabbling in occult practices - nothing heavy, just fringe stuff - and that was how the demons had entered. The entrance of the Holy Spirit at Liz's conversion had stirred up these spirits and they were fighting back.

Occasionally, I'd learned, demons will flee once the Spirit comes in, but more often those messengers of Satan will either try to conceal their presence so as to do damage later on, or angrily protest in order to discomfort the new convert and discourage them in their new faith. This was what was happening to Liz, but I couldn't help feeling that, as so often before, the Lord had allowed such circumstances to develop in order to teach me something. The lesson turned out to be a valuable one, but not one I would willingly have enrolled for. The demons, we discovered, were going to put up a fight for Liz and manifested themselves violently through her body, screaming at us through her voice. Had I been ministering alone I might have hesitated - which was the demons' intention, of course - but evidently Ladin had met this reaction before. He didn't hesitate to take authority over them in Christ's name and to command them to release their hold. I think he must have encountered quite a few demons in the dark places where his faith had landed him. He certainly knew how to handle them.

And that was the lesson: that sometimes we have to get tough with the enemy (but never with the person in whom the spirits dwell) in order to put him to flight. As Ladin told me afterwards, 'When a dog is growling and snarling in your face you don't tell it to calm down and run along - you growl back and kick it in the teeth.' That was what I'd seen Ladin do that night, and I wasn't likely to forget it.

At the same time I was aware that the aggression I'd seen him display was not mere human anger but forcefulness of the Spirit. There was a very great difference, and that difference was the anointing of God. Ladin, I knew, was walking in that anointing. We saw the evidence of it again later that same week when he prayed for Joanna. For a few days our little girl had been off-colour and we had suspected she was in for a bout of the measles that were in fashion among her classmates at school. But we'd not expected the rash to be so severe, and the irritation grew worse until Joanna's eyelids were so swollen she could barely see. Though we had prayed for her in faith, nothing had happened; this was a case where anointed prayer was needed. Which was why Joanna's condition began to improve as soon as Ladin had laid hands on her and prayed for her healing, and why the following morning every last trace of measles had vanished.

The following week Ladin himself left, too, but the blessings we received through his visit lingered. This was true for Joanna as much as any of us, for though we had prayed with her and encouraged her to 'talk to Jesus' from her youngest years, she'd never, to our knowledge, seen a dramatic answer to prayer in her own young life. The miracles we'd seen in the fellowship had mostly gone over her head, and understandably so, but now she had seen that our God, the God of the grown-ups, was the God of her own little world, too.

Later that same year she received further proof of this, and this time she discovered that our heavenly Father loves to grant not only our needs but also the desires of our hearts.

'Mummy, I wish I had a kitten,' she told Cynthia as they drove to school one morning. 'A kitten all of my own.'

'Well, let's tell Jesus about it,' Cynthia replied, and there in the car they told the Lord what was on Joanna's heart.

The following morning, as they were leaving for school again, they opened the back door to find God's answer.

'Mummy, Mummy, look!'

Sitting outside, as though waiting patiently for someone to come to the door, were two kittens. Where they'd come from we hadn't a clue and no one came to enquire about them so we gave one to a friend and the other became Joanna's pet. She called it Twinkle.

'I think kids have a lot to teach us about prayer,' I told Cynthia that evening. 'Their relationship with the Lord is so uncomplicated, so uncluttered.'

'Simple trust and dependence,' she remarked. 'If only all our prayers were offered in child-like faith . . .

And yet in many ways they were. Particularly as far as the farm was concerned. How often, while out working the fields, I'd prayed for wisdom in running the business, seeking God's direction in which crops to develop and which to run down, which stock to increase and which to let go. And when to buy and sell. That, after all, was the key to staying afloat. Farming at the best of times runs on small profit margins. Too many errors of judgment can put a man out of business.

But then I would remember the Lord's promise to me as I'd walked out across the land that first time we came to look at Hollybush. *You just be here, Jim, and I'll prosper you.* That was a comfort, of course, and looking back over the three years we'd been here confirmed that God's hand of blessing had been upon us. Buying and selling at the right time, and trading with the right people, had a great deal to do with that, and the credit for those right decisions had to be the Lord's.

But no man hears from the Lord *all* the time . . .

It was a Monday, and Mondays at Hollybush mean telephone calls. That's the day I do much of the farm's business, ringing around for the best prices on various commodities or tying up contracts for the haulage wagons. There are incoming calls, too; other farmers asking the price of our hay, sales reps fixing appointments, neighbouring farmers passing on some piece of news that will affect us all . . .

It was in this way, on the farming grapevine, that I heard the first rumblings of the trouble that lay ahead. My caller asked if I'd heard the bad news about a certain grain company.

'What bad news is that?'

'Word is they're in big trouble moneywise. Seems likely they'll go under.'

I gulped. Only last month I'd dispatched my wheat to them - every last grain. They owed me £3,000.

'Is this just a rumour, or what?' I asked. 'If they go bankrupt I could be in the soup.'

It was no rumour. A week or so later a rep from the grain company called on me and I knew before he'd opened his mouth that the news was bad. The company had gone to the wall.

'I'm sorry, Jim, but there's nowt I can do about it.'

'Well, do I get my grain back? Will there be compensation? You're talking about a whole year's work down the drain.'

He shook his head. 'All the assets are frozen. Eventually they'll be sold off to help pay the debts.'

'But what about *my* debts? I need that £3,000 to keep the farm going.'

'I'm sorry,' he said. 'You'll be considered, of course, but you'll just have to take what you can get.'

For the rest of the day questions whirled around in my head. Where had I gone wrong? Had I failed to hear the Lord, or had I heard Him only to ignore His leading? One thing was sure, this wasn't part of the blessing God had promised. Somehow I'd managed to get myself outside His will and now I was paying for it.

To my surprise, however, once the initial shock had worn off I found myself taking the whole thing in my stride. There would have to be changes, of course - for a while we would need to tighten our belts a notch or two - but we would recover. Besides, what was the loss of £3,000 compared to the blessings we continued to enjoy? Our health, our family, our friends . . . There was something even more precious - our relationship with the Lord. Nothing could wipe that out, even if we lost the whole farm, or life itself.

And then another thought occurred to me. Was God allowing us to pass through this valley to remind us of that very fact? Perhaps He was, for our loss caused me to think of the many other farmers who had suffered just the same yet didn't know the blessing of being secure in God's love. Maybe to them the loss of £3,000 would seem like the end of the world. How blessed we were to be free of that burden, to know that our God was still in control of our circumstances, and that we were precious to Him. How much we had to be thankful!

There was an extra blessing to come, too. Months later, when the grain company's affairs had finally been sorted out, we received a cheque for £218. And we thought we'd never see so much as a penny.

The following spring, our belts still tightened, we faced another financial dilemma. Our car, an old Ford Zephyr, was due for the annual MOT test and was so shot out that it was bound to fail. We were told it would cost £180 to put the vehicle right and keep it on the road. Realising that probably it would need more spent on it the following year too, we decided to invest our savings - £700 - in another car. So one Saturday I drove out from Hollybush in search of something more reliable. But what reliability could anyone buy with £700 and an old banger in part exchange? It would need a miracle . . . but that was just what the

Lord had in store.

It was a frustrating, humiliating business, going from one second-hand car dealer to another, each time pouring out the same sorry story and each time being all but laughed off the premises, but I was determined to make a trade. By late afternoon, however, having had no success, I thought I might as well pack it in. But on my way home I spotted another dealer's and decided to give it one more try. I wished I'd given it a miss, though, when the manager appeared from his office and came toward me. I knew this man; he was the last person in the world who would do me a favour.

I'd met him a month or so earlier during an outreach we'd been doing in Thirsk on Saturday nights. Among our contacts at that time were two young women who frequented the town's night-club. As a result of our witnessing to them these girls decided to abandon their old ways and commit their lives to the Lord, a move which did not endear us to the club's manager. That man was the same one now bearing down on me with two daggers where his eyes should have been.

'What do you want?' he growled.

'I'm interested in buying a car,' I told him.

He grunted. 'How much have you got?'

'This car and £700.'

He glanced scathingly at the old Zephyr and let out a cruel laugh. 'You must be joking. I can't help you - you might as well clear off.'

I suppose I couldn't blame him. Perhaps it was to be expected. But when I arrived home half an hour later Cynthia had some surprising news for me.

'Some man rang about a car,' she said, and named the garage he'd been calling from.

'That's the place I've just left,' I said. 'What did he want?'

She smiled. 'He says he's got a car for you and can you go down first thing in the morning.'

I wondered what he had in mind. Perhaps he'd remembered some bodged-up old banger he thought he might try to sell me. But nothing was further from the truth, for God was at work.

It turned out that only minutes after I'd left his premises the previous afternoon his boss had phoned him - the boss who owned both the night-club and the car business. Apparently he had a car he had suddenly taken a disliking to and wanted to get rid of as quickly as possible. He wasn't bothered about how much he got for it; he just wanted to see the back of it. Was I interested?

Was I? I did the trade there and then - my old Zephyr and £700 for the boss's car. It was a brand new Volvo, just two weeks old and not 600 miles on the clock.

It never occurred to me to ask what had changed the man's attitude toward me - or why the boss suddenly wanted rid of a superb new car - for I already knew. It was the Lord. I drove home like the king of the road, singing praises all the way.

10/On holy ground

The Volvo was one of several new additions to our world at Hollybush that spring. Another was a new-born lamb, presented to Joanna by our farmer friend Tommy Spence after our little girl's request to have a lamb to raise as a pet. Joanna looked really cute feeding it with a baby's bottle. Its name, she decided, would be Bluebell.

Then there was the arrival of Irene Holt, a young lady who came in each day to help Cynthia with the domestic chores. This was necessary because, with the steady growth of the fellowship, Cynthia was facing increasing demands on her time to counsel people, pray with the sick and take the occasional women's meeting. Irene's assistance released her to spend time in that way.

Such additions to Hollybush were planned, of course. But the biggest change, and the most exciting, was one that none of us had foreseen. Except for Arthur, that is.

It was Easter Sunday and we were enjoying lunch at Hollybush with some friends, Harry and Evelyn Foster from Sunderland. Together we were talking about the work God was doing on the farm and how this might expand, when Mr Foster said, 'Do you know, I have a feeling there's going to be a camp meeting out there in that big field.'

Arthur almost leapt off his chair. 'Hey, that's just the vision I had last year. The Lord showed me a big marquee out there and all the tents and cars.'

Mr Foster nodded. 'That's right. I just feel it in my spirit.' He glanced at me. 'What d'you think, Jim?'

I was still apprehensive. 'Could be. It'd take some organizing.'

'But think of the people we could reach,' said Cynthia. 'I think we should look into it.'

'All right, we'll pray about it and see what the Lord has to say.'

But it was only a matter of hours before I too began to feel that same witness in my spirit, that same excitement. Before the day was out I had caught the vision and was as enthusiastic as the others.

'I suppose mid-summer would be the best time, around the end of July, after the kids have broken up from school. We'd need to advertise, of course - or should we just pray? Where did you say you saw the marquee in your vision, Arthur? Up the top end by the road, wasn't it? I could give Clapham's a ring in the morning and see how much they'd charge for a two hundred-seater - or should I make that three hundred?'

'You'd better ask the Lord,' Cynthia said laughingly. 'If it's what He wants He'll have it all planned out to the last detail.'

But how could we know for sure if the camp was what the Lord wanted? We had Arthur's vision, of course, and the revelation given to Mr Foster had confirmed it - but was that sufficient grounds on which to proceed?

The following Tuesday we shared the idea at the prayer meeting and were encouraged that our friends welcomed the idea and got down to prayer about it that same evening. Yet still we needed more confirmation; we needed to hear from the Lord direct. He wasn't going to let us down.

Over the following weeks, having decided to press ahead with the arrangements in faith, the Spirit showed us two ways in which we would know that the camp meeting was of God. The first of these came to me in a word of knowledge as I was driving down to The Limes one morning.

An American evangelist will be taking meetings at the camp.

It wasn't something I'd been thinking about because I didn't know of any American evangelists other than Billy Graham and my faith didn't reach that far. It was just that suddenly the knowledge was there in my mind. It could have been a human thought, of course - wishful thinking, perhaps - but time would prove it one way or the other and so I spoke out the word at the Friday night meeting.

'Don't ask me to elaborate,' I told the folks, 'but that's what I believe the Lord has said.'

'But where do we find an American evangelist?' someone asked.

'We don't,' I replied. 'If God has spoken it, it will come to pass. We don't have to find a way of engineering it; it'll just happen.'

The second sign of confirmation was revealed to us through prophecy during one of the prayer meetings.

'To give you the sign you seek I will send to the tent a man and his son and I shall save them.'

We could ask for no better proof, and from that point on the fellowship embraced the vision and got on with the organization.

At the same time a couple in the fellowship were seeing God work out a vision in their own lives - something that had nothing to do with the tent meetings but everything to do with the overall purpose of Hollybush: reaching people for Jesus Christ.

Irene and Leslie Lamb had been with us since the earliest meetings at The Limes and, along with Mr and Mrs Hutchinson and Mr and Mrs Allinson, were pillars of the fellowship. Formerly a farmer and later a veterinary salesman, Mr Lamb had now retired and he and his wife were enjoying a more leisurely pace of life. Yet they were as keen as ever in their Christian witness and were not in the least perturbed when God called them out of retirement into full-time service. This too began with a vision.

It came to Mr Lamb during the prayer meeting one Tuesday, a living picture of a cornfield at harvest time, its golden grain shimmering in the sunshine. Standing at the gate of this field, and looking in upon the harvest scene, Mr Lamb saw himself. As he watched, the bright shimmering of the grain grew more and more dazzling until, in the vision, Mr Lamb had to put his hand to his eyes and peer at the field through his fingers. Moments later the vision faded.

That night he told only his wife what he had seen, but when the vision recurred a few weeks later he drew me aside after the meeting and described to me the details. He already knew that the harvest represented the mission field and that God was calling him to a new work. What he didn't know was where that work would be.

'Are we going abroad, do you think?'

The Spirit seemed to give me the answer straightaway. 'No,' I told him, 'this is a home mission. You'll be working here in Britain. You won't be going overseas.'

A week or two later the Lord brought the vision again, this time through a friend, Gladys Greenhowe, whom the Lambs had often brought to the meetings when they'd been living down at Harrogate. She telephoned Mrs Lamb with the news early one morning.

'I've just had a vivid dream about your husband,' she told Irene.

'Oh? And what was he up to?'

To Mrs Lamb's surprise her caller described the shimmering cornfield and told her that she'd seen Mr Lamb on his knees in the corner of the field with his hands shielding his eyes from the glare.

'Then he fell prostrate,' she went on, 'and the shimmering from the corn came and settled on top of him. I know there was more, too, but that's all I can remember.'

'Well, praise the Lord!' Mrs Lamb exclaimed.

'Why, what do you know?'

She explained what her husband had already seen. 'But this time he's *inside* the field. That must mean we're getting closer.'

But they still had no clue as to what sort of work the Lord was calling them. That was to be revealed a few weeks later when they attended the Keswick Convention up in Cumbria. Significantly, the Lord spoke during the missionary meeting.

The speaker that morning was drawing his message to a close and beginning to appeal for Christians to offer themselves for service on the mission field when the vision came again. By now Mr Lamb just had to know what God was asking him to do.

'Lord, what is this thing?' he asked, knowing in his heart that he was quite ready to step out and serve the Lord in whatever sphere he was called to . . . until God answered his question. For, in reply, the vision changed, and coming up out of the corn he saw a bunch of gypsy folk.

'Oh no,' he retorted, 'not that lot!' He would go anywhere but among the gypsies.

But then, as the figures in the vision drew nearer, Mr Lamb saw how lost they looked - as sheep without a shepherd - and his heart softened. The gypsy people, he knew, needed Christ as much as anyone, and if that was the work God had chosen for him, how could he refuse?

'Yes, Lord,' he said, 'here am I - send me. I'll go.'

Then the vision changed again. The corn vanished and in its place Mr Lamb saw plain grass - and as soon as that happened he recognised the field because, on his journeys as a travelling salesman, he had passed it scores of times.

'It's that field where they hold the annual gypsy fair at Brough Field, Cumbria,' he told his wife. 'The Lord must want us to be there.'

From there things moved quickly for them. They traded in their car and bought a motorhome, brought the vehicle down to Hollybush, where we all laid hands on it and dedicated it to the

Lord's service, and then they embarked upon a touring ministry, travelling out from their home several days each week to seek out the gypsy encampments where they shared the love of God with the people they had once thought unlovely.

Back at Hollybush the fellowship regularly supported them in prayer and in practical ways, aware that the Lambs were taking the Gospel to the gypsies as an outreach from the farm.

But that gypsy fair at Brough Field was not their first port of call. A few days before that event began Mr Lamb stopped and spoke to a man whose gypsy caravan was parked beside the road.

'And that was a tremendous encouragement from the Lord,' he told me afterwards. 'This man asked me if I'd ever had any dealings with his people before and I replied that the only time I'd ever been close to a gypsy in my whole life was when I was a lad and my mother took me to a church to hear a famous preacher by the name of Gypsy Smith. As soon as he heard that, he put out his hand and gave me a huge smile. He said, "My name's Smith, too. Gypsy Smith was a distant relative of mine." That was such a seal on the work God has given us to do.'

In the fellowship we were looking for God's seal upon the camp, too. By July we still had no idea where an American was going to materialise from, but the Lord had spoken another word to us. *'Though the vision tarry, wait for it.'*

On the strength of this we had gone ahead with our plans and now had just about everything fixed up. The marquee was booked, the lighting and PA systems arranged, chairs organized, toilet facilities on order . . . and to pay for it all an account had been opened at the bank under the name of Hollybush Christian Fellowship - the first time the name had ever been used officially.

We had advertised the camp locally in one or two newspapers, but we quickly discovered that this was not the way the Lord wanted it done. From the beginning Hollybush had grown simply by word of mouth and that was how it was to continue. The only response we received from each advertisement was the bill!

As for who would preach the Word, we had arranged for Selwyn Hughes and Tom Butler to come and take some of the meetings, allowing room for our American visitor to fit in when he arrived.

But the weeks were fast disappearing and there was still no sign of such a man. Come the last few days and I was beginning to wonder whether that word had been from the Lord at all. The marquee was up, the chairs in, the people almost on their way. . . but still no American evangelist.

By the Friday evening - the night before the camp was due to begin - I was ready to admit I'd been wrong. It was around seven o'clock and I was getting ready to go across to the granary for the fellowship meeting - we'd been meeting in there since the spring - when the telephone rang. It was David Greenhowe, a friend who had ministered at Hollybush many times over the years and who was now up in Fraserburgh helping with a tent crusade.

'It's good to hear you, David,' I said. 'What can I do for you?'

'I understand you've a camp meeting starting tomorrow. Is that right?'

'Aye. What about it?'

'Can you use a speaker?' he asked. 'Our man up here is redundant.'

He explained, that earlier in the week, a young woman had committed her life to Christ at one of their meetings and that this had caused considerable trouble at home. Up till then she had been living with her boyfriend but knew she could no longer continue the relationship and told him that he would have to move out.

'He didn't take kindly to that idea,' David went on, 'so last night he came over here and burned the tent down. We've had to close the crusade.'

I commiserated with him for a moment. 'Well, what's the name of your speaker?'

'Wilbur Jackson,' he said. 'He's an American evangelist.' I

almost leapt for joy. 'He's the man - we're waiting for. Send him down!'

Later that night, after a great deal of rejoicing over in the granary, an army of us marched out on to the site where the marquee stood. We did a complete circuit of the field, singing praises all the way round and stopping in each corner to claim the field for the Lord and to post warrior angels to watch over the camp. There was no doubt about it; this was God's work and it needed God's protection.

Throughout the following day the campers arrived - about 150 of them - and by seven o'clock that evening they were filing into the marquee for our first ever camp meeting. With great relish I recounted the story of how God had told us that an American evangelist would be speaking at some of the meetings and how Wilbur Jackson had come to us. This had taken us all by surprise, of course, but the biggest surprise that evening was Wilbur's voice. We'd never had a speaker with a built-in amplifier before!

But the voice that mattered most was the one that would be heard only by those to whom the Spirit was speaking - that still, small voice calling sinners to repentance. How we had prayed that God would use this camp week to draw people to Himself! And how we rejoiced when, at the close of the meeting, a man rushed forward to the platform to give his life to Christ.

I'd noticed this man earlier because he had sat alone in a section of the tent where there were several empty rows. That was unusual; strangers usually like to get lost in the crowd. But, as we discovered, this man had good reason for sitting by himself - he had mumps. When the Spirit of the Lord moved on him, though, his only thought was to get right with God. When he did that he got blessed beyond his wildest dreams.

His name, we learned, was Brian Sanders, and he had come to the meeting under the direct prompting of God, following an outreach by our young people in Northallerton. There, a tract had been handed to Brian's daughter, who had taken it home and left it for her dad to read. At the time, he was confined to bed and was reading anything he could get his hands on. But this was quite unlike anything else he'd ever read; this told him how much God loved him and challenged him as to whether he had really experienced that love in his life. Wanting to know more, he wrote to the author of the tract, Selwyn Hughes, who sent him further Christian literature, including a newspaper which mentioned that Selwyn would be one of the speakers at the first Hollybush camp. As he read this, Brian heard a persistent voice telling him, 'Go there . . . Go there.'

The voice came at a time when Brian was at his lowest ebb. His illness had kept him in bed for several weeks, and in addition to this he was suffering chronic anxiety, and had been for seven years, since the day a man had stepped into the path of his car. Although he had managed to avoid an accident, the effect of the incident had been devastating. Something inside him had snapped and, from that day, he had lived in fear and terror. He came to Hollybush camp a sick and broken man.

'As I sat there listening to the Gospel message, I just wanted to cry,' he told us. 'Tears were streaming down my face and I just knew God was speaking to me.' When it came to the altar call Brian didn't need prompting; he almost ran to the front and knelt there alone, asking the Lord to touch him. And God did - literally.

'I felt this hand upon my shoulder,' he explained, 'and when I turned to see who it was there was no one there. It was the Lord.'

Moments later he felt a strange but warm power surging through his body, and when he stood up again he was beaming. No one had to tell him what the Lord had done for him. His soul was saved, his body healed, and his mind set free of torment. He was a new man, and when he returned home to his family they barely recognised him.

What a way to begin a series of meetings! What a testimony to the saving, healing and delivering power of God!

The next night Brian was back again, this time with his son Michael, and he too gave his life to Christ. And what rejoicing there was over that. Not simply because another life had been handed over to the Lord, but because we were seeing fulfilled the promise God had given us as confirmation that the camp was in His plan: *'I will send to the tent a man and his son and I shall save them.'* Now we'd seen it happen. Now we knew beyond a doubt that God was with us.

But if we'd needed any further evidence it was to be seen the following day, after the morning Bible study. As usual, once the meeting had finished, I invited people to remain in the tent for meditation and prayer. Among those who stayed behind was Mrs Lamb. During that quiet time she happened to look up and saw the same wonderful sight we had seen so often in our meetings in Hollybush house.

'It was the glory, Jim,' she told me, her eyes bright with the excitement of God's presence. 'It came drifting in at one side of the tent, a fine, glowing mist, and moved slowly across in front of me and out the other side. There's just no doubt about it, God's moving on this camp in a mighty way.'

We experienced this in increasing measure as the week progressed. Each evening we counselled more people than the night before, and each day we heard more stories of how God was dealing with Christians in their quiet times in the privacy of their tents and caravans. Our prayer, of course, had been that every one of our campers would be blessed by being with us, and when it came to the last night and the farewells next morning it seemed as though that prayer had been answered. I'd never shaken so many hands! But the best indication was the number of times I was asked, 'Will there be a camp next year?'

'God willing, yes,' I told them. 'Keep in touch and we'll let you know.' It would have been easy to have said yes right away and to have taken bookings there and then, but we needed to know God's mind on the matter. The barn rallies held in the granary the previous summer had not been repeated this year. Maybe the camp was to be a one-off thing, too. The Lord would let us know in time. Either way, none of us would have missed that thrilling first camp. And when, on the Saturday night, we packed away the chairs and dismantled the tent we sensed a real tearing of the heart. If only the camp could have gone on, if only we could have lingered in that wonderful sense of the Lord's presence . . .

Amazingly, those of us working the farm were able to do just that. Arthur was first to put it into words.

'Have you noticed that tremendous peace out there in the field where we had the marquee?' he asked me over supper one evening. 'As you walk across that patch of ground you can really feel it, as though the Lord's presence is still there, brooding over the place.'

He was right. It was a phenomenon I'd not encountered before, but it was real enough. In fact that peace was still there three or four weeks later.

'D'you know, Arthur,' I said, 'I reckon it's because of those warrior angels we posted in the four corners of that field.'

'How come?'

'Well, we never dismissed them. I reckon they're still out there on duty.'

He laughed that big, hearty laugh of his. 'Y'know, I think you might be right!'

Another blessing to come out of camp week was a new hand. I'd known Ernest Allison for some years, both through the fellowship and the occasional gardening jobs he did for us down at The Limes, when he wasn't working as a long-distance lorry driver. I hadn't seen him for a while so, when he turned up at the Saturday night meeting, I asked him how things were going.

'Work's not so good,' he said. 'I've just been made redundant.'

God's timing is always right. 'Well, for a while I've been meaning to ask if you'd come and work for me. I need another full-time man, basically to drive the wagons, but also to help out around the farm when the haulage side is quiet. The job's yours, if you'd like it.'

A smile creased his tanned face. 'I can start Monday, if that's not too soon.'

And so Ernest came and joined us and quickly proved to be the right man for the job. He also became more heavily involved in the fellowship where, each week, we saw a miracle being worked out in his life.

Being a good Yorkshireman, Ernest was a lover of brass band music and, for some years, had played cornet with Bedale Brass Band. But, with his increasing commitment to Hollybush, this posed a problem: band practice and fellowship night were both on Friday. Ultimately, though, there was no real choice; he knew where he would rather be. Yet there was another snag. Ernest longed to use his gift in the meetings, to help accompany the singing, but he had been trained to play from sheet music; to contribute effectively to our worship he knew he would need to play by ear. Believing God for such a miracle, he resigned from the brass band and brought his cornet to the meetings, providing a welcome addition to our growing 'orchestra' of piano, accordion and guitars.

Music, of course, was only one area in which folk could contribute. Practical skills had a place, too, and when we'd decided to move the Sunday school and Friday meeting into the granary we'd seen God provide our needs through two very capable men, one from the fellowship and one from the local community.

The job in hand was to face-lift the interior of the granary, especially to put in a decent ceiling.

'Looks like a job for the professionals,' I concluded after an inspection. 'Maybe we could get that joiner chap in. What's his name? Lawrence Willis?'

So Lawrence came down and did the job for us. As he was finishing off he told me he'd been thinking about how further improvements could be made.

'I think I've got just the thing for you,' he said. 'How would you like these walls boarded with sheets of wood-grain laminate? There's a builder's merchant closing down and I've been told I can have 30 eight-by-four sheets at half price. If you'd like them for these walls, you can have them at the same price.'

'All right,' I said. 'We'll have them. It'll smarten this place up no end.'

When Lawrence was through we had an attractive new meeting room, plus a number of off-cuts from the boards. It seemed a pity to throw them out, so I approached one of our members, Alan Lawson, about using the pieces to make some sort of housing for a courtesy light over the gateway to the house. Mr Lawson was a retired man and a jack of all trades. I suspected he would welcome such a project, but I could never have guessed what my enquiry would lead to.

After a few days, Mr Lawson came to me with his own idea. 'I've been thinking about those off-cuts, Jim. You say you want a light for the gate, but how about if I use them for another type of light? I've got a sort of pulpit in mind for the fellowship.'

'As you like,' I said. 'We could certainly use a decent stand for the speaker's notes.'

He returned a few weeks later with a construction that surprised and delighted us all. It was a miniature lighthouse, about four feet high, complete in every detail, including a working light set in the dome. With his son Paul, Mr Lawson had spent many hours designing and building a most attractive and original pulpit. It was packed with symbolism, too.

'It consists basically of nine pieces of board,' he explained, 'representing the nine elements of the fruit of the Spirit. Then there's 12 sections to the roof, one for each of the 12 apostles. And see here, this capping piece is made of three pieces of perspex - the three-in-one Godhead. Down here, just one door of admission - only one way to the Father, through Jesus.'

The whole thing was beautifully finished in sand-textured white paint, with the text 'I am the Light of the World' painted around the transparent dome.

But there was a further significance to Mr Lawson's lighthouse - a deep, personal significance.

'I want you to know that everything we used to build this thing was redeemed from the scrap-heap,' he told me. 'Those off-cuts, the timber frame, the dome . . . everything we used had been thrown out. Everything except the light-bulb; that's new. The Lord showed me that was how it was to be, to remind us that He does this very thing with our lives. He takes the off-cuts, the rejects, the bits and pieces - the things men would throw on the scrap-heap - and He makes something beautiful out of them. That's what I've endeavoured to do, to make something beautiful for the Lord, to remind me of how He has redeemed me and taken me off the scrap-heap and placed me in His family, His house, where He Himself is the light.'

A short while later the lighthouse was dedicated and put into service on a Sunday evening. From then on it was to be used every week. It was such a novel pulpit that no speaker visiting us for the first time failed to comment on it, and not a few were amused to find that it had an extendable desk section 'for those with copious notes'.

One of the first speakers to use the lighthouse was our old friend Selwyn Hughes. The first time he preached from it, the first person to give his life to Christ was our neighbour, Eric Bell. Eric and his wife Kathleen were members of the local Anglican church, regularly attending the Sunday morning service. This was the church's only Sunday service, leaving them free to worship elsewhere each Sunday evening. On the Sunday in November that Selwyn was preaching, Eric came to us.

We had been praying for our neighbours, of course, since even before we'd moved into Hollybush, and I'd never forgotten something we'd read in our *Daily Bread* notes that week of the auction. It concerned 'using your home for the Lord' and mentioned some of the many people we might invite in as a means of introducing them to Christ. Among the list was 'your rich neighbours' - and we'd immediately thought of Mr and Mrs Bell. Earlier in the year, Kathleen Bell had committed her life to Christ after a service in David Watson's church down in York. Now it was Eric's turn.

By now the Sunday evening meeting had moved out to the granary and, being one of the last in that night, Eric was found a chair in the centre aisle right next to an oil-stove. But when he began to feel hot under the collar it wasn't only because of the heater.

Selwyn's message that night was based on the story of Abraham sending to a far country for a wife. When his servant found the woman Abraham had described he delivered his master's invitation, but the woman protested that she needed time to think about it.

'But God does not call us to come in three months' time,' Selwyn told us. 'Nor in three weeks. Nor in three days. *Now* is the day of salvation.'

As Eric told us afterwards, he knew without a doubt that God was speaking those words directly to his own heart, for he'd been putting off the call. But no longer. The moment Selwyn had given the invitation for people to come forward, Eric was up out of his seat and down the front, kneeling in front of the lighthouse to give his life to the Lord.

That was tremendous to see and, in coming days, it was to add an exciting new dimension to our daily contact on the farm. Our working friendship was now boosted by Christian fellowship, and that was a blessing beyond price.

11/In His time

In May, 1974, a family dream came true. For years we had cherished the hope that one day we might be able to have a holiday abroad, and since meeting Wilbur Jackson that hope had focused more and more on North America. Wilbur had returned to Hollybush with his wife Jo-An for our second camp the previous year and out of our growing friendship had come the vague notion that the following summer we might visit them at their home in Cincinnatti, Ohio. Come the new year firm plans were being laid. We would stay with Wilbur and Jo-An and spend some of our time ministering at their home church; the rest of our stay would be vacation.

'We might be able to get to a Billy Graham crusade while we're there,' I enthused as we attempted to plan some sort of itinerary. 'I'd love to see how the Americans do it.'

'Or we might get to a Kathryn Kuhlman meeting,' Cynthia added. 'I've always wanted to hear her.'

So we made an agreement with each other and with the Lord. 'Your Word promises that if two of us agree concerning anything we ask for, Father, it shall be done, so we agree on this and ask you that, when we're in the United States, we'll be able to see either Dr Graham or Kathryn Kuhlman. And we thank you that we shall.'

The nearest we'd come to a holiday abroad until now was ten days in Jersey. But that did not even begin to compare with the sheer magic of flying the Atlantic, touching down in another continent half way across the world, and spending two weeks travelling out from the Jacksons' home. To crown it all we were delightfully swamped by the generous American style of hospitality, enjoying tremendous fellowship and fun with strangers who very quickly became our firm friends. Nine-year-old Joanna loved every minute of it, too; it was just a beautiful family holiday. In such an environment taking time to minister at various meetings was simply a joy.

'But we didn't get to see the people we expected to see,' I remarked to Cynthia. It was our last day in North America and, having no special plans, we'd decided to fly from Dayton, Ohio, up to Buffalo to spend a few hours at Niagara Falls. One last splash of sightseeing before we caught the night flight out of New York back to England. A genial cab-driver had taken us on a 20-mile round-trip of the Falls, stopping off every few miles at the vantage points that tourists never normally get to, and now, with our minds still reeling from the stunning spectacle of Niagara, we were relaxing over coffee in the airport lounge as we waited for our flight to be called.

'No,' I said, 'we didn't get to see Billy Graham or – hey! There's the person you're looking for!'

As I'd glanced across at the lounge entrance I'd noticed a tall, slim woman walking by with a young man at her side. Cynthia turned just in time to see the couple disappear from view. In a flash she was on her feet and racing after them.

'Miss Kuhlman!' she called out. 'Excuse me, Miss Kuhlman . . .'

God had not let us down. Instead He had been planning to give us what the Scriptures promised - more than we could ever ask or hope for.' Our request had been that we should get to see either Dr Billy Graham or Kathryn Kuhlman, thinking that we'd be well blessed to get to one of their meetings. Our Lord's plan went way beyond that, and here we were on the last day of our American holiday, sitting in the comfort of Buffalo Airport lounge, having coffee with one of God's very special people. Probably no one in this century had been so consistently and wonderfully used in a healing ministry, and our heavenly Father had lovingly arranged for us to share 20 minutes of thrilling fellowship with this anointed lady and her pianist.

Yet more than enjoying Kathryn Kuhlman, we were jointly enjoying our God, and when we had to part it was with a mutual excitement: our God was the God of miracles and what He had done today He could do again tomorrow. His power was infinite, His compassion endless. All any of us had to do was call upon Him in faith. With this message stirred into new life within our hearts, we returned home with a new enthusiasm, a new joy, a new expectancy. And when at last our car turned off the road into Hollybush our spirits leapt within us, knowing that despite all the wonderful things we'd seen God do here in the past, His work amongst us had barely begun.

Indeed, having been taken out of the Hollybush environment for a while, we'd been able mentally to stand back and take a long look at the fellowship. And what we saw pleased us. Most gratifying was the fact that the 'rose bush' God had pruned so heavily four years earlier had grown up again and that the 'roses' were blooming. Our numbers were back up to 70 at most adult meetings, the Sunday school was catering for up to 40 children each week, and - significantly - our prayer meetings were getting crowded. It was a well worn method of diagnosing a fellowship's strength, of course, but still there was no better way of measuring potential. Long ago I'd learned that the power of God released within any situation is directly related to how many of His people are getting to grips with Him in prayer. From what I saw of Hollybush, as I viewed it from the other side of the world, I expected great things from the future.

What we were looking forward to most of all was our third camp. The previous year we'd had to hire a larger tent than the one we'd used for our first camp, and now we were doing the same again. From 1972 our numbers had leapt to 300 for 1973. This year we were expecting half as many again, and we were also ordering additional marquees for children's meetings.

Alongside the growth of camp week had come the vision for recording the teaching sessions, partly by popular request of those who wanted to relive the meetings at home, and partly because the ministry of our visiting speakers clearly deserved a wider audience.

So 'Hollybush Tapes' was born. Terry and June Brown, one of our young couples, volunteered to take on the project and, with donations from members of the fellowship, we were able to purchase recording equipment and a cassette copying machine. Terry had great fun with this, his spare bedroom becoming an impromptu sound studio, and when at last he emerged from the jungle of wires and tape to announce that he was all set for action it was in good time for camp week.

There was to be some other recording of camp that year, too. Having heard word of what was going on down at Hollybush, the people from Tyne Tees Television contacted me in July to ask if they could come and make a documentary. They were producing a series of programmes entitled 'Faith in Action', each programme dealing with someone whose faith was being worked out in their daily routine. They'd already filmed a doctor, a solicitor and a mechanic, and wanted to include a farmer for further contrast. The series would be shown initially on Tyne Tees with a view to syndicating to other networks.

Naturally we were delighted. Any opportunity to get Hollybush on television meant an opportunity to broadcast the love of God. So down to the farm came a team of nine people with their carloads of equipment and more or less took over the farm for two weeks, the second being camp week. They filmed us at the market, in the prayer meeting, on the land, round the meal-table, on the camp field, in the tent meetings, out driving country lanes, down in the River Wiske, where for the second year running we had public baptisms at the end of camp . . . just about anywhere and everywhere their cameras could go. For two weeks solid it seemed their cameras hardly stopped rolling, and when finally they packed their gear and left they must have had enough film footage to make a *hundred* documentaries.

But had they, we wondered, seen what mattered the most? The hand of God working through the lives of ordinary working men and women? From the moment we'd known they were coming we had prayed that this would not be just another assignment for a hard-nosed TV crew, but a time of personal spiritual awakening; a time for each of them to realise his or her own need of Christ and to make that commitment that would bring them peace with God.

Earlier we had begun to see such an awakening in one of the programme's researchers, a girl whose questions gradually became less professionally probing and more personal. It seemed to us that God had His hand upon her. The following week, however, she was withdrawn from the team and replaced. When we asked about her we were told that her professional judgment had become impaired owing to 'increasing emotional involvement with the subject'. Maybe we'd been too eager to win her for the Lord. It was a mistake we'd made more than once over the years. How long before we learned once and for all to allow the Spirit free rein to win people His own way? So often in our enthusiasm we would charge in with hob-nailed boots, waving a flag and blowing a trumpet, whereas the Spirit would simply tip-toe by and whisper His message into the unsuspecting ear.

Maybe we were doing something right, though, for long after the TV crew had retreated to their cutting rooms, we received a personal letter from one of the cameramen. He had not said a great deal to us during the filming, but several of us had noticed how increasingly committed to the project he had become over the two weeks. Nothing was too much trouble for him; he would go out of his way to get the best pictures for any particular scene. We were sure that when he took off his shoes and rolled up his trousers in order to wade into the River Wiske for footage of the camp baptisms he was acting beyond the call of duty. The letter he sent to us confirmed it.

'In the beginning,' he wrote, 'when I was told about the Hollybush film, I thought, "Another religious assignment . . . treat it with respect and reverence when in church, etc." But on the first Tuesday, something new, something different, something to think about. For the first time, God's blessing asked, God's involvement. Somehow I had never really considered whether He should be asked or not. In fact it never entered my head that He existed in my working life; certainly in my private home life, but not at work! How wrong I was. From that humble moment when I realised God was involved, and that I was involved, a new purpose came over me: I was going to make a film for *Him*.

'How was this possible, I asked myself, to make a film which would be equal to the trust I held? I never found the answer, but what I did find was a new outlook, a new purpose; somehow I had to show *He* existed and this I found was in the faces of those who had truly accepted Him into their lives.

'I hope when you see the film you will be satisfied that I did my best. What I can say is that I think I have now taken the first step along the road in search of God. May the day soon come when I can shake off the shackles, as you have done. Pray that this may be so.'

This letter came to us as a tremendous encouragement, and was a foretaste of the blessing that was to flow once the programme had been shown across the north of England the following spring. Several people wrote to tell us how the documentary had helped strengthen their own faith and witness. Others wanted to book for the next camp. But best of all were the letters from those who, as a direct result of experiencing the love of God shining from their TV screen, had made their own response to that love for the first time.

The documentary, we realised, was not simply something that had happened 'out of the blue'; it was part of the Lord's plan to spread the word of what He was doing at Hollybush, and part of the fulfilment of the prophecy that we would be *'a lighthouse set on a hill, and people shall come and be blessed of me'*.

There was another kind of response, too. Opening Hollybush to the television cameras meant that along with the blessing of touched lives came the buffeting of those who had no time for us and delighted to gossip their own version of what was happening on the farm. One of the favourite stories was that Jim and Cynthia were doing very nicely out of religion. Where does the money go from all those Sunday collections? And think of the packet they must be making from all those tents and caravans parked on the place.'

On the opposite end of the rumours scale was the idea that in fact the farm was bankrupt and it was only 'money from religion' that was keeping us from starving.

But we'd come to expect attacks because ground gained for the Lord meant ground snatched from the enemy, and our adversary wasn't going to sit idly by while so many people were getting saved, healed and delivered.

This three-fold emphasis was now stronger than ever. More and more the Gospel we preached was a Gospel of total freedom in Christ. One text seemed to sum up the whole ministry of Hollybush: 'Where the Spirit of the Lord is, there is liberty.' And the last thing Satan wanted was for people to be completely free. Sometimes this freedom came simply through a prayer of faith, but at other times, where there was spiritual bondage, it had to be fought for. As in the case of John B.

John came to us through a Christian friend and had been

meeting with us for only a few weeks when he committed his life to Christ. Within a fortnight we saw signs of an inner conflict developing and knew that he was going to need help. One evening, as I was counselling him, I suddenly knew what his problem was. He'd already told me that he was a printer.

'John, the Lord shows me that you're allowing evil spirits to trouble your life through your eyes. What sort of books are you printing? What kind of books are you reading?'

The answer was the same to both questions: pornographic literature.

'The Lord can set you free of all that,' I said, 'if you're willing. But you have to want to be free.'

He looked at me with haunted, cowering eyes. 'I want to be free, Jim.'

A week later we met again, this time with Cynthia and three or four other folk from the fellowship whom the Lord had used in deliverance on previous occasions. We hadn't been praying long when the spirits, already exposed and now under pressure to leave, began to manifest themselves, throwing John to the floor where he lay writhing and foaming at the mouth.

'In the name of Jesus Christ we command you to leave this man.'

Baring his teeth and barking like a mad dog, he rolled on to his hands and knees and started to come at us. Then he was up on his haunches, fists flailing.

'We bind you in the name of Christ and forbid you to be violent. Now leave this man. We command you to go.'

For a while nothing seemed to change. The more we prayed and pleaded the blood of Christ, the more ferocious the demons appeared to become. But their show of strength was a sham. We instinctively knew the Lord's anointing was upon us and that if we persevered these trespassers would leave.

'Set him free, Lord. Set him free.'

Suddenly it was done. With one final protest, the spirits threw

John flat on the floor again, and then, in the Spirit, we saw hundreds of shiny green snakes pouring from his mouth.

After a while, exhausted but free, John was helped to his feet, a new light in his eyes. Jesus was victor.

'You'll have to be careful what you allow in through your eyes from now on,' I said. 'And especially watch yourself at work.'

'Don't worry,' he said, still a little shaken. 'I'm changing my job. That place is evil.'

'I've no doubt of it,' I said. 'But you're free now, and what the Bible promises is true: "Whom the Son sets free is free indeed." I believe that's God's word to you tonight.'

Physical healing was a kind of freedom, too, and that was playing as important a part as ever in the Hollybush ministry. 'Miracle Valley' was still living up to its name. This was never more true than during camp week. As this annual event grew and hundreds more people came on to the land during each first week of August, so the number of miracles grew, too.

But we didn't have to wait for the meetings to begin for God to move in healing power. Our Lord was sovereign and, just as the prophecy had promised, some people found themselves receiving a miracle just by being here. It was around this time, in the mid-Seventies, that Peter Binns, one of our regular Hollybush campers, saw a miracle take place in his own caravan; a miracle that no one had asked for or expected.

It was the Friday afternoon before camp was due to begin. Peter and his family had arrived from their Scunthorpe home mid-afternoon, and having parked the caravan and settled in they invited another early arrival over for tea. Their guest was an older man by the name of George, a man whose right arm had been left almost powerless after a stroke.

After tea, a few other campers joined them and they began singing praises together in the caravan. This went on for hour after hour. Dusk had come and gone and now the caravan lights were on.

'Then suddenly the lights went out,' Peter told me. 'Yet I didn't bother to go and find out why because we could still see. Despite being totally dark outside there was this wonderful glow around us and so we just kept singing.'

It was during this time that the miracle occurred. Throughout the time of praise several people had been raising their hands in worship. But George could manage to lift only one hand - until now. Bathed in the glow of God's presence, he felt the power returning to his withered arm and was soon lifting it as high as the other.

'It was lovely to see it,' said Peter. 'One of those wonderful, sovereign healings when God just moves in on someone.'

Late in the evening the Spirit brought their time of praise to an end by withdrawing. The glow was gone; they were in darkness. But as Peter stepped out of the caravan to check the battery terminals the caravan lighting came on again.

'There was nothing wrong with the lighting at all,' Peter said, laughing. 'It was the Lord!'

Once the meetings began we saw many more miracles as people came forward for prayer or as they stood in response to a word of knowledge given to someone on the platform. This was exciting because we knew that when the Lord spoke in this way, pinpointing a particular ailment, the person with that problem was about to be healed, providing they had the faith to receive it. Such was the experience of Dorothy Pettitt from York when she stood to acknowledge that she suffered from circulation problems. With a blood pressure of only 99/50 she had been receiving medical treatment and also taking herbal medicine. Neither had produced any significant relief. But when our speaker asked those with blood pressure problems to stand and receive their healing, Dorothy shot to her feet, quietly asking the Lord that He would restore her pulse to 110/70. On her next visit to her GP Dorothy's blood pressure was exactly that.

Hearing from the Lord in this way, through a spiritual gift, was a tremendous asset and reminded us how important it was for those leading the meeting or bringing the message to be in tune with the Lord.

Sometimes, though, the speaker wouldn't have to wait for the word of knowledge to operate in his spirit. Occasionally he could *ask* the Lord who needed a healing and the answer would be given by direct reply.

This happened shortly after camp had finished one year. Once again Wilbur and Jo-An Jackson were with us (by now they were almost part of the Hollybush camp fittings) and I had asked Wilbur if he would speak at our Friday evening meeting. He agreed, and as he was preparing he asked the Lord, 'Is there anyone you have a special word for tonight?'

Immediately he heard that silent voice replying. *Yes, there's someone who has a deteriorating ear-drum. It's in the left ear. I want to heal them tonight.*

When Wilbur announced this toward the end of the meeting one of our members came forward. Ruth Krieger had tears in her eyes.

'Only this morning,' she said, 'I asked the Lord how long before he restored my ear-drum.'

Nine years later Ruth told Wilbur that, from that day on, she'd had no further trouble. Her ear had been made whole.

Occasionally healing had to be administered at a moment's notice in what were emergency circumstances. One such instance occurred when a woman with heart trouble slumped to the ground during a camp meeting. Within seconds she was being carried outside where a group of Christians laid hands on her, rebuked her condition, and through faith released healing to her body. Despite a bleak history of similar attacks she made a full and instant recovery which she confirmed to us at camp three years later.

In the majority of cases the miracle needed was this type of physical healing, but now and then we found ourselves battling against more than straightforward physical affliction. It happened one year when Wilbur had just launched into his message. His subject was 'Himpossibilities'.

Suddenly there was a disruption: an elderly woman seated in a wheelchair collapsed to the floor and began haemorrhaging at the mouth. Wilbur's first reaction, he told me afterwards, was to go to the woman immediately and to minister healing to her. But then the Lord spoke to him.

You don't need to do that. Just speak to the spirit of death that has come upon her and command it to go. Then release the spirit of life to her.

He did exactly that - and within five minutes the woman was back in her chair, delivered and healed. She had been suffering from a weak heart.

After the meeting we learned that during those few moments after her collapse the woman appeared quite dead. One of the first people to reach her was a medical technician who had checked her life systems and found her apparently clinically dead.

It was a lesson for us all. We had not encountered a 'spirit of death' before - a demon with the ability to simulate clinical death within a human body - and the episode only underlined how subtle is our enemy and how vital are the gifts of the Holy Spirit which enable us to receive life-giving truth direct from our loving Father.

From time to time, however, a very different kind of healing was needed: the healing of a broken heart.

Paul and Wendy Lawson were still rejoicing in the safe arrival of their second child, Stephen, when at nine weeks old the baby died. The doctors said it was a 'cot death', but explanations didn't help. Wendy was devastated.

Naturally, the fellowship rallied round in prayer and practical support, and one member in particular, Dorcas Willows, drew alongside Wendy and committed herself to helping the family through the heartache.

But human hands could do only so much; what Wendy needed was the healing touch of Christ. God had it in hand.

It was the following year at camp, almost exactly a year since the tragedy. Paul and Wendy were in the meeting, seated at the back in case they had to slip out with their daughter, Sarah.

But it was Wendy who wanted to leave the tent. Unable to enter into the joyful spirit of the meeting she had become more and more miserable and was about to get up and go out. Just then, however, it began raining heavily. Wendy had no coat, so she stayed put. It was all in the plan.

A few minutes later, with Wendy now crying quietly to herself, a couple went up on to the platform to tell how God had brought them through the deepest hurt they'd ever experienced . . . the hurt of losing their daughter.

Paul and Wendy glanced at each other, their own sadness now mingled with expectancy. Was the Lord speaking to them?

Soon the couple on the platform returned to their seats . . . incredibly, in a gathering of over a thousand people, directly in front of Paul and Wendy.

Then our guest speaker that night, John Hutchinson, stood up.

'Friends, God did not permit that testimony without a purpose. There is someone here who has been through the same experience. Will you stand up and let us pray with you?'

As Wendy turned to Paul in amazement another woman in the congregation stood up.

'No, sister,' said John, 'it's not you; I spoke with you earlier.'

Without further hesitation the Lawsons got to their feet.

From that night on, Paul told me, the hurt subsided. It did not disappear completely - each year around the time Stephen had died Wendy would go a little quiet - but the deep, gaping wound had been healed.

We know this to be true because along with the hurt Wendy had also known the fear of having the same thing happen to another baby. For that reason she'd said she would never have any more children.

A year or so later, however, we were rejoicing with them over the birth of their new son, John.

But as some healings begin so others come to an end. For ten years, since the day God restored her weak heart, Mother had enjoyed wonderful health. Now, in October, 1975, she was ill with silent pneumonia and the doctor told us her lungs were filling with fluid. It was only a matter of time, he said, and we should be prepared for the worst.

'Well, Lord,' I prayed, 'if this is Mother's time I've just one last request. I'd like to be there when she goes.'

Mother didn't go into hospital; she was being nursed at home by her companion, Miss Lilian Jefferson. But before long additional help was needed. The tablets Mother was taking had caused her to be confused about time and she was getting up at all times of the night, thinking it was morning, and retiring to bed in the middle of the day. A few days of this soon tired Miss Jefferson and so my brothers and I volunteered to take it in turn to do a 24-hour watch.

A week later I went up to Mother's bungalow at midday to begin the next watch. Mother and Miss Jefferson were having lunch. With that over, Mother declared, 'Well, I must be off to bed. I mustn't stay up too late.'

Once she was settled I went into her room to sit with her. She was sitting up in bed so I picked up her hair brush and went and sat on the edge of the bed. I put one arm around her shoulders, and sat gently brushing her fine, long hair. Just once I glanced at her face: she looked supremely happy and at peace.

Then, without any warning, she breathed out ... and was gone.

I went quietly to the door and called out: 'Miss Jefferson?' She came immediately with another of Mother's friends, Margaret Ashbridge.

Before we did anything else we stood and had a time of prayer, a time of rejoicing. For there was nothing gloomy about Mother's going, and when the doctor had told us to prepare for the worst he could not have known that for Christians death is but a doorway into the very best. How thankful I was that, in Christ, death is swallowed up in victory. How good to know that Mother was with the Saviour she loved.

But did I say that Mother's healing had come to an end? No, that isn't true. As I drove slowly home to share the news I knew that at last her healing was complete.

The timing, too, was perfect. We had the assurance that our heavenly Father does not bring us into this world or lead us out a moment too soon or too late.

Timing was a crucial factor in another work which the Holy Spirit was doing at this time, a work with which I was to become closely associated. Ever since that day back at The Limes when I'd first heard those tapes of Full Gospel Business Men's Fellowship International meetings in America I'd nurtured the hope that one day such a movement would be started in Britain. Again, in the natural I would have liked it to happen straightaway, for the potential of such meetings to win men for the Lord was enormous. To my knowledge, we had nothing in Britain to equal the FGBMFI approach. Why couldn't we have something similar right away?

But God knew the right time - 1975 - and that was now. Monthly meetings of the first British chapter had just begun at Altrincham, Cheshire, and the moment I was invited to attend I jumped at the chance. For like Demos Shakarian, who had started the Fellowship back in 1951, I too had noticed that the number of women who committed their lives to Christ far outweighed the number of men. Yet it was the men who were needed in the church for positions of leadership and counsel. And it was the men we wanted to see taking up their rightful role as spiritual head of their families. Even so, little was being done to win them, which was why I wanted to support the only major movement whose members were committed to this aim.

The way they went about it seemed so very right. Steering well clear of churches and mission halls for their meetings, the Full Gospel Business Men arranged all their outreach events in the relaxed atmosphere of restaurants and hotel dining rooms. The idea was that members of the Fellowship should invite their business contacts for a meal, after which a guest speaker - a layman and a businessman - would tell how he had become a Christian and how Christ had helped him in his business life. The word 'businessman', however, was not meant to denote only professionals and executives; it was to be interpreted in its widest sense: any man who was trying to earn a living was considered a 'businessman'. Indeed, Demos Shakarian himself was no company tycoon - not to begin with, anyway. At the time he founded the FGBMFI he'd been a farmer like myself. Maybe that was another reason why joining the Fellowship appealed to me. And from that first meeting, over roast chicken at the Excelsior Hotel, Manchester Airport, I knew I belonged. Not because the Fellowship offered a good excuse for an evening out, but because here was a credible means of introducing my Lord to those farmers, sales reps and other farming contacts who wouldn't come within a mile of the Hollybush meetings. The only drawback was the distance; Altrincham was quite a trek. If only we could have a Full Gospel chapter in Northallerton or Thirsk.

But that was the aim, we were told by the Altrincham chapter's first President, Leslie Hailes. The vision behind FGBMFI was to have many local chapters, so that the Fellowship could fulfil its proposed role as an arm of the local church.

It didn't take me long to grasp the vision; with others I began praying for such a local chapter that very week.

Such was my enthusiasm for the FGBMFI that when a second opportunity arose for us to visit North America the following year I had a Full Gospel chapter meeting at the top of my list of 'things I'd like to do'. But that wasn't to be, at least not yet. Instead God had it in store to bless me in another way. In fact our whole family was going to get blessed, for after a meeting at which I was speaking in Baltimore, Maryland, our daughter Joanna, now 12, gave her heart to the Lord. That was an unexpected thrill, but of course one for which we'd been praying since the day she had come into our lives. We were so thankful, then, that we'd never pressed her into 'making a decision' but had left her to find the Lord in her own way and her own time.

And yet, as we'd seen in so many other areas of our lives, that time was not really ours to choose, but His. In that fact lay great security - and in the next development at Hollybush that security was something we were all going to need.

12/Only the best

Wednesday, 19 April, 1978, was a red letter day; a day when I had an extra spring in my step. For this was the day when Hollybush Farm finally became ours. Every penny of the loan - £34,500 plus interest - had at last been paid off. That was good news indeed. But best of all was the fact that all the money had been repaid in just ten years, not 25 as expected.

'It's the goodness of the Lord,' I told the folks at the Friday meeting. 'We came here in 1968 without a penny in our pockets and God said, "You just be here and I'll prosper the land." Well, that's exactly what He's done. The success of the farm hasn't been our doing; we haven't grown because Jim's a canny businessman. No, 'tis the Lord. He's the one with the wisdom and the loving heart that delights to bless. We've just sought to follow Him. And now we say, "Thank you, Lord"- it's good to be free!'

But our freedom was to be short-lived. We were soon to be back in debt again, though this time the debt was to be the fellowship's, not ours alone.

I suppose it was inevitable. For the best part of a year the granary had been too small for the numbers now regularly attending the meetings and it had become only a matter of time before we would be obliged to make some other arrangement. But where to go? Into one of the barns? No. Though Eric Bell had finished renting them and their use had returned to Hollybush there was nowhere suitable for holding meetings. A few years earlier we might have considered converting the old farmhouse - the original dwelling before Hollybush house was built - but Arthur had been living there since he'd married Jane back in 1975.

We were left with only one possibility: erect a new building specifically for the fellowship. The most suitable position was that presently occupied by the old barn and stables adjoining the original farmhouse. Those buildings were derelict, anyway; an improvement was overdue.

'But would we get permission from the authorities?' Arthur wondered. 'It seems unlikely that any council would allow a church to be built in the middle of a farmyard.'

'There's only one way to find out,' I said. 'What's the name of the planning officer up at Bedale?'

His name was Mr Daley and within a week I was sitting opposite him in the offices of the Hambleton District Council. Back at their homes or jobs, members of the fellowship were praying.

'We need bigger premises,' I told Mr Daley. 'For one thing the building we're using at present has no fire escape.'

'I wondered about that,' he said. 'I've been keeping an eye on you folks for quite a while. I pass your farm almost every day, you know.'

I nodded. 'Well, what are the chances of obtaining planning permission for a meeting hall?'

'You haven't a hope,' he said flatly. 'It just wouldn't be allowed.'

I suddenly remembered the folks praying back home.

'All right, but if you were me, and you were applying for a building for Christian work on a farm, how would you word it on your application form?'

He grinned faintly, as if to say, 'It'll do you no good.' But then he said, 'If it were me I'd apply for a building for religious purposes on agricultural property. But I'm afraid there's no way you'll get it.'

I smiled. 'I'd like to try, anyway. Could you let me have the forms?'

Perhaps I should have felt despondent, but somehow I couldn't. Anything was possible with our God.

We applied the following week, covering the forms with our prayers as we sent them off, and then put them to the back of our minds. It was up to the Lord now.

The next thing we knew an advertisement appeared in the local paper announcing the application and asking if any person had reason to object to the proposals. Apparently no such objection was made and several weeks later we received the Council's reply: permission granted. The usual conditions pertaining to fire doors and the like had to be met, of course, but apart from these normal requisites the Council's only stipulation was that the new building be constructed of the old bricks from the derelict barn. This would ensure that the new structure blended in with the established farm buildings.

Our God had done it again!

Over the following weeks we prayed and planned together, inviting the full involvement of the fellowship and particularly giving a listening ear to anyone with ideas as to how we might save money. The fellowship was in no position to lay out vast amounts of cash and if we could save by cutting corners here and there it would be sensible to do so.

We decided that the most economical way of doing the job would be to knock down the old barn ourselves and to hire a bricklayer and joiner to construct the shell of the new hall. The labouring - mixing mortar and fetching timber - could be done, at no cost, by ourselves. Likewise we could do most of the finishing, calling in skilled professionals only when necessary. This way we could save thousands of pounds on the sort of fees we would have to pay out to a building contractor.

So we agreed that this was how we would proceed and set things in motion by commissioning a set of plans for a local architect. (If we'd known the first thing about drawing plans we would have saved money in that area, too.)

By September the plans had been approved and we were all set to get to work. The only thing we needed now was God's blessing.

But we weren't going to get it. In our enthusiasm we had forged ahead with ideas that, on the surface, appeared sensible and honouring to God. But we had omitted to ask Him how *He* wanted the job done. Now He wasn't going to leave us in any doubt about it.

It was a Sunday evening service up in the granary. The meeting was over, the benediction announced. Everyone was ready to get up and leave. Then a lone voice broke out above the buzzing of a dozen conversations. I recognised it at once as that of Roger Teale, a friend who was visiting us from his home in Scarborough. Roger was an itinerant evangelist and had presented the Gospel message at Hollybush many times. But the words coming from his lips now were something very different. This was prophecy. It could have been nothing else, for Roger was unaware of our plans for the new building.

'. . . concerning the finances of this venture, surely it shall come, and it shall come in large and small amounts. Thou shalt have no lack, and thou must not skimp in anything that thou shalt do, but thou shalt have the best for me, says the Lord. I will require the best - the best carpet, the best chairs and curtains, and all that thou shalt see and behold with thine eyes. And, behold, thou shalt not tempt the Lord thy God by saying, "We cannot afford it."

'I will provide for my house and there shall be meat and drink, and there shall be honour. People shall walk in and open their eyes and say, "Such beauty, such glory, such things - surely the Lord has done great things." For would I have my testimony to be abased? Would I have that which is impoverished? Would I

have that which is faulty? No, it would not bring glory to my name. For surely thou must not bring the lame and the halt and the blind. I require the best, and thou must bring of the choicest things.'

I was stunned. The Lord's word to us completely opposed all that we'd planned for the new hall. Particularly significant was the phrase 'thou must not *skimp*'. Though we had not used that word in our discussions it certainly summed up our intention. And it hadn't seemed wrong to us; indeed, we'd thought it wise stewardship. But no longer. Now, all at once, we realised that we had indeed been tempting the Lord by saying, 'We cannot afford it.' How dare we proceed with our original plans now? How dare we plan anything other than 'the best . . . the choicest things'?

So we began all over again, even from the planning stage. Laying aside the drawings from our local architect, we contacted Mortimer, Barnett & Partners, award-winning chartered architects based in Northallerton, and commissioned a whole new set of plans. As for the building work, we asked the architects' advice and they put us in touch with the firm they considered to be the best around, John Malcolm Ltd at Darlington. No one from Hollybush would be mixing mortar or fetching timber; the Lord was going to have the best. The furnishings and fittings would be the best money could buy, too. No expense would be spared.

And here was where we needed the security of knowing we were moving in God's will. To run up such debts without the assurance of God's leading would have been folly. In fact as a fellowship we would have been back where the farm was ten years earlier, for the total cost of the new building, including every last seat-cushion, was £34,500 - exactly the same amount we had borrowed to buy the farm. There was no way a fellowship of around 100 people could pay off such a loan in the short term unless God was with them. And it was that factor which enabled us to press ahead, regardless of the mounting cost. Where the money would come from we had no idea, but what we did have was the Lord's promise through that dramatic prophecy that the money would 'come in large and small amounts' and that we would 'have no lack'.

But what was our role to be in helping that promise to be fulfilled? Someone outside the fellowship suggested we should make every possible effort by organising jumble sales, raffles, bring-and-buy fayres and such like. Well, perhaps if we'd got ourselves into debt on our own account we might have been obliged to get that desperate. But knowing what the Lord had told us we did only two things. The first was to surround the entire project with prayer through every stage of development. The second was to arrange an overdraft facility at the bank. (And that later proved to have been prompted by our lack of faith, for not once did we need to make use of that reserve.)

And so we pressed ahead, excited at the prospect of the new building, and encouraged yet again to see how the work was growing.

But it was not all joy. There were pressures, too. Expansion brought increased responsibility. Though I'd never considered myself a pastor in the usual sense of the word, there was no doubt that the people looked to Cynthia and myself for their leadership. And here we learned a painful fact of fellowship life: leaders are not allowed to have days off. Those closest to us were more understanding, of course, but some folk had the idea that Jim and Cynthia were 'super-Christians' who ought always to be on call, as though we never had need of an evening off or time for our family. To those people our door should always be open, day or night. In a sense, of course, it was; we would never turn anyone away in an emergency. But we were a family, too, and needed time for one another. Joanna particularly seemed to suffer in this way. Hollybush was 'our home', we had told her when young, but at times, with so many people passing through, it must have seemed to her as though she was growing up in a railway station.

Weekends especially were sometimes difficult. While other

children freely had the attention of their parents on Saturdays and Sundays, enjoying the weekend as a family leisure time, Joanna would have to take second place to our visiting speaker. As the prophecy had promised, these came from north, south, east and west - many from overseas - and in order to take advantage of their ministry we often invited them to come for the Friday meeting and to stay over for the Sunday services. This meant entertaining them throughout the weekend, which we were happy to do, but it carried its price. It sometimes brought trepidation, too, as when we had Graham Kerr, TV's 'Galloping Gourmet', to stay. Poor Cynthia was in turmoil. What do you cook for an internationally famous chef? And will he scrutinise every mouthful? When he and his wife Treena arrived for dinner on Friday evening, Graham put Cynthia's mind at rest by explaining that the 'gourmet' was only a TV image. 'Treena's the real cook,' he said, grinning. 'She's the brains behind the programmes. The only thing I can cook properly is an omelette.'

Occasionally the pressures would overtake us. In my own case, the thing that brought me grinding to a halt was a fierce headache that came on late one Saturday night. It wasn't a migraine - I knew the Lord had healed me of those long years ago - but the pain was just as debilitating. For the first time in years I found myself reaching for the aspirin bottle. But not even two lots of tablets would shift it. At four o'clock in the morning, the pain still thumping away, Cynthia prayed over me and commanded the affliction to leave. Nothing happened. Next morning we called in some members of the fellowship to lay hands on me and pray the pain away. Again nothing - until I realised that this 'affliction' was in fact a message from the Lord. No one told me so, but deep in my spirit I sensed the Lord speaking to me. *You've got to slow down*, He was saying. *You must stop doing so much*.

Oddly, I'd not even been aware of pushing myself, but here was the proof: my body was crying out for mercy.

It was important to heed such warnings and to seek to reduce the pressures we were under because living in top gear all the time meant there were no reserves for those times of crisis that occasionally come to us all.

For Cynthia, the biggest crisis came in the summer of 1977 during camp week. The telephone jangled late one afternoon and Cynthia answered it to hear her mother's urgent voice on the other end. Could she come quickly? Father had suffered a stroke. That was Tuesday. Two days later he died. The funeral was fixed for the following Monday.

All this would have been hard enough to bear at any time, but the pressure was intensified with over a thousand holiday-makers on the farm. When your heart is breaking the last thing you need around you is hundreds of rejoicing Christians.

Not long afterwards, Joanna experienced her first real sadness, returning home from school one afternoon to find that Mally, our old labrador, had been put down. Old age had simply overtaken her.

'It was for the best, love,' Cynthia assured her. 'The vet said she'd never be able to walk again.'

But words would not console and Joanna disappeared down the fields to walk the paths she had so often walked with Mally, her eyes brimming with tears.

In fact we all missed Mally and to fill that void we purchased a labrador pup that we named Sally. A similar name, but there the similarity ended. Perhaps we made the mistake of going for a labrador with a distinguished pedigree.

'She'll make a marvellous companion and a fine gun-dog,' we were told, but this proved to be only half true. A marvellous companion Sally certainly was because she would never leave the house, preferring to stretch out in front of the kitchen range all day. As for being a gun-dog, she showed not the slightest inclination to chase after rabbits, even dead ones, and was so frightened of sudden noise that she would hide under a chair even if someone burst a paper bag.

'Sally, you're hopeless,' I told her when at last I gave up trying to train her as a sporting dog. 'A real disappointment.' In reply she gave a waggle of her ears, blinked her big eyes at me, and headed back to the range.

There was nothing disappointing about the new church hall, however. Begun the previous November, the building was now ready for use and was everything we'd hoped for. It was roomy - 1300 square feet of floor space - comfortable, modern and bright: quite a contrast to the basic accommodation of the old granary. But the real test was yet to come: how many people could the building hold? - We'd bought 220 chairs, but were our calculations correct? And what were the acoustics like for recording? This was important because, having seen the growing demand for tapes of the camp week meetings, we realised that we could further enlarge the ministry by taping our guest speakers, many of them gifted men of God whose messages were too good to keep to ourselves. With this in mind, we had included in the design of the building an audio control room and tape library - a boon to our tape man, Terry Brown, and an absolute necessity now that his growing family was requiring the use of that spare bedroom.

Everything was put to the test on 14 April, 1979, at the official opening service, and the results were tremendous. With extra seating, and with some of the young people sitting on the platform to either side of our lighthouse pulpit, we managed to cram in over 300 people, many of them visiting from other churches for the occasion. The sound, too, was first class, as was the message brought by our guest speaker, evangelist Eddie Smith. How much we had to be thankful for.

'But the building isn't paid for yet,' I reminded the folks. 'We've a long way to go. Praise God, the money has been coming just as He said it would, in large and small amounts, but don't stop praying yet.'

Even as I said it, I knew the Lord would not allow us to fall behind with the regular payments we were making to the builders because He had promised that we would 'have no lack'. Over the past year we had marvelled time and again at His provision of this need. We had not advertised our building project or in any way asked for people's support; the money had simply come in. Gifts ranging from £10 to £1,000 were trickling in week by week, and each time we had to pay a bill we had just the right amount of cash to meet it. Only the Lord could have arranged it so neatly - and only He could have prompted people to be so generous.

Many of our furnishing suppliers had been generous, too. Without asking for them, special discounts were given once the companies knew where their goods would be used. The company that supplied.and fitted the carpeting, for example, insisted we have the carpets at cost price plus a nominal charge for labour.

We had also benefited from generous loans. Members of both our own and other fellowships had made large sums of money available - in one case £4,000 - and so we never once fell behind with our payments. God saw to that. He also saw to it that almost exactly one year after our opening service every last penny had been paid off - all £34,500.

'God did it all,' I told the folks. 'It wasn't our doing; all we did was sign the cheques. The glory - including the glory you see around you in this new building - is all His.'

The key, of course, was in obedience. Despite the apparent risks of going all out for the very best money could buy we had never had a single shaky moment. The Lord had honoured us because we had honoured Him. Equally, if we had disregarded His instructions and settled for the seemingly safer course of a much cheaper building, we could have landed ourselves in debt up to our necks. And even if, financially, we had sailed through, we still would have been the poorer for we wouldn't have had God's blessing. That couldn't be bought at any price.

It was the same lesson we had sought to put into practice throughout our years on the farm; and, as it turned out, we twice had occasion to prove that divine principle the same year as we opened the new church.

The first incident concerned our corn. As usual, I had asked the Lord when was the best time to sell. As a general rule, the later the farmer sells, the better the price he gets; corn usually increases by one or two pounds per ton per month. On this occasion I sensed the Lord telling me not to start selling until January - and in January the price took an unexpected leap of £4 per ton. 'Thank you, Lord.'

I then started to get smart. Maybe I ought to hold the rest of my corn back till early summer; there should be even better increases by, say, June.

But the Lord knew better. *You need to sell all your corn before April.*

The Lord doesn't make mistakes. By 1 April there was not a sack of corn left on the farm.

Ten days later, for no apparent reason, the price of corn crashed by £12 per ton.

I wiped the sweat off my brow and said again, 'Thank you, Lord.'

The following month He blessed us once more, this time with our potato crop. I'd started selling on 24 April - again a late start to fetch a better price. But two weeks later I knew I had to get shot of the entire crop. *Don't hang on to it, Jim*, the Lord seemed to be saying. *Sell it now.* So, a little begrudgingly, I sent the rest of the crop off to market. On 16 June the entire potato market collapsed. Because I'd listened to the Lord I picked up the best price all season.

But allowing the Lord to get us the best prices was easy. Being obedient when it involved giving money away was something else.

I heard the voice - that still, inner voice - as clear as day.

I want you to send a cheque to somebody, Jim. And He named the person He had in mind.

'Fine, Lord. How much?'

He dropped a figure into my spirit that almost knocked me off my chair. It had a lot of noughts in it.

'But, Lord,' I protested, 'that's a lot of money. I really don't know how things are going till next April.'

He reminded me that *He* doesn't settle His accounts in April.

'It's still a lot of money . . . '

And I'm still your God.

So I wrote out the cheque, gulping as I scrawled all those noughts, and sent it off.

'You, er - you won't forget to make it up to me, Lord?'

He didn't answer that time.

The following May, when our accountant had finished the books, he called me on the phone to express his surprise at the year's profit.

'It's remarkably high,' he said. 'We can't understand it.'

Nor could I, at first. But a few minutes later, as I returned the receiver to its cradle, it suddenly struck me. That unusually high figure was exactly ten times the amount I'd sent out on that cheque. Believing as I did that the Scriptures require us to set aside one tenth of our profit for the Lord, all He had done was to ask for it in advance! I couldn't have known, of course, that this was going to be a bumper year and that our profit would be so high. Or was it that our profits increased because I had been obedient when asked to give? Certainly God's Word promised, 'Give and it shall be given to you, pressed down, shaken together and running over.'

And yet it would have been a mistake to think that every gift I gave would be returned to me tenfold. Indeed, the following year proved it. A second time the Lord spoke to me, naming a figure He wanted me to send to someone in need. Again it was a nail-biting amount. This time, however, I didn't protest for quite as long and duly sent the cheque off in the post.

Come accounts time there was no sign of a bumper profit. No ten times the amount given. Clearly that was the exception not the rule. But did it matter? Our heavenly Father would look after us, and He would never ask us to give more than *He* could afford. No, the lesson here was merely a reminder of the one I'd had to learn back at The Limes: the business was the Lord's and so was the money. I was just a steward. As long as I kept things in that perspective we would continue to walk in blessing; we would never be in need.

Being a steward brought other responsibilities, too; not least was the question of who was allowed to work the Lord's farm. Over the years I'd nurtured a vision to see our land tended by a team of godly men who would feel a real sense of commitment to Hollybush and The Limes; men who would see their labours not merely as a job but as an integral part of the ministry of the fellowship. But this wasn't something I felt I had to strive to achieve; if it was of the Lord it would be realised in His time. After Arthur and then Ernest had joined us in the early Seventies I felt we were close to achieving the sort of team I had in mind, but in fact it wasn't until the summer of 1979 that another man with this same vision signed on. And the way he came to us confirmed that he was indeed God's man for the farm.

I'd known Edwin Gill for some years. He and his wife Elsie were familiar faces at the meetings, and knowing that they travelled over 200 miles each week to be with us left me in no doubt about their commitment to Hollybush. But it had never occurred to me to offer Edwin a job; I knew him to be a hard and ambitious worker who in the space of just three years had progressed from dairy hand to farm manager. As far as I knew he had his career nicely mapped out.

Yet the Lord had other plans and for no apparent reason Edwin became unsettled in his job. At the same time he started to wonder about working with me at Hollybush. Was this what the Lord wanted?

'If so, Lord,' he prayed, 'you'll have to get me both the job and a house to go with it.'

Nothing happened for two years, except that he became increasingly disillusioned with his own career plans. At camp week 1979 he asked me if I had any jobs going.

'As a matter of fact, I have. I've a man leaving The Limes in a couple of weeks. How d'you fancy working down there?'

'I'm very interested,' he said. 'But what about accommodation?'

'That goes with the job. I'd want you to move in down there, if you could.'

We fixed a time for Edwin and Elsie to look over the place the next day, but afterwards Edwin confessed he wasn't sure about it.

'I'd like to think it over for a day or so, Jim - to see what the Lord has to say about it.'

'Fair enough,' I said. 'It's only right that you should be sure.'

The following morning Edwin was listening to the radio while working in the dairy. It was the morning service. He didn't pay a lot of attention, knowing how dry some of those services could be, but for some reason one of the Scriptures from the lesson stuck in his mind. It was from the book of Acts: 'And they went out of the prison, and entered into the house of Lydia.'

Edwin had no idea why that should be significant, and he put the text out of his mind . . . until that evening when he was sitting in the marquee at camp. Suddenly he was hearing the verse again. Our speaker that night 'just happened' to refer to it in his sermon.

'Are you trying to tell me something, Lord?' Edwin asked. The following evening he almost fell off his chair: that same verse was the speaker's text and he kept referring to it over and over again. But it was the way the speaker interpreted the wording which convinced Edwin that God was speaking to him through it.

'And they went out of the prison, *and entered into the house of one of God's servants.*'

Edwin was in no doubt. That just had to mean Jim - and the house just had to be The Limes.

'I'd like to take that job,' he told me later that evening. 'The

Lord's made it plain that I'm to work with you.'

'Great,' I said. 'Can you start in a couple of weeks?'

He hesitated. 'The boss won't like it, but if that's what the Lord wants . . . '

The following morning he handed in his resignation - and he was right: his boss was most upset.

'I'll never get another man in just two weeks; I'll need a month's notice at least.'

Edwin shook his head as the Spirit stirred the gift of knowledge within him.

'You'll have a man here in two weeks - I'm sure of it.'

Two weeks later the new man arrived and Edwin left. He was a great asset to us from his first day. And now that he was living so much closer to Hollybush he was able to contribute to more of the meetings, too. We saw the Lord's hand in it all.

Someone else who was contributing more to the meetings these days was Joanna. For some years we had been aware that she had inherited Cynthia's gift for singing, and now, with another girl from the fellowship, Tracy Tinsley, Joanna was occasionally singing in the meetings.

'She's developing a fine voice,' I remarked to Cynthia after hearing the girls sing one Sunday evening in the new hall. 'And it just thrills me to hear her using it for the Lord.'

Cynthia smiled. 'She'll soon be taking over from me. I'll have to move over.'

'No, you won't. There's room for both of you; you've different styles. Joanna's voice is modern. Yours is – well . . . '

Cynthia laughed. 'Square?'

'Traditional,' I said. 'The fellowship needs both. Anyway, you could never give it up; people get blessed when they hear you singing - and that includes me.'

She nudged me in the ribs. 'After all these years?'

'After all these years,' I said.

It was true. Cynthia's gift continued to delight and inspire, and barely a month passed without her being invited to sing at some meeting or other. Most of these were straightforward fellowship meetings, but occasionally there would come the invitation to sing at some special event - like the time Cynthia was guest soloist at the Annual Festival of Male Voice Praise in Carnegie Hall, Dunfermline (where her top C shattered the microphones); or, more recently, when she had sung before an audience of 500 businessmen gathered in London's Lancaster Gate Hotel for the inaugural meeting of the City chapter of the Full Gospel Business Men's Fellowship International.

I was delighted when that invitation arrived for it gave me an opportunity to increase my links with this visionary movement and to share with the national leaders my own vision for a chapter in Northallerton. Their advice was simple: 'Keep praying.' Which we did.

My resolve had been further strengthened the following year when attending the Fellowship's first national convention in a Glasgow conference centre, where I was pleased to meet the man who had started it all, Demos Shakarian. His advice was not much different: 'Keep praying, brother - and believing.'

Within 12 months plans were being laid for the first meeting of the Northallerton chapter. The venue was not unfamiliar - the place where we'd clinched the deal to buy Hollybush - the Golden Lion Hotel.

First, though, we were to see how the Americans did it. This dream, carried over from our last trip to the States, was finally fulfilled in September of 1979 when we went to stay with our friends Melvin and Irene Good in Williamsport, Pennsylvania. There, Melvin had arranged for us to visit the local Full Gospel chapter during our vacation. In fact he went further than we'd expected. Calling us long distance from Williamsport about a week before we were due to fly out, Melvin announced, 'I've got you booked in at the Full Gospel dinner, Jim - and the folks have asked me if you'd like to give a testimony. How about it?'

'Well, glory!' I said. 'That's fine by me. Just ask the Lord to give me a special word for the occasion.'

There was a great deal I could share at such a meeting, of course - already I had enough material with the story of Hollybush to fill several evenings - but I was looking to the Lord for a word that was right up to date.

It came to me in the most unlikely of places: a television studio on Huntley Street, Toronto. We had flown to Canada, rather than entering the United States direct, in order to spend a few days with our old friends Bob and Brenda Britton before motoring down to Pennsylvania. Brenda was a local lass, originally from Heighington near Darlington, who had gone out to Labrador as a medical missionary some years earlier. There she had met Bob and they were now married and settled in Toronto. In 1977 they had visited us at Hollybush and now we were looking forward to renewing the fellowship on Bob's own soil.

When we arrived we discovered that they'd arranged a few outings for us, one of which was a visit to 100 Huntley Street, the TV studios from which a Christian programme of witness was regularly beamed out to the nation. The programme, we discovered, was being sent out live, and on hand to receive viewers' comments and questions was a bank of 24 telephones, each manned by a volunteer counsellor. To our astonishment, within five minutes of the programme going on the air every one of those 24 lines was busy with people wanting help. . . people whom the counsellors were able to point to the Lord.

The potential as a form of outreach was clearly enormous and, as I watched, I envied a country whose broadcasting system allowed live television evangelism. If only we had something like it in Britain . . .

It was then the Lord spoke to me - not in an audible voice, or even in silent words, but simply through an impression in my spirit:

We could send out live television programmes from

Hollybush. The new building was ideal.

We didn't know the first thing about cameras and lighting, of course, but we'd observed television techniques during the two weeks the Tyne Tees people were with us back in 1974. It didn't look that difficult. And what we didn't know we could always learn.

Too ambitious? Not for the Lord. And I spoke out the vision by faith, first to Bob and Brenda, and later to my audience at that Full Gospel dinner.

'If it's God's will,' I told them, 'it'll come to pass. If not, we won't be worried if it doesn't happen. But I've a feeling something will come of this . . .'

Flying back home, relaxing in my seat way above the clouds, I began to turn the idea over again. Maybe live broadcasts *would* come from Hollybush, but what could we do *now* to set the vision in motion, to use television as a means to reach people for the Lord?

Gradually the idea formed and it was so obvious I wondered why it hadn't hit me before. We could video-record our meetings and camp sessions as a service to the people, just as we'd been taping the sound for cassettes all these years. It made sense. Video systems were something of an innovation at this stage, but there was no doubt that in years to come the home video would be as common as the cassette player. Was that what God was saying to us? There was only one way to find out.

Back home we got people talking and praying about it. Was this one of Jim's crackpot ideas, or was it something vital that the Lord was leading us into? Was this the next stage of development for the work of Hollybush? One thing was for sure: video cameras and copiers were expensive equipment. If it wasn't in the Lord's plan we could be making a costly mistake.

But the vision only increased; the majority of our members felt we should go ahead.

'Well, Lord, you'll just have to show us what to buy and how to set it up; we haven't got a clue.' Which was true; the nearest we came to a technical expert in the fellowship was a Hoover salesman. It didn't seem likely he would know much about the workings of video cameras.

But having decided to press ahead we came face to face with a big decision. In Britain, we discovered, there were two major video systems, VHS and Betamax. The tapes and players were not interchangeable. So which system should we go for?

'We need to know, Lord. Should we buy VHS equipment, or Beta?'

His answer sent shivers up our bank balance.

Both of them. You'll need both VHS and Betamax.

Swallowing hard, I went to see the bank manager. I told him about the vision of live television being broadcast from Hollybush, and about our desire to help things along by installing two video cameras in the church, together with copying equipment, radio links between the programme producer and camera operators, and all the other bits and pieces needed to put such a system into operation.

'We reckon it'll cost a few thousand pounds to finance,' I told him. 'Will that be all right?'

He was used to Jim Wilkinson and his God by now.

'Will you require all the money at once?' he asked.

13/Celebration

It was the morning of 26 July, 1982. Early sunshine was streaming into the kitchen and bouncing off the polished pine table as I settled myself in the big bay window with notepad and pencil. Before me lay an unusually tricky task: I was making notes in preparation for a special event the next evening; little reminders of what I should talk about.

On the face of it there shouldn't have been anything difficult about it for a man who was used to speaking in public, but this time it was different. The special event was a thanksgiving dinner to celebrate our 25th wedding anniversary and the notes I was compiling were for my speech. I'd already crossed out six unsuccessful attempts at making a start.

'I don't know,' I groaned as Cynthia brought me a coffee, 'I just can't seem to get off on the right tack. Stand me up in front of a couple of hundred Christians and I could spout all night - but ask me to write a speech for a roomful of cousins . . .'

The prospect was made more daunting by the fact that few of our relatives shared our faith in Christ and fewer still understood what the ministry of Hollybush was all about. Some, we knew, didn't care, and a number of others thought we were positively crackers. Even so, we were determined to share this celebration with the family. Having sent out 72 invitations and received only two apologies we'd gone ahead and booked the dining hall of the Spa Hotel in Ripon. But as the hour approached, I wondered more and more how I could share the essence of the past 25 years with our relatives without sounding as though I was warming up for a Gospel appeal.

'I just long to tell them about the Lord,' I said, 'but I don't want them to switch off.'

'Can't you start off with a joke?' Cynthia suggested.

'Some of them think Hollybush *is* a joke,' I said.

'Well, we can't help that. I think you'll just have to tell them how it is, Jim. Tell them what these 25 years have meant to us as a couple. That's what they'll expect to hear, anyway.' She glanced at the kitchen clock. 'Do you want anything in town? I've got to dash.'

But all I wanted was a generous portion of inspiration. Now alone in the house, I lifted my pencil and began to write once more, this time jotting down headings and highlights.

Wedding day. 26 July, 1957.
The Limes. Early days of farming at Sandhutton.
Expansion. Buying further 50 acres.

Yes, there was a good story there to share with the folks. Probably some of them would remember that time back in 1963 when some acreage adjacent to The Limes had come on the market and Dad and I had gone down to the auction rooms to try to buy it. We thought it unlikely that anybody else would want it; the land had been used by the military as an extension to Skipton-on-Swale Aerodrome during the last war and the concrete runways running through it were enough to put off most farmers.

'But we could use the soil between the concrete strips,' I'd told Dad. 'And later on we can break up the concrete and haul it away; that'll be a good 50-acre field then.'

We didn't think anyone else would be daft enough to buy themselves so much hard work so we went to the auction expecting to pick up the land at a bargain price.

It had never occurred to us that someone might actually be interested in purchasing the land because he *wanted* the concrete strips, but the man we found ourselves bidding against had come to the auction with just that in mind. And compared to his vast wealth our resources looked like the contents of a piggy-bank. It was Mr Guy Reed, the owner of the Buxted Chickens company. He was after the runways to put chicken-runs on. And there was just the two of us bidding.

We did our best, of course, taking our bid as high as we dare, but Mr Reed constantly topped our price and in the end we retired and left the 50 acres to the man with the money.

But that wasn't the end of it. At the close of the deal Mr Reed approached me with a genial smile on his face.

'I take it you're after the land?'

'That's right, but I know when I'm beaten.'

He nodded thoughtfully. 'Well, look - I only want the runways. If you're interested, I'll sell you the land between the strips for the same price I just paid for it.'

'That's great,' I said. 'I'd really appreciate it.'

Then he laughed. 'If only you'd stopped bidding sooner,' he said, 'you could have got it cheaper.'

I smiled at the recollection. And then another little incident tugged at my memory.

It had happened a year or two earlier than the runways story, but it too had concerned additional land. On that occasion only five acres were involved, but I wasn't likely to forget the fun and games we had in making that land suitable for farming. Like the other 50 acres, these five had been used by the authorities in wartime but along with the stretches of concrete went a mass of bomb-dumps. This land, however, had remained the property of The Limes and we were able to secure a government grant to enable us to reclaim the area for farming use.

The task required specialised equipment, of course. There was no way ordinary farm machinery would be able to dig up the massive slabs of concrete - some of it reinforced and two feet thick - so we called in a contractor with the necessary bulldozers and demolition gear. It was a long and sweaty job but, working side by side with the specialists, we cleared yard after yard of the smashed concrete, levelling the earth mounds of the bomb-dumps back over the holes where the concrete had been until the whole five acres had returned to something resembling a field.

Even then the job was not finished. As we ploughed that land ready for sowing we found left-over chunks of concrete and small stones coming to the surface and all of these had to be picked from the soil and carted away. The same happened the following year after ploughing, and the next year, too. In fact it was five or six years before all the stones had been ploughed out; only then could we regard that acreage as good, clean soil that could be fully cultivated. Reclamation, we discovered, was a long and demanding process.

The same was true of our own lives, I mused. Once we'd yielded to the Lord, He sent in His own specialist - the Holy Spirit - to begin the work of reclaiming us. And as I looked back at the changes He had brought I realised that, in my case at least, He'd had more than a few 'bomb-dumps' to deal with in those early days. There'd been plenty of 'stones' to pick over the years, too . . .

But wait. I put down my pencil and leaned back in my window-seat. This wasn't what my cousins wanted to hear. It wasn't even relevant.

Yet a voice from somewhere deep inside told me otherwise. There was something meaningful to my family here - not on a personal level, perhaps, for no one wanted to hear Jim rattling on about his own experiences - but the fact of Christ's power to reclaim spent and broken lives was relevant to every man, woman and child across the world.

And that brought me to my next heading.
Hollybush.

How could I talk about Hollybush without mentioning changed lives? That was what these last 14 years had been about: people meeting Jesus and never being the same again. Disillusioned people finding fulfilment. Sad people discovering joy. Guilty people experiencing forgiveness. Broken people being made whole. Sick people receiving health. Oppressed people being set free . . .

And there was so much more. What a story I could tell them if only I had the time and they the inclination to hear . . .

I stirred in my seat and lifted the pencil. Maybe I should headline these events, too, just to collect my thoughts. But where to begin? The prophecy? Yes.

The prophecy. It had taken our breath away to hear God promise that Hollybush would become known as a place of miracles, and that even as the sick stepped upon that holy ground they would be made whole. That promise was still bang up to date, too. Only last month, a man who had been taken ill in the car bringing him to Hollybush for the Friday meeting had been healed as the singing coming from the new hall reached his ears and encouraged him to step out of the car in faith.

And then there was that other staggering assurance that the Lord would bring people to us 'from the north, south, east and west to minister to you and to be ministered to'. No one could have guessed the vast sweep of that promise in its fulfilment, for over the years we had been privileged to welcome to our pulpit Bible teachers, evangelists and just plain excited Christians from every continent of the world and from scores of countries.

I jotted down the ones that came readily to mind. We'd had visitors from the United States, Canada, Australia, South Africa, China, Thailand, the Philippines (16 converted pagans), Paraguay, Uruguay, Greenland, West Germany, Romania, Hungary, Czechoslovakia . . . The list seemed endless, and with each country came the memory of smiling faces. What a wide cross-section of God's family we'd been privileged to learn from and have fellowship with over the years. Some were well known names, like author and Bible teacher Judson Cornwall, and Chico Holliday, the former Las Vegas night-club singer; some were pastors whose names had reached us perhaps only once before; but most were 'God's unknowns' - ordinary men and women who had been quietly serving the Lord in their own corner of the world until, for one reason or another, they found themselves at Hollybush. Many such people had been sent specifically to minister to us; but, as the prophecy had foretold, there'd also been those who had come amongst us to receive.

I paused for a moment. If I had to choose, which of our hundreds of visitors would I pick out as examples of the fulfilment of that prophecy? There were so many memorable occasions, so many tremendous evenings to choose from . . . But perhaps the most startling was the appearance of those former pagans and animists, now Bible college students at Luzon in the Philippines. Whoever would have thought that God would be teaching us about His love and power through such men; men whose very looks and actions left us in no doubt that they were truly brands plucked from the burning.

And what about those whom God had sent to Hollybush to be ministered to? Who would I choose from the countless folks who had become our friends in this way? Here there was no contest; springing to my mind came the name of a sweet lady from South Africa who had simply turned up at the beginning of camp week three or four years earlier. She had come, she told us, because she had heard the voice of God saying, *Go to England, to Hollybush Farm*. Having no other directions, and never having heard of Hollybush, she obediently boarded the next plane to Manchester where she enquired how to find us.

'Is that the only address you have?' asked the blank-faced airline official. 'Hollybush Farm, England?'

But before she had time to answer someone was at her elbow with the directions. He was another passenger who 'just happened' to overhear her question and who 'just happened' to have heard of us.

She arrived in time for our first camp meeting that year and stayed all week.

'But why have you come?' we asked her, intrigued.

She shrugged her shoulders. 'God wanted me here,' she replied. 'He told me if I came to Hollybush I'd get blessed, so here I am!'

We had just laughed. Who could argue with such faith?

I paused again; there was something missing. All these thoughts tended to suggest that Hollybush was introspective, only concerned with who came to us. Yet, over the past ten years or so we had seen many people reaching out into the world for Christ and using Hollybush as a home-base. I scribbled some names.

Liz Nutt. A former teacher, Liz was with us for about three years before God called her to join German evangelist Reinhard Bonnke and his team in South Africa. Now affiliated with the Christ for All Nations team ministry, Liz's main work was evangelism in schools.

Mark Teale. An itinerant evangelist who had been associated with Hollybush since the earliest days. Mark's trademark for many years was an enormous van in which he transported all the equipment needed for mini-crusades. Painted in bright colours, the vehicle carried the legend: 'Jesus saves, heals, delivers!'

Steve Gill. A young man who had first come to Hollybush about eight years ago. After working in various mission situations, Steve went to study at Capernwray Bible College, later stepping out in itinerant evangelism.

John Mattison. John's links with Hollybush went way back to the days when every meeting was in the house. It was he who drove down from Bilsdale with Arthur each week on petrol financed by rabbits. Now John was serving the Lord overseas in a practical capacity, supplying technical aid to Kenya and

Uganda through the Church Missionary Society.

Other names came to mind, too; people who were no longer directly associated with Hollybush but who had roots here of one kind or another.

Brad Thurston, for example, came to Hollybush from America. He was with us for two years as an itinerant evangelist before marrying a local girl (our first marriage at Hollybush) and moving on to a fellowship in Scotland. Later he accepted a calling to outreach work in the Ruhr area of Germany.

Jonathan Dunning was among those who committed their lives to Christ during the early years of the fellowship. After leaving school, Jonathan worked locally for a while and then went into training for Christian service at London Bible College. Returning to the north, he later took up the role of Assistant Pastor at Altrincham Full Gospel Church. Recently he had moved back home to become our administrator.

Eddie Lamb, Leslie and Irene's son, had been heavily involved in the ministry of Hollybush for about three years when he and his wife Shirley were invited to visit the United States. From that visit came the call of God and since April, 1981, Eddie had been ministering in Cottage Grove, Oregon.

Even among those who remained at Hollybush, I reflected, there was an outward vision, and over the years many members of the fellowship had travelled abroad expressly to meet and encourage believers in difficult circumstances. Many such trips had been made to parts of Eastern Europe where it was known that Christians were suffering hardship because of their faith. Where an interpreter was needed, and when the geography was right, our people would call on Mary Feldy, our little Yugoslav potato picker. Mary, of course, was a story in herself . . .

I checked myself. Next heading?

Hollybush Camp. None of us could have envisaged how this would grow - not even Arthur, who'd seen the busy camp-field scene in his vision. In a day or two we would be erecting the marquee for our eleventh camp, and with over 1,500 people booked in we would be seeing the camp-field full and tents and caravans spilling into the overflow area down toward the river.

As always, we were excited about camp week because, having received the go-ahead from the Lord once again, we knew we could look forward to His blessing permeating all the activities: the morning Bible studies, the women's meetings, pastors' and leaders' groups, the children's meetings and youth work, the evening fellowship sessions, the river baptisms . . . In every area we anticipated the life-changing touch of the Spirit.

Hollybush Tapes. This less conspicuous arm of the ministry had also grown. From its fairly tentative start in the Browns' spare bedroom, we had watched this audio service go from strength to strength, confirming our belief that much of the Bible teaching we received at our meetings deserved a wider audience. Our annual output, originally 500 tapes, was now in excess of 5,000. Included in this figure were dozens of regular orders, many from overseas, from Christians who for one reason or another were not receiving regular Bible ministry in their local situation. This included Christian workers in various countries and it was very gratifying to know that, through the tapes, we were able, indirectly, to support them in their work.

There was a problem, however. Because the tape ministry was largely an impersonal one, there was rarely any feedback. Plenty of tapes were going out each month, but were they really being used? A few months earlier this had become quite a challenge for Terry. After years of running the service, and only occasionally receiving any encouragement to carry on, he was seriously considering handing over to someone else.

'I just wonder if it's worthwhile any longer, Jim,' he told me. 'I never get any response. If the Lord's using the tapes I'd like to know.'

The following Sunday evening, having returned home from recording yet another Hollybush service, Terry answered the phone to hear a stranger on the line. It was a young soldier serving in Northern Ireland. He was ringing to say that, having come off duty earlier that evening, and looking around for some tapes to play, he had come across one of ours.

'I just wanted you to know that God spoke to me through that tape,' he said. 'I don't know how it got here in the barracks, but I'm glad I found it. And I've done what the fella on the tape suggested - I've given my life to Christ.'

For Terry the crisis was over, just a few words of encouragement was all it took.

Television ministry. This was one of those surprise areas of the fellowship's development, for none of us would ever have anticipated, or even imagined, that the Lord would open doors for us to tell people about His love for them through this powerful medium. But how glad we were that this had been possible. Following the showing of the 'Faith in Action' documentaries on Tyne Tees television, the series was then purchased by first one and then another regional company. Eventually it was taken up by every independent network in the country so that, within two years of the original showing, that little film about Hollybush had been seen right across the nation. The result, we discovered, was that following the showing on each regional station, at least one person committed their life to the Lord.

And the film was to have an ongoing ministry. Seeing the potential, International Films, a film hire service, had purchased 12 copies. Those copies continued to be used by churches and fellowships across the country and abroad.

Now, remarkably, we were making our own video programmes. Peter Snowdon and his wife Meri had taken on the responsibility for this, and under Peter's direction each Friday meeting and Sunday evening service was being video-taped. Each meeting during camp week was recorded, too. Those who wanted a permanent reminder of a particular meeting or series of meetings could now have it in living colour and sound to play at any time on their TV screen. And for those who could not afford to buy the tapes there was a short-term hire service.

Now, of course, we were able to see the Lord's wisdom in instructing us to buy both VHS and Beta systems; the two had grown side by side and if we'd gone in for only one system we would have cut our potential audience in half.

As for the future, I continued to believe that the day would come when we would be broadcasting live to people's homes. How it would happen I had no idea, but I was sure of the Lord's mind on the matter: 'Though the vision tarry, wait for it.'

I paused, glancing down the growing list of headings and notes. Something wasn't right. My headings were too . . . impersonal. This was supposed to be a speech for our Silver Wedding, not a potted history of the fellowship. It didn't say anything about us as a family. Our cousins would relate to Hollybush only if Hollybush was seen to relate to us - Cynthia, Joanna and myself.

And then it came to me: tell them about Joanna's music.

Of course! Nothing thrilled Cynthia and myself so much as to see the way Joanna, now 17, was developing her own witness as a Christian through her singing. She was on her own now - she and Tracy had parted about a year ago - and as we watched her ministering to the Lord in this way we were so thankful for the encouragement she had received to enable her to progress.

Looking back, I was aware that the turning point for Joanna had come four years earlier at a weekend camp where she was baptised in the Holy Spirit. Previously a very shy, self-conscious girl, that Pentecost experience had instilled within her a boldness we knew, she never would have started singing in public.

But that boldness needed nourishing from time to time, and encouragement had come in a variety of ways. Perhaps the most consistent source of inspiration had been our good friend Betty-Lou Mills who, with her husband Russell, had been a frequent guest at Hollybush Camp over the past few years. Being such a firmly established Gospel singer with so many albums to her name, Betty-Lou had been able to encourage and advise Joanna in a way that none of our other friends could have done.

Then there had been encouragement through the Scriptures - significant texts brought to Joanna's attention at just the right time - as well as through the gifts of the Spirit. The previous summer, a friend in the fellowship said she had seen a vision in which Joanna was singing before a vast gathering of people, which for Joanna at that time was unthinkable.

Similarly, another member of the fellowship was given a word of prophecy concerning Joanna's ministry. This was spoken out at the close of one of the Sunday evening services and declared that in coming days Joanna would be singing on radio and television, and that her voice would be heard by many nations. This word, however, carried the warning that she was not to look to men for the fulfilment of these things, but rather to trust the Lord and to be still in Him.

Practical support came from our fellowship pianist, Philip Sowerbutts. An accomplished musician, Philip had been able to help Joanna develop her musical expression, and it was he who often accompanied her on singing engagements.

Philip had also had a great deal to do with Joanna's latest project - a professionally produced cassette tape of her favourite songs. This was in production even as I wrote, and the rush was on to get it released in time for camp the following weekend.

Producing this tape, I reflected, had been a useful exercise in more ways than one. Embarking on such a project had obviously stretched Joanna both vocally and in regard to her faith; vocally, because all 12 of the songs had to be recorded in just one day instead of over the usual two or three weeks, and faith-wise because Joanna had been working for only eight months and her investment in the recording was over £1,000. In order to recover that money she would need to sell every one of the 250 tapes being made.

'It'll be quite a test for you,' I'd told her, 'but if the Lord's in it you'll not lose a penny.'

Wisely, she didn't rush in but took time to think about it. But once she'd made up her mind to go ahead she threw herself into the project, confident that God was with her.

'But what are you going to call this album?' Cynthia had asked her. 'I mean, what will the title be?'

Joanna's firm reply had brought joy to our hearts.

'That's easy, Mum. It's the title of one of the songs - "Living for Jesus".'

The following evening at the hotel, happily surrounded by all but three of our cousins and our one remaining aunt, we sat down to roast turkey, followed by lemon sorbet - a superb celebration dinner. But, as I told the folks a little later, this was more than a celebration.

'It's also a thanksgiving, for we've much to be thankful for these past 25 years. And I want to declare it here and now: God's been good to us.'

Before me on the table my notes were open and, from time to time, I glanced down at them, but soon they were forgotten for I found that the things I wanted to say were written not on paper but on my heart.

Hollybush was mentioned, of course, for the fellowship was so much a part of our lives, but it wasn't prominent. And why should it be? For Hollybush and all it stood for was but a channel, a means to an end.

No, it was the *God* of Hollybush who was worth talking about. For everything good that had taken place on the farm, and everything of merit within our own lives, was His doing and His alone.

'If you see anything good in us,' I told the folks, 'it's not because of Jim and Cynthia but because of Him, our Lord Jesus Christ whom we've sought to serve these past 25 years.'

Yes, His was the glory, His the praise. Ours was but the joy of knowing His loving touch upon our otherwise empty lives.

14/The secret

It was September, 1982, and we were in Canada again, this time with a team from Hollybush. At the invitation of local Christians we were taking meetings in Vancouver churches and, on this particular evening, we were ministering at the Bible Life Fellowship on Kingsway/Commercial Street.

It was, I suppose, a routine meeting - plenty of rejoicing and welcome opportunities to share our faith - but in fact this was to be a special evening; an evening when God would show us just how far-flung was the ministry of that Yorkshire farm we called home.

It happened after the meeting. I was standing talking with some of the regulars when I noticed a swarthy-faced young man pushing his way toward me through the crowd. Moments later he was gripping my hand and saying, 'You know, you folks sing just like on the tape.'

'Oh?' I said. 'Which tape is that?'

He grinned widely. 'A tape of Hollybush choruses. Someone gave it to me and I get real blessed every time I listen to it.'

'That's great.' I said. 'I didn't realise any of our tapes had reached Vancouver.'

'Oh no,' he said. 'I am not from these parts. I am only visiting.'

It turned out that he was an Eskimo Indian from the frozen

north, in Vancouver for the weekend. Wanting to attend a Sunday service he'd been glancing through the church advertisements in the local paper and discovered that Jim Wilkinson and a team from Hollybush Farm, England, would be ministering at the Bible Life church.

'I just had to look you up,' he said, grinning. 'Your tape means a lot to me.'

And hearing him say that meant a lot to us. Whoever would have believed that our songs of praise, echoing from the gentle Yorkshire Dales, would be heard so many thousands of miles away in so remote a place?

But this was typical of the moments of encouragement with which the Lord continued to bless us. We received another on that same trip.

It was a week or so later. With a few days left before we were due to return home, Cynthia and I decided to fly down to Oregon to visit Eddie and Shirley Lamb. While waiting for our flight to be called in the boarding area of Vancouver Airport, we noticed a man standing with his back to us, wearing a stetson hat.

'Don't we know him?' I asked. 'He's got silver hair just like Rev. Tom Butler, but Tom's with the Lord.'

'And he didn't wear a cowboy hat!' chuckled Cynthia. 'No, you know who that is - it's Demos Shakarian.'

Of course! I went and tapped him on the shoulder. 'Demos?'

He turned with a big grin on his face - the same grin he'd been wearing on the one and only time I'd met him, at the Full Gospel Business Men's convention in Glasgow three years earlier.

'Jim Wilkinson,' he replied. 'Well, how are you, Jim? What brings you to Canada?'

It was quite remarkable that a man who had travelled more than two million miles on Full Gospel business and who had met many thousands of Christians around the world should put a name to my face without a moment's hesitation, but we just put it down to the Lord. Certainly it was the Lord who had lovingly arranged for Cynthia and myself to be in that boarding area at the same day and time as Demos, and booked us on the same flight to the same destination. What sweet fellowship we had on that trip, all the way to Oregon.

Spending time with Demos in this way was, of course, a spur to my own involvement with the Full Gospel Business Men's Fellowship. Not that I'd allowed my interest to slip. Since that first Fellowship dinner at Altrincham in 1975 I'd been privileged to give my testimony at more than 30 chapters in Britain and North America, and occasionally I was involved in the regional and national conventions. Though commitments at Hollybush had prevented me from ever taking office in the Northallerton chapter, I was always ready to contribute to a work of God that had evangelism of this kind at its heart.

But then, to my delight, in the summer of 1983 the opportunity arose for these two interests to come together - Hollybush and the FGBMFI. Having heard that we were video-recording our fellowship meetings, members of the Full Gospel executive asked if we would be willing to film the teaching sessions of the forthcoming national convention at Blackpool. We didn't need to be asked twice.

And this wonderfully confirmed another of the impressions I'd brought home from that Canada/US trip the previous September. The Lord, I believed, had spoken to me about moving on with the video ministry; that this was going to be increasingly in demand and that we should improve the system wherever we could. But that meant spending big money, and so, as a fellowship we asked the Lord about it. Confirmation was not long in coming and, by December, we had invested £8,000 in two new high-technology cameras and ancillary equipment. That had been a big step, of course, but only a few months later, with our commission to record the Full Gospel meetings, we knew we'd done the right thing.

But it was God's wisdom, not ours. Just as all the other right steps we'd taken over the years had been His leading. Whether on the farm or in the fellowship, if it had been blessed we could only say, 'tis the Lord!

Of course, there were still those in whose eyes we could do nothing right; those sharp-tongued critics who said, 'It's not what it's cracked up to be' - that in fact the fellowship was subsidising the farm because, in truth, Jim and Cynthia were bankrupt. And, in a sense, who could blame them? The experts maintained that in farming today it took 200 acres to support one family, yet at Hollybush and The Limes they saw a total of 220 acres keeping *four* families. There just had to be a catch.

But there was no such thing. And it was no credit to us as farmers either. It was simply the goodness of God. All we had done was to trust Him and take Him at His word.

And yet, to be fair, there was a secret. It had come home to me one evening a few years earlier, the night we'd been taking a service in the little village of Nidderdale. There in the congregation sat an elderly lady, a Mrs Harrison, whose face I remembered from many years ago when I used to take services there with the Mission Band.

'Would you like to come back for a cup of tea before you rush off home?' she had asked at the close of the meeting.

Time was against us that evening but we had said yes, and I was so glad we had. For while we were drinking that tea in Mrs Harrison's cottage home, she had gone to a chest of drawers in the living room and taken out a little notebook, dog-eared and faded from years of use.

Opening the book in front of me she had said, 'This is my prayer list. See, there's your name, Jim. I pray for you at 9.30 every morning - have done for years.'

That was the secret of Hollybush - the prayers of the saints. Simple, believing prayer that released the power of God into our lives and kept the vision of revival fresh in our hearts. So long as that power continued to flow, and that vision burned bright and clear, we would go forward.

And the next step? In the spring of 1984 we completed work on our latest project: a cafeteria, built behind the hay-barn on the edge of the camp field. This was erected mainly with our campers in mind but we also envisaged it as a means of attracting passers-by on to the premises. Once they were here - as so many others had discovered - almost anything could happen. If they were looking for a miracle they would have come to the right place.

'But it isn't the miracles we want people to see,' I occasionally remind our folks. 'For miracles alone never met anyone's deepest need. Only Jesus can do that; only He can bring new life and write my name in heaven; only His love can set me free.'

As for ourselves, who can tell where Jim and Cynthia will be tomorrow? We hold the farm with a very light hand and if the Lord called us to another place we should find it no great hardship to pack up and go. All we ask is to be where He wants us to be, and so we shall be ready if and when He decides to move us on.

In a sense, of course, we are always pressing forward, for those 'stepping stones' that led us to Hollybush Farm all those years ago stretch out before us as surely as the waiting seasons, and by faith we place our feet upon them day by day. It's a winding path, of course, and sometimes steep, but we would choose no other. For this is the way that has stood the test of time. This is the King's highway. It is the path of blessing . . . the road to high adventure!

Part II

15/First harvest

I had only one prayer for the book which made its debut on Friday 16 May, 1984. 'Lord, if just one soul comes to know you through our story, it will have been worth all the toil.'

I'd thought that in time we might hear of someone being blessed through *Miracle Valley* - indeed, I would have been very surprised if it didn't happen - but even in my wildest dreams I couldn't have predicted just how quickly this prayer would be answered. At 8.30 on Saturday morning, just hours after the book had first come on sale, our telephone rang and I found myself speaking to a woman who had been cleaning a church in Birmingham the previous afternoon when she'd stopped by the bookstall and been drawn to one of the new paperbacks on display. In a voice bubbling with excitement she told me how she had taken the book home with her and read it in one sitting, so gripped was she by the Lord's dealing in our lives.

'I finished reading around half three this morning,' she told me in her broad Brum accent, 'and was delighted to see that you'd included your address for anyone who wanted to contact you. I got your number from Directory Enquiries and was so excited I wanted to ring you there and then to tell you I'd asked Jesus into my life, but I decided I'd better wait till morning.'

'Glory!' I exclaimed. 'Thank you, Father!' And to our early

caller I said, 'I appreciate your letting me sleep, sister, but on this occasion I really wouldn't have objected to being woken in the night.' For there's no better reason for getting a pastor (or an author) out of bed than to tell him that his words have been used by God to help someone pass from the kingdom of darkness to the kingdom of light. And there was no doubt in my mind that this dear lady had taken that step of faith. When the Holy Spirit moves on your heart to help you place your faith in Christ as Saviour, and you just know that something real and wonderful and lasting has happened to you, the first thing you want to do is share it with whoever will give you their ear.

As I recounted the conversation to Cynthia over a late breakfast, and as we thanked God for confirming so soon His blessing on the book, I was reminded of someone else who had a late night encounter with Jesus. His name was Nicodemus, a name familiar to Sunday school students everywhere as 'the man who came to Jesus by night'. As a simple Yorkshire farmer who had learned a thing or two about human nature over the years, I rather liked Nicodemus, but I'd always been amused by the Bible scholars and professors of theology who had committed all sorts of mental contortions in order to suggest a reason for such a man (he was an academic with more than a passing knowledge of the Scriptures) to visit the Master after dark. 'They try so hard to read all sorts of meaning into it,' I chuckled as Cynthia passed me the toast, 'that they overlook the obvious. It never occurs to them that Nicodemus might simply have been so excited about meeting Jesus that he just couldn't wait till morning.'

It was good to know that God's hand was upon the book. There is no better proof that you've sown the right seed than the first evidence of your harvest. Looking back, I suppose our hopes for *Miracle Valley* were somewhat limited, our prayer for 'just one soul' rather tentative. But not any longer. Our joyful early morning caller had given us a massive injection of faith-adrenaline and now we were ready and waiting for more good news. 'Do it again, Lord!' was our cry. He did not disappoint us.

As the days ran into weeks and the weeks grew into months, letters and phone calls prompted by the book became a feature of almost every single day. As word of the Hollybush story spread, and more folk got hold of the paperback, so the correspondence increased and the calls mounted. God was busy honouring our efforts and using the story of our own steps of faith to help others place their spiritual feet on the path that leads to eternal life. By the time we stopped counting, hundreds of readers, some of them in faraway lands, had been prompted to put pen to paper. We never listed the phone calls, so we have no record of how many people rang us as a result of God touching their life through the pages of our story. Likewise, we lost count of the number of people who showed up at the farm, either while on holiday or having made a special trip to track us down, and told us they had read the book and just had to find 'Miracle Valley' for themselves. Others turned up or wrote to us as a result of reading about Hollybush Fellowship in the various publications which had picked up on the story - publications as diverse as the *Daily Express* and *Farmers Weekly*. The latter, under the heading 'Centre for saints and sinners', succinctly plotted the growth of the fellowship from our first house meetings at The Limes in Sandutton to the opening of our 220-seater church building on the farm at Hollybush. Even then, the feature noted, our numbers were increasing beyond the capacity of the new hall. And that growth was to continue as more and more people, some from as far as 60 miles away, came regularly to the meetings, making Hollybush Fellowship their spiritual home.

Some, not surprisingly, came looking for a miracle. We encouraged them to believe for one, according to their particular need. Certainly they had moved into the right environment, where the faith of individuals was strong, and the experience of many bore testimony to the love and power of our wonder-working

God. Often those seeking God's touch on their lives would tell us their story over a cuppa in the cafeteria after the Friday night meeting or Sunday services. And that was a most appropriate spot in which to offer encouragement; as I've pointed out more than a few times, the very place in which we were sitting had been provided as a direct result of the Father's loving intervention.

The cafeteria was the Lord's idea, of that I was convinced. I'd been aware of a clear impression in my spirit that He wanted me to build it, and so, after prayer and a sense of confirmation, we forged ahead. Once we'd agreed the plans we knew we would be looking at costs of around £15,000. Previously, when we'd had a financial need, we had prayed about it within the fellowship and invited folks to make a donation, if they felt so led, and by this means, without adding any pressure and trusting in the Lord to provide, we always met our financial goals, often much earlier than schedules demanded. So, as we got underway with the cafeteria, I mentioned the costs to our congregation one Friday night and asked folks to consider making a donation. 'Mark your gift "cafeteria",' I told them, 'and we'll make sure it goes into that account.'

To my surprise, not to mention my disappointment, not one gift was forthcoming. In consternation I went to the Lord. 'Please, we want to build the café, but no one seems interested.'

With that the Lord pulled me up sharp. *I didn't ask the people to build the cafeteria - I asked you to build it.*

I swallowed hard and got off my knees. I stood corrected. And concerned. I didn't have the £15,000, and at that point I was struggling with the possibility of a loss on my potato crop. There was a glut of potatoes and prices were way down. At best we could expect no more than £30 or £40 per ton. I decided not to sell right away - to hold off and see if the market might pick up. It looked unlikely at that time, but as I talked to the Father about this I sensed I was right to wait. Amazingly - miraculously? - within a few short weeks there was a shortage of potatoes.

Suddenly my crop was in demand. The price shot up to £150 per ton. I sold, not at a loss as originally seemed likely, but at a substantial profit. And the difference between my break-even and the price I received? £15,000. Or one cafeteria. Thank you, Jesus!

The Scripture says that without a vision, the people perish. As with the cafeteria, so it had been from the earliest days of the fellowship, that the work grew as we held fast to the vision that had been granted to us. In fact, without that vision and our exercising faith in reaching for it, Hollybush might simply have run out of steam. The same was true of us as individual believers. The year that we added the cafeteria to the facilities here on the farm I was prompted to exhort the fellowship with a message on the subject. Vision, Vitality and Vocation were the three words the Lord gave me to pass on.

'We need a vision for building His kingdom,' I told the folks. 'As the old hymn says, you in your small corner and I in mine.

'We need the spiritual vitality that comes from His strength within us as we spend time with Him and make ourselves available to Him.

'And we need a sense of vocation, of His personal calling to that work.'

Confirmation that we are heading in the right direction will come in due course. In fact, the prophecy which encouraged us in the early days of the fellowship had a great deal to say about direction. The Lord's promise that *I will bring people here from the north, south, east and west* was both exciting and motivating, and its fulfilment over the years continues to amaze and bless us as men and women of God from around the world show up here, most by arrangement but some unannounced, some from the next town and some from the other side of the world. But no one has ever come quite as far as Charlie Duke, who as Charles M. Duke the astronaut came all the way from the moon! I met Charlie in Dublin, where he was the principal speaker at an international meeting of the Full Gospel Business Men's Fellowship. I was one of five earth-bound souls sharing the platform with the intrepid space traveller, who, as I learned, holds the record for time spent on the moon's surface. As a lunar module pilot he was up there for 71 hours and 14 minutes, inspecting, surveying and gathering rock samples from the rugged lunar highlands. It was an experience that changed Charlie's life. But, as he himself says, being part of the first scientific expedition to the moon pales into insignificance when compared to the dramatic experience of knowing Christ at work in his life. It's been our privilege to hear his testimony from our rostrum on two occasions. I suppose if you can find your way to the moon, you can negotiate the North Yorkshire hills and dales without too much difficulty.

In another sense, Hollybush exists to help those who've lost their way. To paraphrase Jesus, it's the disoriented who need a map, not those who think they're on the right road. During the Eighties we had occasion to present that message to those who truly had lost their way and ended up incarcerated at Her Majesty's pleasure. Jonathan Dunning, then our administrator, led many meetings in prison chapels in the area. At one time a team of fellowship members was heading out every two weeks to take the Gospel to no fewer than six prisons.

But, as we've been reminded on many occasions, not all the 'prisoners' in this world are behind bars. There are many more people 'in chains' walking about as free citizens than could ever be accommodated behind lock and key. One such 'captive' was a businessman named John. He and his wife had attended meetings at Hollybush and we'd got to know them quite well. At that point we had no idea that John had a dark secret, but one Monday afternoon a phone call from his wife alerted us to the fact that John was not a free man.

'His face is all twisted,' she told me, sounding deeply concerned. 'He's had the doctor in and been examined but he says there's nothing wrong with him.'

I said I'd come over as soon as I could get away, and a couple of hours later I picked up Brian Sanders, one of our prayer team members, and headed out to their place.

We found John upstairs, fearful and strangely disfigured, one side of his face distorted. For three days he hadn't been able to eat or sleep, and couldn't understand what was happening to him.

In the natural we wouldn't have had much idea what to do - John's condition looked as though it might be an unfortunate affliction - but, in the Spirit, God enlightened us. As Brian and I prayed and laid hands on John, I asked if he'd had any dealings with the occult. It eventually came out that he was a long-serving Freemason and was second-in-command at his lodge. We didn't need to delve any deeper. The affliction was clearly demonic. Taking authority in the name of Christ, we prayed for John to be set free, and free he became. Almost instantly, his face returned to normal and we rejoiced together.

John came downstairs with us to show us out, but as we were about to leave he called us back. 'Don't go,' he said. 'There's something else I need to deal with . . .'

He told us that he believed God had been speaking to him about his involvement in Freemasonry, and he wanted out of it. 'I believe I should get rid of all my suits and masonic gear. Will you wait while I pack it up, so you can take it away with you?'

His wife decided that she too should be shot of connections with the Masons and set to turning out the dresses and gowns she had worn at the various ladies' nights, so we ended up taking away two large suitcases of expensive suits and gowns, with John's instructions to 'burn the lot'. They were finished with Freemasonry. Christ had set John free from physical affliction; now they were ditching what they recognised as the devil's work and were throwing their lot in with the Lord.

Back home, after dropping Brian off, I told Cynthia about the evening's events and showed her the suitcases. 'It's all quality stuff,' I said. 'Seems too good to burn.' Being a Yorkshireman

I've always been cost conscious, and I wondered if these outfits might be sold and the money used to benefit the Lord's work in some way. While I thought on it, I put the suitcases in the garage. No need to be hasty in carrying out John's instructions, I thought. Besides, I mused, he might change his mind and then he wouldn't thank me if I'd put a few hundred quids' worth of garments on the fire.

Two days later, John showed up at the farm. 'Have you burned those clothes yet?' he wanted to know.

I'd had a feeling he might change his mind. There was a lot of money in those suitcases. 'They're still here,' I said. 'Do you . . .'

'Good. Because I want to burn them myself.'

We took the clothes to the other side of the camp field, poured on some petrol and set them ablaze. It was the right thing to do. The look on John's face told me that. Burning those clothes carried a lot of symbolism for him. He was sending 'smoke signals' to both the enemy and the Lord. Putting a torch to his past, he was now determined to be 'on fire' for Christ. To this day, John has remained free.

Expensive clothes featured in the testimony of another man who crossed our path. Like John, Frank was a businessman whose life had been turned around by the Lord. Financial problems in his business had brought him to the point of despair when a friend invited him to lunch and told him about the love and power of God. On the way back to the office, Frank felt such a conviction of the Holy Spirit that he had to pull off the road. Shortly after that he handed his life over to the Lord, and he told me about it on one of his subsequent visits to Hollybush. He was now so thankful for the peace that God had brought into his heart that he wanted everyone to know. Well, he was to have his opportunity in due course. Hearing that we would be holding public baptisms during camp week, Frank asked if we would include him as one of the baptismal candidates. I said we'd be delighted to baptise him and we arranged a date and time.

When he turned up at the riverside I was surprised to see him in his best suit and shoes, wearing a crisp shirt and smart tie, along with a fine watch and expensive cuff-links. Usually folk turn up at the water's edge in their swimsuit or their jeans, ready to go under, but although Frank had some other clothes with him, he explained that those were for changing into later, after he'd dried off. He intended to be baptised in what he was wearing.

'But . . . that's a fine suit,' I protested. 'And those shoes . . .'

He dismissed my concerns with a smile. 'This is what I was wearing when the Lord saved me,' he explained, 'and this is how I'm going into the river.'

'Right-o,' I said, but he could see that I was dismayed.

'The clothes don't matter,' he added, cheerfully. 'Only the best is good enough for the Lord, and I want Him to know I mean it.'

And so we baptised Frank in his finery. It caused quite a stir among the camp folks gathered on the banks when this figure stepped into the water dressed like he was ready for a meeting with the bank manager, but once we'd baptised him they heard his story. And they weren't the only ones. A crew from Yorkshire Television was there that day, filming for a programme about Hollybush, and naturally they seized the opportunity to interview a man who had put himself through this 'strange' Christian ritual in his best togs. Frank was delighted, of course; he was so thankful to have found the Lord that he was eager to grasp any opportunity to tell his story, to the glory of God.

In both cases, these men had been challenged about their priorities - who was to be first in their lives - and the Lord had won.

The same lesson was driven home through an incident on the farm at that time. The utilities people had approached us about putting two 42-inch gas pipelines through our land at Sandhutton. We agreed the terms and the diggers moved in, carving out a huge trench across the fields. As they did so, they placed the topsoil on one side of the trench and the subsoil on the other.

When it came to filling in the trench, however, they made the mistake of putting the topsoil in first and covering it with the subsoil. Any farmer or gardener knows that there's a reason why topsoil should be on the top; without it, nothing grows. You can't produce a crop from subsoil. In the same way, it's essential that our own priorities don't become confused. As the Lord's people, the spiritual issues in our lives should be 'on top' as our priority; the 'subsoil' of our lives - our human concerns - should remain a secondary consideration. If that order is upset, and human concerns take priority, we find that nothing grows.

On the land, the correct balance will eventually be restored, for Nature has a way of righting itself, but it took a good 12 years before that land was productive again. In our lives, no such process will come to our rescue; the choice of priority is left up to us. Not that there's much of a choice, in my view, as I remarked to the folks when I recounted this parable one Friday night. I felt God had given me a clear message for the fellowship at that time. 'Quality of life, quality of direction and quality of power are the issues that should concern us,' I said. 'God's quality of life is holiness; His quality of direction is about vision; and His quality of power centres on the anointing. If we are willing to take up His priorities we'll see growth in our faith, in our dealings with others, and in our relationship with the Father.'

16/Come rain, come shine

The agricultural rep stood in the cornfield, studying our crop and shaking his head. I'd called him down because slugs were eating our corn, nibbling into our new young plants of wheat and biting great chunks out of our potential profit.

'Slug pellets,' he said. 'That's what you need here. I'll drop some off.'

I nodded, doing a quick calculation in my head. It seemed we couldn't escape some sort of loss on this crop. If the slugs stayed they'd cost us money; to get rid of them would also be expensive. But at least the pellets would give us a chance of saving part of the crop. I turned to the rep. 'How soon can you deliver?'

He promised to return the next day, and as he drove off I glanced again at the slug-ridden field. *We could use your help here, Lord*, I silently prayed. But I took the matter no further. I would have appreciated some divine intervention but acknowledged that, even in Miracle Valley, we had to contend with the results of a fallen world. We are not immune. Crops would be blighted. Bank balances would feel the effect.

Cynthia reacted quite differently. I'd no sooner told her about the problem that evening than she was off across the yard, heading for the fields. Reaching the corn, she moved among it, praying, as she later told me, that the Father would send His own solution.

That night, while we slept, a sharp white frost descended, a frost that was unusually severe for October.

Next morning, when our supplies rep showed up, I asked him to take another look at the crop and let me know what was going on there. Minutes later he was calling back from the field: 'These slugs are all dead!' Our crop was out of danger. Cynthia and I already knew that and we were still rejoicing in God's goodness. But the rep, understandably, was less enthusiastic. He suggested we keep the pellets handy in case the frost had failed to completely eradicate the pests. I agreed, on the understanding that he would take them back if we didn't use them. Three weeks later he came and collected the pellets and our bank statement gave a sigh of relief.

There wasn't another sharp frost until well after Christmas.

A coincidence or 'God-incidence'? We believe that on this occasion God stepped in and responded to Cynthia's prayer, using the weather to provide His answer. We have no idea why He should choose to respond in this way, other than that He is God and His thoughts are far above our own.

At other times it would appear that our prayers for His intervention go unheeded, even when large numbers have prayed for a change in the weather. We could have used such an answer during our main camp week that summer. Over the years both the youth camp and family camp weeks had grown, so that we were now seeing around a thousand folks on site for the last week of July. On many occasions we had been blessed with good weather, but this year the rain started to fall on the Monday and continued virtually non-stop through Tuesday and Wednesday, finally easing up late on Thursday. The resulting mud was so bad that we had to ask folks not to take their cars on to the field. And at the entrance to the marquee, where we held the meetings, buckets of water were provided so that boots could be washed off. Within a very short space of time, not a single pair of wellingtons was to be found in the Northallerton shops, and even a special stock of wellies, brought personally from Harrogate by the owner of our local Army & Navy Stores, soon sold out. Those who didn't manage to secure a pair - or who didn't like walking around in wellingtons - went barefoot.

Weatherwise, that camp was a washout, and none of us would wish to repeat that soggy experience. But it says something about the God of Hollybush - the one who always shows up for camp week, whatever the weather - that none of our campers packed up and left during the downpour. All returned home on the Saturday, duly blessed.

On another occasion we could have used some rain. Some years earlier, the sun had shone with a vengeance and no one could get cool. It was particularly hot inside the marquee, even with the sides of the big tent rolled up. No wonder more than a few folks availed themselves of an ice cream from the van of an enterprising driver who arrived on the field during one of our meetings. While his business acumen was to be applauded his timing was unfortunate, for the American group who were ministering at that point were astounded to see folks leaving the meeting for ice cream. Perhaps our American visitors were more used to the high temperatures, or maybe they just thought it sacrilegious that anyone would leave a Christian meeting in order to purchase refreshments. Whatever, that sun-baked camp week gave new meaning to the phrase 'hot Gospel'!

Camp weeks became an increasingly popular feature of Hollybush during those years, with little need to advertise as word of mouth ensured that each year we would have to turn folks away. This was none of our doing, of course, for of ourselves we have nothing to offer the people who turn up here. No, 'tis the Lord. And He was the reason numbers continued to grow in our Friday night and Sunday meetings till the 'new' church, built in '79, was creaking at the seams.

There was nothing for it but to move out into a bigger building, and with the farm we had that option, although the barn we moved into was somewhat basic, being little more than a shell of steel and asbestos, with concrete blocks forming the lower walls. This move more or less doubled our capacity, providing seating for 400, but even with insulation it still would have looked like a farm building, so we regarded the solution as temporary. Its short-term use was confirmed by the fire regulation people, who came along and informed us that, in order to bring the building into line with current standards, we'd have to spend around £12,000, and to fully equip it for our purposes would have cost considerably more.

We decided to start afresh and ask permission to put up a new, purpose-built structure - a brand new church - adjacent to the cafeteria. Believing we would see further growth, and assured by the Father's answers to our prayers, we planned an 800-seater. This would accommodate not only the growing 'family' that met at Hollybush but also dispense with the need for a marquee at camp weeks, with all the problems, or potential problems (especially the vagaries of the weather), with which we'd had to contend previously. To our delight, though not our surprise, for we felt strongly that this was the Lord's will for us, we were granted permission to begin work on the new church late in 1988. Estimates put the cost at around £120,000 - a huge amount of money, even for those of us who'd been used to the Lord supplying our needs - but we moved ahead in faith, knowing that our God cannot fail.

While scaling up on the church front, on the domestic side we scaled down. Joanna, now 26, had flown the nest. The main farmhouse, with its 16 rooms, was becoming more than we cared to manage. Even with our friend Irene as live-in helper, the chores were now simply too demanding. Added to this were some health problems - perhaps an indication of our ages - so we decided to sell the house. We would keep on the farm and continue to be as committed as ever to the fellowship, but we would no longer live on the premises. Irene moved into one of the cottages behind the first church building, while Cynthia and I found a more manageable property - a large, newly-built bungalow - in the nearby village of Newby Wiske.

We were pleased when a Christian came forward to purchase Hollybush farmhouse, or Hollin Tree House, as it was originally known, and which name the new owner reinstated. Bob Gordon of Kerygma Ministries managed a number of buses - 'King's Coaches' - which were used in evangelism across the country. That the house was to remain 'in the family' and continue to be used to God's glory gave us no small measure of satisfaction. Seeing the one bus that was stationed here coming and going gave us a little thrill and kept us on our spiritual toes in praying for this worthy outreach. Later on, Kerygma was to decide to run all buses from one depot, so Bob, his team, and the bus moved down to Norwich, and the house sold on, this time to an army officer, who rented the place to Norman and Jean Pattison, a young couple from the fellowship. They made good use of its facilities as a 'bed and breakfast' until the new owner decided to move back and live there himself.

Changes were taking place in the fellowship, too. After so many years as an informal group of Christians, we decided to establish Hollybush Christian Fellowship as a church, with a membership and basis of belief. In addition to the benefits which would come with being officially recognised as a Christian body (rather than the 'sect' or 'cult' we'd been labelled by disgruntled individuals in the past), this step would enable us to register as a charity, which made good sense from the financial angle since we would now be able to claim back the tax on donations, effectively topping up each gift to the church by almost a third of its value. With our largest building project about to get underway, the extra income would be welcome and well used.

Finances on the farm, meanwhile, continued to tick over, our total acreage of The Limes and Hollybush continuing to support four families. There was no cash to spare, however, and we needed wisdom in our decision making. One of our biggest challenges in those years was whether or not to continue in potato farming. Despite the occasional 'windfall' situation, such as we experienced when we needed the capital to build the cafeteria, there had generally been no great profit to be had from potatoes. Even so, with the old system of manual planting and picking we had been able to keep pace. Now things were changing, supposedly for the better, with the implementation of a mechanised system. This was to become obligatory for potato production, so we had no choice but to tool up or get out. Since the 'tools' would have set us back £40,000 we decided to move on. We would stick with sugar-beet and cereals.

Thankfully, Cynthia and I have never had to make such decisions about the other sort of seed and harvest in our lives. For, unlike farming the land, sowing the seed of the Spirit - planting the Gospel, so to speak - is an ongoing, unchanging commission. As opportunities arise, we continue to delight in telling forth the love of God not only at Hollybush but also in other churches, fellowships and meeting places, wherever we are invited to lift up the lovely name of Jesus.

Non-church events in particular usually present a welcome opportunity to proclaim the goodness of God and the Gospel of Christ because there, I find, I'm most likely to be addressing some who have yet to place their trust in the Lord. FGBMFI (Full Gospel Business Men's Fellowship International) meetings are a particular favourite of mine, and as the years have rolled on I've been privileged to share my story and commend my Saviour at more than 40 such meetings both here and in North America. Many of those have been memorable occasions, but the one which gave me the biggest buzz was the 10th anniversary meeting of our local Northallerton chapter, which I helped to get started.

Cynthia, meanwhile, rejoices in the opportunities she has to speak and sing at various women's meetings, and sometimes I get to join her on the platform, or at the head table, as was the case when we shared the ministry at the Women's Aglow Christmas dinner in Morecambe. At about the same time we were able to share our story, and our blessings, closer to home, with a gathering of our families. Almost a hundred of our clan were there, and though not all our relatives share our faith, and some continue to believe we are off our heads, they always give us a good hearing as 'family', and we continue to pray for them, that they will join us on the narrow way that leads to life eternal.

Now and then we are privileged to commend the Lord to someone else's family gathering, as was the case when evangelist Melvin Banks and his wife invited us to attend their twenty-fifth wedding anniversary down in Chippenham, Wiltshire. Melvin has been a guest speaker at Hollybush on a number of occasions, and over the years we've become good friends, so I was glad when he and Lilian asked me to preach the Gospel after the meal. Before I got to my feet, however, Melvin signalled for the cutting of the cake, and that, I discovered, was a signal for the doors to be thrown wide. The anniversary couple had invited anyone from their home town to join them for cake, which on this occasion came with a Gospel message. A true evangelist never misses an opportunity to proclaim the Good News! It was a first for me, at Melvin's request, preaching at someone else's anniversary celebration, but six people responded to the appeal, which gave me a fresh reason to appreciate Paul's exhortation, 'by all means save some'.

On such occasions I am pleased to relate how God takes care of His children, and at that time I'd recently received yet another reminder of the detail that goes into His planning, and which confirms that He has been watching over us. We had received an invitation to take some meetings in the Middle East, where some friends were running an underground fellowship. Expenses were not mentioned, but we felt it right to make the trip, so Cynthia and I, along with fellowship member John Pierson, made the arrangements and duly set off for a state on the Persian Gulf.

John is a meticulous book-keeper and kept a detailed record of all that we paid out, right down to the cost of sandwiches we bought on the train to Heathrow. During our three-week stay we took many meetings but received no expenses. On the final night, however, an offering was taken on our behalf and John was handed the cash, which was made up of various currencies, including Malaysian, Indian, Philippino and Quatari coins and notes. We were grateful, of course, but had no idea what this assortment of monies could be worth. Only when John paid it all into the bank back in Northallerton did we discover that the amount donated on that last evening covered all our costs, with a few pence left over. God is no man's debtor, and He has some delightful ways of proving it. As the old hymn declares, 'Great is Thy faithfulness' - in all matters, financial or spiritual.

17/Home and away

Back at the bungalow, refreshed by a much-needed cuppa, we set to unpacking, warm memories of the East tumbling out of our suitcases along with the gifts and mementoes.

'I've a feeling we'll be going back to the Gulf sometime,' I said as Cynthia headed for the laundry basket, her arms overflowing with clothes for the washing. Her muffled agreement from the next room confirmed what I felt. During three weeks of meetings, conversations and prayer times in that distant land we had seen and sensed God at work in individual lives. And somehow we knew there was more to be done. But neither of us could have guessed at just how soon we would return. The following weekend we accepted the invitation of friends to join them for a meal. Harry and Rosalind Vincent were frequent visitors to Hollybush and always keen to know what we had been up to in the Lord's service. On this occasion they were particularly interested to hear about our exploits in the Middle East, and they confirmed our own thoughts about a second visit. 'I believe you'll be going back there quite soon,' Harry declared, and handed a cheque to us across the meal table.

He was right. To our surprise, we felt impressed in our spirits to book our tickets for a couple of weeks' time. This was made possible by the very generous gift from these friends. Their cheque covered all our costs, this time in advance. Praise the Lord!

Those two trips to the Middle East gave us much evidence of the Lord's loving care, and not simply in terms of our financial needs. His protection was evident, too. At one point, John and I decided to fly down to Saudi Arabia to visit friends there, but the authorities decided that I was a suspicious character and needed interrogating. Airport police escorted me to a small room where I was questioned about my presence in their country, my movements and my intentions. The fact that I was a preacher and pastor did not thrill them. I suppose they were concerned that I might spread 'dangerous' Christian doctrines and try to convert some of their subjects. But, after a while - presumably long enough, in their view, to warn me off any idea I might have of proselytising - they let me go. By this point we had missed our flight, so we left the airport. Later that afternoon, discussing the situation with Cynthia and friends, we decided it was time to leave the country. Ian, our host, suggested we go to the airport at its busiest time, around noon, the next day. The theory was that, with so many passengers to process, the authorities would not bother with us and we could leave unhindered. And so it was. Ian's guess now seemed inspired and as our plane took off we were able to lean back in our seats and relax. We may have been leaving sooner than planned, but we trusted God for His timing and thanked Him for the opportunities we'd had for ministry and fellowship, and especially for the encouragement we had been able to bring to our fellow Christians in that difficult situation. I was thankful, too, that I had been spared first-hand experience of 'hospitality' in one of that Muslim state's penal establishments. I'm not sure how close I'd come to being detained, but I was certainly now more aware that our friends' involvement in the underground church in that country was not without risk.

Back in Britain we rejoiced in the freedom we continue to enjoy to preach the Gospel, something I returned to with more than my usual relish. Over the ensuing weeks, as I headed out from Hollybush for preaching engagements in various churches, hotels, prisons, village halls and other venues, I thanked God that we are still free to disseminate the life-giving Gospel of Jesus Christ without fear of losing our own freedom.

I am thankful, too, for opportunities to take that message to various church groups. As I reflect on speaking engagements over the years, I'm pleased to know that we've been welcomed into every Christian denomination in Britain, even the Methodist Church! There was a time, of course, when our friends in the Wesleyan brotherhood gave us the left foot of fellowship, but, thankfully, rifts have been healed and we are once more on good terms with our Methodist neighbours.

I continue to thank God for my roots in Methodism and always find it particularly gratifying when I have the opportunity to stand up and hold forth in one of its chapels. Even more pleasing was the opportunity I received a few years ago to speak to ministers-in-training at the Methodist-run Cliff College. My theme that day was 'Raising the Living and the Dead'.

Perhaps even more surprising (to some) was the invitation to address the faithful at the Roman Catholic church in Formby, Lancashire. But I have no problem with that, provided I have freedom to preach the whole Gospel of Christ crucified, risen, ascended and glorified, with Christ the only one who can take away sin. And on these occasions - a series of Saturday afternoon and evening meetings - I had the joy of seeing a number of regulars coming to full salvation in the Lord. It's good to see lives firmly planted in the love of Jesus, regardless of the container which holds the soil. As for the growth we look for in the lives of new converts, God is well able to care for His own. Our responsibility is to be willing to take the Word wherever it will be received, regardless of denominational or doctrinal differences. Plant the seeds and the Gardener will look after the young plants.

Back at Hollybush, we were pretty heavily involved in our

own programme of growth. The new church building was coming along, having received planning approval and a first influx of gifts which enabled the foundations to be laid. In fact, on the financial front we were to witness that same pattern of need and supply as the money came in to keep pace with each stage of the building process. No jumble sales were necessary. No bring-and-buy stalls. No arm-twisting or cajoling. God's people were advised of developments and lovingly gave to the cause. And, later on, as the basic structure was completed and the specialists moved out, so folks gave of their time and talents as we laboured at the hundred and one jobs that needed attention.

Meanwhile, growth continued on the spiritual plane, too. Our facilities at that point, when we met in the barn, were basic, but there was nothing sparse about the movement of the Spirit in our midst. As people came, reaching out to God, so He reached out to them, pouring out His love 'in accordance with His riches'. Graham and Sheila Housam were typical of those who received in this measure. They turned up at Hollybush one day, brought by Sheila's cousin and his wife, Peter and Shirley Binns, who were members of the church fellowship at Scunthorpe.

Sheila was in a wheelchair, having suffered a recurrence of a back problem which had begun in childhood. She was diagnosed as suffering from infantile paralysis, or polio, and spent four years in hospital, during which she spent periods confined to an iron lung. When eventually she was allowed home her parents were informed that, because of a weakness in her spine, she would be very limited in what she could do and probably would never bear children.

But, as Sheila says, God knew different.

At 16 she went to work in a corn factory, where she often lifted sacks weighing ten stone or more. Later, having married Graham, she gave birth to four bouncing babies.

As her family grew, however, Sheila's health began to deteriorate. She had long been a strong Christian, but her body was displaying signs of the weakness which dogged her early years. Arthritis began to take hold of her body. By the time she and Graham arrived at Hollybush, she had been in the wheelchair for nine years and expected to remain in it. When Shirley was showing Sheila around outside the barn she explained that, during camp week, baptisms were held in the river which ran through the land. Sheila joked, 'When God heals me, I'll get baptised there!' Though her faith in the Lord was sound, she didn't believe she'd ever walk unaided again. But, again, God knew different.

It was on a second visit to Hollybush, during camp week a couple of years later, that He proved it.

'I was sitting in the aisle, in my wheelchair, enjoying the meeting,' Sheila says, 'when I started to shake. Suddenly I could feel some unusual movement in my body and my bones started to make a loud cracking noise. I felt a bit embarrassed, afraid I was disturbing the people around me, but as the sensation was subsiding, my leg began to move, and before I knew it I was leaping out of the wheelchair. Suddenly my back was straight and the pain in my back, arms and legs all but disappeared. Praise God, from that moment I was free to walk and run around!'

Realising what was going on, our speaker called Sheila to the front of the meeting, to share with everyone what had just happened to her, and, with tears flowing and Graham at her side, she walked unaided up the steps to testify to God's healing touch.

'I later walked back to our caravan,' she says, 'rejoicing in God's miracle-working power. It was holy freedom.'

Still rejoicing the next day, and in playful mood, Sheila gave Graham a short piggy-back ride.

The following day, she fulfilled her own words of two years earlier and stepped down into the River Wiske, where I had the joy of baptising her. Graham joined her in the water to make his own declaration of faith, resulting in a memorable day for both of them. 'I felt a newness and lightness all around me,' she later recalled, 'and found myself back on top of the bank before I realised what had happened.'

Today, with the passing years, Sheila occasionally has to use her wheelchair, but for ten years she enjoyed full mobility, happily testifying to the love and goodness of her God.

Graham has his own reasons for rejoicing. At about the same time that he and Sheila first visited Hollybush, he attended the eye clinic at their local hospital for tests. There the specialist told him that he had a full reverse cataract in his right eye, and that this would require surgery. He'd not had sight in his left eye since childhood.

'During our first visit to Hollybush,' Graham says, 'prayers were offered for the restoration of my sight. Then, some time later, a handkerchief was blessed at the fellowship and brought to me at home by Peter and Shirley. Peter placed the handkerchief over my right eye and all four of us prayed for my sight to return in the Lord's time.

'I had no doubt that it could happen because nine years earlier I had been diagnosed with Cushing's Syndrome and told I had only two years to live. The Lord had healed me then and I believed He would heal me now.'

Over the next few months, however, Graham's eyesight grew worse and he was given a white guide stick and a braille watch. He was virtually blind.

But God could see Graham's future very clearly.

Two years later, around the same time that Sheila was so wonderfully healed, they both attended an 'abundant life' weekend at a local church.

'Then things began to happen,' says Graham. 'During one of the meetings a man who had noticed my disability came up to me and asked if I would like a large-print hymn book. I thanked him and accepted but really did not expect the larger print to help. To my amazement, the words appeared in front of me. I couldn't understand how I could suddenly see.

'Back home, while Sheila was preparing lunch, I was in the

lounge and realised I could see the hands of the clock. I called to Sheila that I could read the time and she thought I was joking, till I told her that I could see the marks on the wall calendar. Sheila rushed into the room, realised that I could indeed see, and we thanked the Lord for restoring my sight.'

The following month Graham attended the eye clinic again, where his improvement astounded the specialist. 'I could read even the smallest print,' Graham recalls, 'and he couldn't understand what had taken place, so I was given exhaustive eye tests to try to find what had caused my eyesight to return. But no reason could be found and I was told I'd made medical history. Despite still having a full reverse cataract, my name was removed from the surgery list. It was agreed that God had healed me. Praise Him for His blessings.'

I like Sheila's description of her healing as 'holy freedom'. Over the years, so many have entered into that special place of divine liberty here at Hollybush, and not only through physical healing. Sometimes healing of a very different kind is called for, as was the case when we were approached by three people who had been coming to the fellowship for a while. The circumstances were rather unusual. Dot had brought her friend Edith, who brought Barry, her ex-husband. In time, all accepted Christ as Saviour. Then things began to get a bit complicated when Barry and Dot became close. Clearly, Edith was still fond of Barry, and she began to feel a little awkward with the new friendship. And when Dot and Barry decided that they wanted to become engaged, things became rather tense. It was at this point that they came to me, wondering what they should do.

'Perhaps Dot and I should find another church,' Barry suggested. Edith, too, offered to move on.

That didn't seem like a good idea to me. It would make for an easy remedy, I told them, but that would be just what the enemy would want. 'No matter what's in the past,' I said, 'if you love the

Lord, as I know you do, we should be able to work this through together.'

And that's what happened. We took the matter to the Lord in prayer, and then we talked about it, trusting God to help us find a way forward. And He did. In time, Dot and Barry married, and all three remained in fellowship at Hollybush. Better still, they remained friends. I believe that was a significant victory and a notable healing, which would not have been possible outside of God's grace.

Such testimonies speak louder than any sermon. The triumph of God's love at work in an otherwise intolerable situation is, I believe, more powerful than any physical healing. Indeed, while folk may be drawn to Hollybush by the miracles, we know that signs and wonders will not be enough to keep them. Only love can do that - the love of God, as evidenced in individual lives as it reaches out to others in warmth and welcome.

A couple from Chesterfield came to us for the first time and said they would return because of the love they had experienced here. Well, you don't feel love simply by shaking hands; the warmth they encountered, and which blessed them, may have begun with a cheery greeting, but it certainly didn't end there.

Such love brings people back time and time again. A lady who comes to us from Tanfield is typical. A regular at her local Anglican church, she likes to visit Hollybush now and then because, as she put it, 'it feels like family'. That's something we can't organise. We can't engineer it. But we can allow it to flow, as we give the Holy Spirit access to our lives and are willing to be channels for the love that streams from the heart of God.

A couple from Bury, Ron and Margaret Hancock, come to Hollybush every weekend, driving 70 miles across country on Friday afternoon in time for the evening meeting, and staying on in their caravan for the Sunday services, returning home late on Sunday night. They say they wouldn't miss it, which blesses my heart. And they're not alone. One member of the fellowship,

Michael Neiland, drives a round trip of 50 miles on a moped each week for the Sunday services. He has been doing this for more than 25 years. Along with George Wood and Mike Stewart, he has been faithfully and lovingly giving a welcoming handshake at the door and although many visitors cannot remember his name, they ask the question, 'Is that smiling Irishman still with you?' He and so many other members of the church have unobtrusively been doing what would appear to be menial tasks, some for two or three decades. They are the unsung heroes, the faithful who make Hollybush tick.

Why do they do it? 'Tis the Lord, of course. He alone creates the feeling of family. He alone is the attraction. He alone is worth the journey.

18/Getting it right, getting it wrong

We opened the new church on Saturday, 2 May, 1992. The total cost was £140,000, which was more than we had expected but not more than God had planned. Not once did we fall behind on paying our bills. But that day the finances were of little consequence; the building, its interior warmly finished in pine and open brickwork, with green carpeting and matching chairs, buzzed with an excitement about the work of God on a farm in North Yorkshire. The place was packed, with more than 800 fellowship members and guests filling both the main auditorium and galleries, and with such a crowd of God's children we had quite a celebration. It was, after all, an exciting moment in our history - a giant step forward for a relatively small group of people, some of whom could remember how all this started more than 30 years ago in Jim and Cynthia's lounge at The Limes, a few miles down the road in Sandhutton. The passage of time had claimed a number of our friends from those early days, dear ones we'd rejoiced and prayed with over the years and who had now been promoted to Glory. But some from that pioneering group still remained, including two of the folks who had been with us from our very first meeting: Mr Hutchinson and Mrs Allinson. Their partners were among those now with the Lord, but Cynthia and I were delighted that these two faithful friends were with us still, and we happily honoured them by inviting them to take part in our little opening ceremony. Gathering outside the main door of the new church, we rejoiced as Mr Hutchinson cut the ribbon and Mrs Allinson unlocked the door.

My, we'd come a long way since those early meetings, and we reflected on the same during our afternoon celebration.

To put things in perspective, but making the point that it had never been our practice at Hollybush to count heads or compile statistics, we reflected on how many people had passed through Hollybush since the fellowship's inception. Erring on the side of conservative estimates, lest we exaggerate, we reckoned that over the preceding ten years more than 75,000 visits had been paid to various fellowship meetings by non-members, and that at least 6,000 of those were by first-time visitors.

Over the same period, more than 10,000 people had stayed on the field during camp weeks or special weekend events. During camp week alone, we estimated, the cafeteria had produced more than 170 full meals each day, plus 400 portions of chips and thousands of cups of tea and coffee.

During those ten years, we reckoned, we'd produced at least 25,000 audio tapes and 2,500 video recordings of the meetings. Sales of youth camp worship tapes had exceeded 5,000.

The number of meetings taken by teams going out from Hollybush each month was thought to be around 30 but it could well have been more, since on Sundays alone there will usually be three or four teams in action.

As for the number of people who had made a first-time commitment to the Lord Jesus Christ at Hollybush, estimates ranged between 1,000 and 1,500.

These figures and other reflections were presented to us by Jonathan Dunning, who was then our administrator, and by Meri Snowdon, the wife of one of our trustees at that time. In closing, Jonathan reminded us that whatever we had achieved, all was to the glory of God.

Meri picked up the theme as she rounded off: 'And that's the purpose of this presentation - simply to say that this new building is not for us to sit in and enjoy and be proud of, but to be used for others, just as the other rooms and buildings have been used down the years.'

She then made an important point, reminding us, and anyone who might think otherwise, that 'most of what we have described has just happened as, week by week, we have worshipped here'.

That was a key phrase, for we acknowledged the fact that, without our prayers and worship, we would not have been celebrating the opening of a brand new church with seating for 800. Worship, we had learned, opened our hearts to God and allowed Him to reach out through our lives to touch others. If, all those years ago, we had been an inward looking group, intent on doing our own thing and asking God to bless our own agenda, we would still be sitting in a small room, a holy huddle that would have been of little use to the community and of even less use to the Lord.

Thankfully, we'd discovered early that the gifts of God are meant to be shared with others. This divine principle never alters. Hold on to the gifts and they will crumble in your hands; give them away and both they and you will flourish.

That joyful day was shared with friends from all over the country, and with visiting preachers from America and Canada - Wilbur and Jo-An Jackson from Cincinnati and Arthur and Greta Sheppard from Vancouver. Together we rejoiced that, with His help, we had managed to walk in the will of God at least some of the time. His blessing on this latest building project proved that.

We had been helped, of course, by the prophetic words, or words of knowledge, which had given us direct leading, and much needed encouragement, in seeking to follow the Lord's directions. Clear leading from the Holy Spirit at crucial times had enabled us to take important foundational steps. But such leading was not always given and many times when God had been silent we'd had to feel our way forward through faith and prayer, trusting that we were making the right moves.

Let it be said now, and clearly. We have not always got it right. Despite what some sarcastic cynics might say, Jim and Cynthia do not have a hot-line to the Almighty. For us, as for any Christian, the question of discerning the will of God is the hardest part of the walk. Believing in and practising the gifts of the Spirit can help, but only if we truly hear from God.

There have been many times, I'm glad to say, when I have heard correctly, or discerned rightly, such as the occasion when I was visiting our friends, Fred and Joan Lee and Kelly and Anne France, at Littledale Hall near Lancaster. I felt led to speak a word prophesying the way in which the Lord would use that place - a large house and grounds situated deep in a fertile valley - for His glory. That word, as they will tell you, was fulfilled and today, under the direction of Stuart and Wendy Rushton, Littledale Hall is well known as a retreat centre and much loved as a place of peace, comfort and healing.

Yes, on that occasion I heard aright. Sometimes, however, our natural eagerness to offer a word of encouragement or direction to brothers and sisters in the Lord gets in the way, and we find that what we have spoken out, believing it to be inspired by the Holy Spirit, is nothing more than wishful thinking. It may sound right, it may feel right, it may even strike a chord with those who receive it, but if it hasn't come from the Lord then it is just a bunch of empty words.

This was the case when I gave what I thought was a word from the Lord to a couple visiting from Australia. Neal and Noreen Hall were farmers like myself but their business was going through a rough patch and they'd come forward for prayer at the close of one of our camp meetings. As I prayed with them, and as I tried to hear what the Lord might have to say to them, I felt I should tell them that within a month of returning home their finances would pick up and the expenses for their present journey would be met by a miracle. A few months later, when they'd been back in their own country for a while, I heard that no such improvement had materialised.

I was perplexed. Clearly I'd got it wrong. Understandably, the couple felt disappointed. I'd spoken out a positive word that I believed was Spirit-inspired, but it was just Jim.

I could have left it there, I suppose - swept it under the carpet in the name of experience - but I knew I had a responsibility to this couple. It was bad enough that they'd had the disappointment of seeing their business in the doldrums; now I'd inadvertently added to their trial by telling them that all would be well. At best, having to question my spoken word, they would have felt discouraged; at worst they might have questioned their faith.

I did the only thing that seemed right in the circumstances. I apologised. I wrote and admitted I'd got it wrong. 'Sorry,' I told them. 'Please forgive me.' And I was forgiven. Thank you, Neal and Noreen. And thank you, Jesus.

Physician, heal thyself!

Some would say I'm giving ammunition to those who hold the gifts of the Spirit in disdain; those who believe, as I once did, that the gifts were for the Early Church alone; that God no longer speaks to or through individuals. But I've seen words of prophecy and knowledge come true often enough to know that God still uses this medium to reveal His plans, to guide His people, to bring blessing into the lives of individual believers.

There is nothing wrong with the gift or the giver, only occasionally with the channel. We can get it wrong because we are human. God knows this, yet He continues to trust us enough to speak through us. Our difficulty is in learning to know when the message is from our own heart, rather than the Lord's. And when I get it wrong I need to have the guts and the grace to say so. That is honesty, that is truth, and the Scripture says that our Father requires truth in the inward parts. We readily accept the pat on the back if we get it right. Honesty demands that we be as quick to offer the apology if we get it wrong.

Sometimes, of course, Cynthia and I, along with the fellowship, are on the receiving end, and we too can be perplexed by words of prophecy. One evening the following was given:

'There will be a going and a coming. There will be a building up and a pulling down, a holding and a letting go, and the Lord will have His way.'

There is no formula for testing the veracity of such pronouncements. The only sure-fire test is time. But something rang true with those words, and I instinctively felt that, at some time in the future, we would be in for a bumpy ride.

19/Sending out smiles

I'm thankful that our vision at Hollybush has never been self-centred. We have always been aware that we are but a tiny part of God's world, and that we have a responsibility to help promote the Lord's work in other lands. The many national flags which hang from the balconies of the new church are not there simply for decoration, and they're not there simply as a statement, either. Each flag speaks of a part of the world in which Hollybush members or friends are, or have been, actively engaged in mission. In fact, most of the flags have been provided by those folks as a reminder that we have a stake in the countries where they serve, in terms of preaching the Gospel - or, where that is not permitted, as a means of quietly demonstrating the love of Christ. This is usually in conjunction with some sort of practical work, of course, for most countries will now accept mission workers only if they can make a tangible contribution to the practical welfare of that land.

The day of the missionary dedicated to nothing other than converting the natives is long gone. Thus God's people have needed to find new, productive ways to justify their acceptance into foreign communities. Under God's direction, many from Hollybush have done just that. For example, as I write . . .

Margaret Evans, called alongside the Jewish people, works as a nurse in Jerusalem.

Philip Walters is serving the Lord with YWAM in Thailand.

Lowell Sheppard and his wife Kande, once youth workers here, are in Japan with the Asia Pacific branch of Youth for Christ.

David and Sue Prosser are back home after running a children's home in Zimbabwe.

Eddie and Shirley Lamb pastor a church in Florida, where Eddie's parents, Leslie and Irene, are also now resident. You may recall that it was Leslie and Irene who were called to minister to Gypsies in the north of England. That work continues to grow, with several Romany evangelists employed full-time.

Ian and Sylvia Leck are now back in this country after serving out in the Gulf, lifting up Christ among ex-patriots and foreign nationals.

Astrid Leck, Ian and Sylvia's daughter, is an eye specialist currently working in Africa, bringing relief through cataract surgery and other treatment. Her husband Peter is studying Arabic and both have a vision for reaching out to the Arab world with the Gospel and medical aid.

Pam and Tony Burn recently returned from Jerusalem, where they worked as volunteers, reaching out to both Jewish and Palestinian communities.

Twin sisters Maggie and Fiona Askham are in Egypt, teaching English to students at a language school, as well as to Sudanese refugees.

Peter Gregory, our retired vicar, and his wife June have been active for the Lord in various provinces of China, helping to support a literature campaign.

David Raine and former Hollybush member Steve Cowie have been instrumental in establishing a new outreach, the All India Mission, which supports the work of Indian evangelist N.J. Varughese. N.J., as we call him, visits us each year to update us, to renew fellowship, and to inspire us in our commitment to mission.

Barry and Dot Dearlove, returning from Bible college in

Canada, are about to take up a post with Teen Challenge in Wales.

Colin and Carey Towers are soon to return from studying at Hills Christian Life Centre Bible School in Sydney, Australia, and are looking to the Lord for direction in service.

The list goes on, as does our support for these folk. We are aware that they need our prayers, especially those who find themselves in a difficult or hostile situation. In areas where there is political unrest the lives of foreigners especially can be at risk. Barbara Ashworth, for example, recently returned from Africa after fleeing from her home and church, which were ransacked and destroyed during an uprising. She had spent 24 hours hiding in a ditch before escaping to safety. How much that safety had depended on our prayers we'll never know, but Barbara's experience has reminded us all of how much we constantly need to lift our co-workers to the Lord.

We in Britain are sheltered, compared with our brothers and sisters in other countries, where hostile situations are not uncommon and Christian martyrdom is a present danger.

Despite the risks, the Lord's people continue to 'go', and Hollybush continues to 'send'. And if we're not sending people we're endeavouring to send money to support mission in its various forms.

Based here on the farm, in the barn which we used as an interim church before the new building was finished, is a little gem of a venture known as Missions Mart. It's a simple idea, raising funds for overseas missions from the sale of second-hand clothes, books, toys, etc. on Friday evenings and special sale days, but it wouldn't happen without the enthusiasm and dedication of two of our members. June Arrowsmith and Jackie McEwan launched the project with a single table of second-hand items during camp week in 1984. That initial effort raised £199, but these days the ladies and their helpers generate around £6,000 each year to help finance the work of the Gospel overseas and to assist in sending containers of clothing to Africa and Eastern Europe.

Hollybush regulars Terry and Wendy Bousfield have been equally productive in sending out the love of God in the form of aid to Eastern Europe. Northern Aid for Romania, as the charity is known, has made something like 20 trips, taking clothes, toys, food and medical aid to the needy folk who have become their friends and second family. Few of us have seen the happy faces of those who receive this aid, but the folks who've helped pack the wagons have shared in that joy. No wonder the slogan on the side of the trucks declares that they're 'Sending Out Smiles'.

Reaching out across international borders is something for which one of our members is particularly grateful. Tom Walters, a regular at Hollybush for the past 17 years, was born in Germany to a Jewish mother in 1932 and only saved from a Nazi death camp by a scheme which enabled a British couple to adopt him.

Born Thomas Baumann, Tom was among thousands of Jewish children who were admitted to Britain in 1939 in an attempt to rescue at least some of the youngsters whose lives were in danger. A Christian couple, Chris and Eva Walters, moved by compassion, and no doubt concern for God's chosen people, applied to adopt one of these children, and Tom duly arrived in England.

His extraordinary and moving story - from refugee to successful businessman, from the Jewish faith to faith in Christ - is told in the book *The Boy from Berlin* by R.M. Burt. Tom's life was also the subject of a television documentary, some of which was filmed at Hollybush.

Cynthia and I got to know Tom and his wife Judy when they moved up from London to open a Christian holiday centre, Elm House, in Redmire on the edge of the Yorkshire Dales National Park. In that lovely place, doubtless encouraged by the warmth of Tom's gentle spirit and fervent love for the Lord, many have passed from spiritual death to eternal life, their own journey echoing that of the nine-year-old German lad who escaped from the shadow of the gas chamber to flourish in a new and welcoming land.

Perhaps it's hardly surprising that today Tom has a lively interest in mission…or that Tom and Judy's son Philip is serving the Lord overseas.

Occasionally the flow of missionary traffic is reversed, with visitors from overseas turning up here at Hollybush. On one memorable, and humbling, occasion we were given the opportunity to play host to a group of pastors who had travelled all the way from Chernobyl in the Ukraine.

These quiet, unassuming men arrived with no clothes other than those they stood up in, and we suspected that they lived just as simply. We showed them around the place and noticed that they seemed impressed by just about everything we had. But it was the stock of household items which awaited sale in the Missions Mart building which seemed to amaze them more than anything else on the premises.

'You can help yourselves,' we told them. 'Take anything you want.'

Their English was not good, but when the message finally got through to them it brought out a rash of East European smiles which did our own hearts good.

But they didn't rush in and plunder the place; they didn't grab up what they could while they had the chance. Slow and thoughtful, they chose carefully, and not at all extravagantly.

I was touched. And humbled. I don't suppose any one of them had ever been faced with such an array of free gifts.

A little later, when I saw one of them stepping out into the soft sunlight of that autumn afternoon, I noticed that he was clutching nothing more than a few items of crockery, all oddments.

'Have you got what you want?' I asked, returning his cheery smile.

'Saucers,' he said, holding up his booty. 'My wife has no saucers.'

The tear that escaped down my cheek took me completely by surprise. I felt humbled at the action of this man, who could have chosen all sorts of things for himself - there were racks of men's clothing there - but who thought only of his wife's needs.

I wondered how I would have reacted in his position and was moved by the joy of these dear pastors who had nothing in terms of wordly goods but everything a person could need - the peace of the Lord. I was reminded of the words of my Saviour, 'What shall it profit a man if he gains the whole world but loses his own soul?' As I slid my handkerchief back into my pocket, I reflected on the parable I'd been shown through a smiling face…and a few saucers.

20/Family matters

The Nineties proved to be the most difficult decade for the fellowship. What was that about a bumpy ride?

It had started well, with much promise and an abundance of enthusiasm. This was, after all, the so-called Decade of Evangelism. With the Gospel at the heart of Hollybush, we were buzzing with an expectancy. This doubtless had begun with the building of the new church, a major project that had drawn us together as a family in Christ, and which now found new expression with the excitement generated by a national evangelistic initiative. Working under the umbrella of that initiative, knowing that countless other churches and fellowships across the land were engaged in outreach programmes, gave us a real sense of being part of the wider family of God. Thus we were encouraged and motivated and eager to get out there with the Gospel. Special meetings, village evangelism, street outreach, prison visits . . . in a wide variety of ways we embraced the vision and threw ourselves into the job of harvesting souls with renewed fervour.

There was only one problem. No one wanted to know. The message fell on deaf ears. Our efforts seemed in vain. We prayed the harder but there was no response.

After a while we began to flag. Toiling in the fields is not easy without some sign that your labour is bearing fruit.

Then along came JIM. No, not yours truly, but 'Jesus In Me', another national outreach initiative, this time with badges and stickers and plenty of back-up. Do you recall it? If not, where were you? JIM attracted a good deal of media attention and provided witnessing Christians with a novel means of speaking to friends, neighbours, workmates and passers-by about faith in Christ - the benefits of knowing 'Jesus In Me'. At Hollybush we climbed on board. Signed up, prayed up, praised up and spoke up.

But no one wanted to know. JIM received the cold shoulder. To the best of my knowledge, not one person came to faith as a result of our efforts with that particular programme. Our shining enthusiasm was beginning to look a little tarnished.

Then evangelist Reinhard Bonnke introduced yet another initiative. His 'Minus to Plus' literature campaign, in which a Gospel booklet was delivered to every home in the country, fired us up again and once more we got stuck in. Surely this would open up some opportunities for us to share our faith and help folks turn their lives around as they moved from minus to plus, from darkness to light, from eternal death to everlasting life.

But no one wanted to know. It was the old story. Now and then we'd meet someone who was interested in turning over a new leaf, but not, it seemed, in turning over their life to Christ. What was going on? How were we to interpret this extraordinary lack of response to the Gospel, this singular apathy, the likes of which we'd never encountered in all our years of taking the Good News out on to the streets? Our prayers brought no answers. What was God saying? *Or not saying*?

A little battle-weary, not to mention foot-sore, we returned to camp and took stock. It was all rather discouraging. Somehow we had to keep on keeping on, but we're only human and humans like to see results. On the farm, if you keep sowing seed but see no harvest, you'll eventually think, Is it worth it? But in the Kingdom, despite seeing no fruit, you have to keep going. We would do that, of course, because the Kingdom is the only reason we're here, but at that point it was a little like walking through treacle. Never mind, we told ourselves, things will pick up. This is just a dry period. Blessing will follow in due course.

But that didn't happen. At least, not right away. In fact, things were to get a little more uncomfortable before they improved. With many of our young people reaching the age when they head for university or employment or marriage, our youth group began to look sadly depleted. Those that remained found themselves being drawn to other churches where there were more Christians of their own age. Not surprisingly, many found a new spiritual home at the New Life Church in Northallerton, where our friend Rodney Breckon is pastor. Rodney has strong links with Hollybush, having spent much of his time here as a lad. His dad, George, was of course a key figure in the development of this fellowship, and in my own growth in the Lord. Now George has been promoted to Glory, but he is remembered with a great deal of affection and it is gratifying for us to know that his son is leading a thriving church just down the road. We are glad, too, that strong links with the Breckon family continue through our fellowship with Rodney. As for many of our young people attending there…well, if Rodney's church was able to offer them what was not available at Hollybush at that time, we were not about to complain. As long as the youngsters were growing in the Lord, what did it matter where they were being fed? As I've said before, Hollybush has never been about numbers.

Even so, it was rather disconcerting when we found that we were losing the children in the Sunday school, too. Some of the young families followed the young people to New Life Church and other fellowships, and for the first time in many years there was a noticeable reduction in the decibels which once indicated very clearly that this was a family church.

Perhaps if I'd been anything other than a farmer I might have begun to feel concerned. But farmers are used to change - we see it all the time on the land and through the seasons, and even with the size of the crops we cultivate. So the reduction in our numbers did not phase me. Cynthia and I had learned to live with change, even to expect it, and we took the new situation in our stride.

Besides, there were many bright spots to lift us, not least Joanna's wedding. We had watched with pride as our lovely daughter had grown from a little girl into a young woman, and now she was to marry. There was, of course, much feverish planning by the female Wilkinsons, followed by endless letters, phone calls and personal visits in order to secure all that needs to be in place for the Big Day. As a mere male I was excused involvement in many of these duties, but I was nonetheless exercised in my thoughts as we moved ever nearer the day when I would be walking down the aisle with my only daughter to give her away. This sobering thought was my companion as I went about my work on the farm, a strange cocktail of joy and sadness giving rise to my own version of pre-wedding nerves. Our girl had given us much joy over the years, and I was proud to be her dad, proud to have been the main male figure in her life. It's not easy for a man to let go of that. And I admit that I had one or two reservations about her choice, but those thoughts were eased by the knowledge that Joanna would be marrying a man she loved, and who loved her. So, on balance - and accepting that it's quite natural for a father to wonder if *any* man is entirely good enough for his daughter - I laid my concerns to one side and simply continued to pray that Joanna's choice was the right one. At the end of the day, our main concern was that she should marry a man who would cherish his wife.

Before Joanna's wedding, however, I was to have the joy of conducting a marriage service for one of our long-time fellowship members and his bride.

Kevin Hammond first came to Hollybush when just a lad of 12, brought each week by his parents. His girl, a lovely German lass by the name of Inge, had come to Britain on a student exchange programme and the two had met at university.

Naturally, he brought Inge along to the meetings at the fellowship which had now become his own spiritual home, but at that point his beloved had no idea that her reaction to Hollybush might determine whether or not they had a future together. As Kevin told me later, even before meeting Inge he had drawn up a list of what he would look for in a wife, and that she should love Hollybush as much as he was one of the prominent features. So, after her first visit, as they were driving out of the gates, he was delighted to hear Inge say that she had been truly blessed that night. 'Bathed in God's love' was how she put it, and that was good enough for Kevin.

The only dark spot in connection with the fellowship was when one of our members reacted negatively to hearing that Kevin was dating a German girl. The disgruntled brother soon changed his tune, however, when eventually he met Inge. Realising that members of her family, like his own, had been called up to go to war helped him put things in perspective. It's all too easy to jump to conclusions and activate old prejudices. Thankfully, that one was quickly defused.

The wedding was to be my first overseas. Inge came from a little village not far from the Black Forest, so a day or so before the big event I found myself on a plane to Stuttgart, along with another fellowship member, Eileen Cranfield. Cynthia stayed home, finalising the details for Joanna's wedding, which was now just a week away.

From the airport we took a train to Spiegelberg, the bride's village, which we found to be beautifully decorated with flowers from the woods. That was quite enchanting, as was the pre-wedding procession through the village streets. The local children led the way to the church, followed by the bride and groom, with the guests bringing up the rear. I shared the walk with Inge's pastor, known as Frau France, though I can't say we exchanged many words because I knew no German and she was not strong on English. We were, however, speaking the same language in our desire to give the young couple a glorious, godly wedding service, and, to our delight, we found that the language situation created no real difficulties. Indeed, Frau France and I found ourselves flowing so naturally - or supernaturally - together, that I even found myself dropping in the odd word of German. I hadn't a clue what I was saying, but no one complained so I took it as a lovely grace-touch from the Lord.

Grace was at work in other aspects of the service, too. I liked very much the way our time in the church had begun, with Inge and Kevin standing in the doorway, shaking hands with their guests as they filed into the building.

I liked, too, the fact that the couple had included communion in the service, and that, once Frau France and I had served each other with the bread and wine, Kevin and Inge served everyone else. That was a nice touch, and one which involved the Lord in the marriage service in a profound and moving way. And that gave me cause to think that these young people were getting off to a sound start in their married life. For in the best Christian marriages there are not two but three partners. With Christ at the head, such a union should have every chance of succeeding. Watching this young couple serving the bread and wine brought a smile to my face and a warm glow to my heart. Inge and Kevin would do just fine, of that I was sure.

Once the ceremony and photographs were over, we headed for the village hall, where a tantalising buffet had been laid out, and of which I took full advantage. The villagers had provided all the food, I was informed, and I intended to extend to them the courtesy of tasting as many of their tasty dishes as possible. This meant that I was soon feeling full and warmly appreciative of German hospitality. Unfortunately, however, I had made the mistake of thinking that this sumptuous spread was the main meal. In fact, as it turned out, these dishes were but tasty titbits for folks to dip into while they were waiting for the main meal, which was equally delicious but sadly beyond my capacity to enjoy to the full. I did, however, manage a slice of real Black Forest gateau, which was an experience in itself as well as an eye-opener. Tucking into that locally made sweet, I discovered a real treat for the taste-buds. The British versions I'd sampled just didn't compare.

And, as I reflected later, there was a little sermon there. This present age offers all sorts of alternatives to faith in Christ, from the sturdy, dependable respectability of traditional religion to the tantalising, cultish charms of so-called New Age mysticism. But the Scripture invites us to 'taste and see that the Lord is good', and those who do so find in Him a sweetness beyond compare. Once you've tasted the real thing, nothing else will satisfy.

Back in England, I got the wedding suit out again a week later and proudly walked Joanna down the aisle before giving her away in a ceremony conducted by our local vicar, Rev. Ted Spiller. For all of us it was a very happy occasion, tinged with sadness of course as Cynthia and I handed on responsibility for our daughter to her groom.

At the reception, we sat back and sighed. Joanna looked radiant, the blushing bride with a beaming smile. Her new husband looked like a prospector who'd just struck gold. Indeed, as far as her parents were concerned, he had.

'They look happy enough,' I remarked to Cynthia as we watched them leave for the honeymoon. In fact they looked so happy that I wondered if I'd been wrong about my reservations. Probably dads just worry too much about their daughters, I reflected. Our little girl had long dreamed of being happily married, and from the look on her face that day it seemed her dreams had come true. Or, to put it in the Bible's terminology, it appeared Joanna was receiving the desires of her heart.

Within the wider family of the fellowship, despite the loss of so many young people and young families, individuals were being blessed with the desires of *their* hearts.

Pam Burn was thrilled when her husband Tony committed his life to Christ during our Easter celebrations a while back. We'd been adding our prayers to Pam's for some years and rejoiced with her when Tony finally came through. That boost to her faith helped when hospital tests revealed that she had an ovarian cyst. Years earlier she'd had the same problem, resulting in a traumatic operation. 'I dreaded the thought of going through the whole horrendous experience again,' she says, 'but we turned it all over to the Lord and trusted Him for healing.'

The fellowship added its prayers to theirs, believing for a miracle, but six months later a scan revealed that a second cyst was present. Again we prayed.

When Pam went for a third scan she was sent home because the machine had broken. An appointment was made for the following week. 'A couple of days later,' she recalls, 'another fellowship member, Sylvia Leck, came to me and said the Lord had shown her a picture which she felt was for me.' The picture was of a balloon, deflating, shrivelling.

'And I've a message for you,' Sylvia added. 'The Lord says to tell you that it's not going to be like last time.'

And it wasn't. On her next visit to the hospital, Pam was told there was no sign of the cysts.

Our book-keeper, Hal Russ, rejoices in being reprieved from a death sentence. Cancer had invaded one of his lungs and the condition was said to be inoperable. He was given only months to live. But the fellowship prayed and, after three courses of chemotherapy, Hal was given the all-clear. As a bonus, having lost his grey hair three times during treatment, it eventually grew back jet black, the colour it had been when he was a young man!

At the same time, Hal's wife Colleen had been praying for healing from angina. She too was now looking for a miracle. It came during one of our Friday fellowship meetings. Our speaker that night was Brian Sanders, the man whose conversion, along with that of his son, confirmed that our first camp was in God's will. Brian had grown in faith and ministry along with the fellowship, and was a man whom God had used in healing, so when he started to call folk to the front as the Lord revealed to him various illnesses and infirmities within the congregation, Colleen was all ears. *If he mentions angina*, she thought, *I'll be out there.*

But the minutes ticked by and heart problems were not mentioned. Colleen felt disappointed, especially when we wound up the prayer session and I got up to close the meeting. But suddenly Brian was on his feet again, saying he had just one word on his mind - a word he couldn't shake. Angina.

Colleen flew to the front, where we prayed for her, and where she fell to the floor as the Spirit moved upon her. When at last she got to her feet, she said she felt as though a great weight had been lifted from her chest. 'I felt free,' she told me later. 'Free…and healed.'

But, despite her relief, Colleen could not truly believe she had been healed, and for the next three weeks she lived as though she still had her heart problems. She continued to avoid exerting herself, resting often, taking things easy. But one day, as she was hanging out the washing, the Lord spoke to her. *Do you believe I healed you?*

She didn't hesitate. 'Yes, Lord, I do.'

Then prove it, He challenged her. *Set to and do the things you couldn't do before.*

Suitably chided, she obeyed. Immediately she set about cleaning the house from top to bottom, hoovering, dusting and polishing with the sort of vigour she'd not risked for months. And she didn't collapse in a heap because God doesn't do things by halves. He does, however, ask us to *act* on our healing, stepping out in faith, living in the belief that He has touched us. Healing is a gift from God, and, like the gifts of the Spirit, we use it or lose it. Colleen's story could so easily have ended differently. Had she failed to act on the Lord's prompting that day, she probably would have forfeited the healing. The Scripture is very clear: without faith it is impossible to please God. It may not always be necessary to exercise faith in order to receive a healing, but it is essential if we are to keep it.

Sometimes our healing may be one of relief rather than release, as was the case for Jean Allison. Jean and Ernest have been with us at Hollybush since the early days, and when I was making notes for this book they reminded me that when we had meetings in the big house, they used to bring their five children - toddlers at the time - and tuck them up in our bed, which was directly above the meeting room. Apparently our singing used to send the little ones off to sleep, and they would carry on sleeping right through the meeting. Perhaps that early exposure to the preaching of the Word and the singing of praises did some good, since all five of those kiddies have grown up to love and serve the Lord. Some of them have seen miracles, too. Which hardly surprises their mum and dad, who over the years have witnessed more miracles than most.

At this particular time Jean was seeking a miracle of relief from arthritic pain in her hip. She'd seen the doctor, who told her she needed a hip replacement operation and added her name to the waiting list. But while she waited the pain increased to the point that she could barely move without discomfort. Over the years, Jean and Ernest had seen numerous answers to prayer, so their faith was strong and their hopes high. Which is how Jean came to ask the Lord to give her hinds' feet - 'So that I could skip and leap and run!' she told me. And, during one of the meetings, He did just that. Suddenly Jean felt something good happening within her hip and leaped from her seat in expectation. Moments later she was running around the church at such a speed that one brother declared that *he* couldn't run that fast, and he didn't have a dodgy hip!

I was conducting the meeting that night and rejoiced with everyone else that Jean was getting blessed. 'Are you better?' I asked when she'd completed her circuit of the church. To which she replied, 'No, Jim, I'm still limping.'

'Then run round again!' I encouraged her. To our amusement, off she dashed once more, her healing increasing as her faith abounded. Well, she'd asked for hinds' feet, and the Lord had given them to her!

Eventually Jean went in for the operation, and we all gave thanks to God for her new hip, but in those intervening months she was pretty much free of pain. God is good.

Further encouragement came to us as visitors to Hollybush were blessed. People like August Ericson, who runs a fish and chip shop - 'Sign of The Fish' - in Lincoln. At that time August's business was in trouble and he needed to put in all the hours God sent. The son of an Icelandic sea captain, he wasn't afraid of hard work, but of course he needed to be fit to do it. It was then that his right hand was horribly burned in an accident with the boiling-hot fat from the frying range. Jill, his wife, called the ambulance and he was rushed to hospital. As if he wasn't in enough pain, his agony increased when he was told that healing would take six months, and even then he may never recover full use of the damaged hand.

Well, August thought this was the end of his business. And it might well have been, but for the God of the impossible. The day after the accident, two American friends brought him to Hollybush for the Friday meeting. I had met August before and, seeing him in the congregation, asked him to explain to the folks why his arm was in a sling, and to give us the opportunity to pray for him. In fact, we asked God to heal our brother there and then, so that he could return to his business and the work of providing for his wife and children.

Eleven days later, August was back frying fish and chips. His hand was completely healed, without a trace of the injury and with new skin as smooth as a baby's. Glory!

Healing of a very different kind came to another visitor to the fellowship on the farm - professional singer John Gaughan. John began his musical career with the Sixties beat group The Hermits, but his prospects later dwindled and ultimately vanished when a taste for drink led to alcohol addiction. The demon drink eventually broke him, so that he lost his wife, his work and his self-respect. A failed suicide attempt, when he leapt from an upper window, left him with a badly damaged back and broken feet.

'While I was recovering,' John told me, 'and still drinking, my auntie used to call round to check on me and clear away the bottles. She reminded me of something my grandmother used to say to me when I was a kid - that "there's a God and it's no use hiding under the table"!'

That stayed with John while he made various attempts to break free of alcohol. 'When the clinics and hospitals failed to cure me,' he went on, I came to the conclusion that the only way out was through God.'

The lovely thing is that, while John was still thinking about searching for the Father, the Father was already searching for him.

'A man who was an elder at a local church came to my house because, as he says, God had told him to come and tell me about Jesus.'

Before long, John committed his life to the Lord and gradually, with the support of other Christians, he began to pull his life back together. Healing of his back and feet followed, and eventually he was able to start singing for a living again. It was at that time that John came to Hollybush, brought by his cousin, Ian Bretherick, a professional chef who'd had his own problems and found the answers in the God of Hollybush. Ian now helps to run our cafeteria, producing some wonderfully mouth-watering meals.

But it was food for the soul that John needed when he turned up here during camp week of 1994. He found plenty of that, along with the first step toward a new direction in his life. It was at that camp that John first got up and sang for the Lord. As a result, he was invited to sing and give his testimony at other churches, which he gladly did, with the support and encouragement of Hollybush friends Colin and Judith Henley, who took John under their wing and nurtured him in the faith.

An album of Christian songs, recorded with the help of our friend Rodney Breckon, helped to promote John's talents, and, following a season working with Pastor Ken Gott at Sunderland Christian Centre, John branched out on his own as a full-time Christian singer.

Now happily remarried, with a family (and Tommy the cat!) to support, John is busy with engagements, singing and testifying for the Lord. We see him from time to time, for whenever his travels bring him this way he calls in at the farm and we renew fellowship. He drops in at the meetings, too, when he can, just to recharge his batteries.

'I love this place,' John tells me. 'It was here that the Lord set me on a new path, gave me a new purpose, and made sense of my life.' Thanks be to God!

Release and renewal - we've been privileged to see it time and time again. Sometimes it seems to fall from heaven at the whisper of a prayer, and at other times it's hard-won, wrenched from the enemy's hands through the power of the blood, because that's the only way.

This was the case with a couple who came to us from Middlesbrough. The husband was particularly concerned because some unpleasant things were happening in their home.

'The house is cold,' he informed us, 'even when the central heating is full on.'

Short of there being a hole in the roof, another explanation seemed likely, so some of our folks drove over to the house and set to praying, asking for the peace of God in every room. But the low temperatures persisted and it soon became clear that there was some sort of dark presence in the place. This was rather disconcerting for the couple, as you'd imagine, but we resisted the urge to jump to conclusions; it wasn't necessarily a reflection on something these folk had done, or something they'd unwittingly brought into the house. Sometimes the dark phenomenon may have been there long before the house was built. But eventually the wife owned up to the fact that she had been making occult paintings. She was an artist, and this was her subject.

Our folks took one look at her work, based on occult images, and declared, 'These will have to go.'

'But this is my living,' the lady informed us.

'Then you have a choice,' she was told. 'Either get rid of these pictures, in which case you can expect the place to start warming up, or carry on as you are.'

'But there's £20,000 worth of paintings here,' she protested.

What price, we wondered, did she put on having the peace of God in her home?

Thankfully, reason prevailed. Before many more days had passed the couple turned up at the farm with a van packed out with the paintings and we drove down to the aerodrome at Sandhutton, piled them up in a bonfire, and set light to them. Together we rejoiced in the liberating power of Jesus Christ, and that couple went home free. The troubled husband found peace, and his wife found new purpose. I understand that these days she uses her brushes to glorify God…and that their home is filled with the warmth of God's love.

Our own home felt pretty warm at about that time, too. Cynthia had broken her wrist, and I had taken some time off to look after her. It was December, a quiet month on the farm, so I was able to be around to do for Cynthia what she couldn't do for herself. In fact it had been many years since we'd spent so much time together, and with the long winter evenings we had time to sit and chat, to watch a video, or just to enjoy being together, holding hands. It turned out to be quite a precious time, to the extent of our falling in love all over again. We thanked God for that, and for a marriage that had lasted.

It was ironic that, not long after that happy interlude, Joanna turned up at the bungalow, far from the beaming bride we'd seen off on her honeymoon two years before.

'I've been to see a lawyer,' she announced. 'I'm getting a divorce.'

21/Constant change is here to stay

Trouble, we learned, had been brewing for quite a while. Our son-in-law apparently had a drink problem, which caused him to be violent. Joanna had put up with his behaviour for as long as was reasonably possible, and now she'd had enough.

I couldn't blame her, of course, and it was essential that our daughter should remove herself from what had become an increasingly dangerous situation, but I was dreading having to tell the fellowship that our daughter's marriage was over. I had always believed, and still do, that marriage is for life, and I had stated my conviction publicly. Never had there been a marriage break-up in the Wilkinson family and I'd been proud of that. Now I had to swallow that pride and tell the folks that, sadly, my own child was divorcing.

The thought came to me that perhaps I was to blame; that I should have listened to the reservations I'd had about this union. But there was no mileage in that. What was needed now was for the family to rally round and support the lassie. She had already endured a lot of pain; we did not wish to see that added to. Our hope, of course, was that the church family would also rally round, and in fairness many were sympathetic and supportive, allowing the love of Christ to flow through their hearts in a measure of caring and concern. But not all felt that way. As the news got out, tongues began to wag, hands were thrown up in horror, and the brickbats started to pile up.

'You obviously haven't brought her up right.'

'It's your fault; you shouldn't have let them get married.'

'It's shameful. How will this look to the people we're trying to reach?'

At such times it's not easy to keep a smile on your face or in your heart. But this is life; sometimes it will be tough, and Jesus told us so. It's particularly tough because we have a formidable opposition in the world, the flesh, and other people. If that implies that some folks act like the devil - well, that's true. Going through a divorce - and it hurts the whole family, not just the couple concerned - is difficult enough, but the hurts are multiplied when criticism comes from other Christians. As the Lord's people we will receive opposition from the world, but we can put up with that because the Bible tells us to expect it, and even to rejoice in it, when we're vilified for Christ's sake. But the spiritual armour doesn't always work against the barbed words of your brothers and sisters. The poisoned arrows sent out by our own seem to strike home with stinging effect, stabbing us in the back, for which the armour of God provides no protection (see Ephesians chapter 6).

I have never understood why Christians should sometimes be so hurtful to one another. As someone has said, the Lord's army is the only army which shoots its own soldiers. It's ironic but true that Christians occasionally do the devil's work for him, and probably we've all been on the receiving end. The only redeeming factor in this, or in any attack, is the assurance from Scripture that all things work together for good to those who love God. In other words, what the devil intends for harm, the Lord uses for our good. That doesn't take away any of the pain, but it does give us hope, as well as the assurance that God knows and cares what is happening to us.

As the Nineties rolled on, we had cause to reflect on this

principle quite a bit. As I've already indicated, we experienced something of a cloud in the fellowship with the loss of so many from our youth group as well as a number of young families.

At the same time we became aware that we weren't seeing quite so many miracles as we had in the past, and those we did see often required persistent knocking on heaven's door. Previously, we'd often asked just the once and seen the Lord answer right away. Thus our little corner of North Yorkshire had become known as a valley of miracles. So what had changed, and why?

The answer, I believe, is that we were growing up. Seeing so many miracles, so often, was exciting and faith building, but, as we have matured, the Lord evidently wants us to walk by faith rather than by miracles. He also wants to see the fruit of the Spirit in our lives, and fruit has to be cultivated. As a farmer, I know that fruit, or a crop of any kind, comes at a price. Nothing worth having appears overnight, as if by magic. So when I read about the fruit that God wants to see in our lives - love, joy, peace, patience, kindness, goodness, faithfulness, gentleness, self-control - I know that, at some point, there will be a cost involved. We should not be afraid of that. The changes which God sends or allows in our lives may not be welcome, but Father knows best. Or, as our friend Selwyn Hughes has said in *Every Day With Jesus*, Not one shaft can hit, till His love sees fit.

Enduring the trial may be difficult, but we remember what Paul had to say about us all being parts of the one body, and that if one part of the body suffers, all parts suffer. At Hollybush we've learned this first-hand as we've stood by members of the fellowship who have been struck down with long-term illness. This is hard to bear in any circumstances but particularly so when those who are suffering have previously played such an effective role within the body.

Such has been the case with our friends Stuart and Christine Dawling. For many years they had been active in evangelism, at first part-time, as their work commitments allowed, and then in full-time service. As a singing duo they often accompanied Cynthia and me on outreach trips to the United States, as well as here at home.

Then, in the early Nineties, Christine began to experience back pain, along with occasional numbness in her limbs. After exhaustive tests, she was diagnosed as having Multiple Sclerosis, which shocked us all and prompted us to pray all the harder.

As the months and years passed, though, our prayers seemed to have little effect and the disease took a firm grip. Gradually, Christine lost the use of her legs and one arm. At the time of writing she is bed-ridden and requiring 24-hour care, which Stuart provides, in conjunction with the various home helps who call each day. Christine remains cheerful, for the most part, and always manages to encourage me when I visit her and Stuart at their little cottage in Masham. Others say the same. All of us go with a prayer that we will be a blessing to this couple, but, more often than not, we are the ones who get blessed. The secret, I've learned, is that her illness has enabled Christine to spend much more time with the Lord than my own life allows, and thus she has become a channel for His peace and love.

Christine was not always at peace about her condition, however. 'I used to strive,' she says, 'and particularly missed being able to sing and dance before the Lord. But then one night, when I couldn't sleep, I felt the Lord say to me, very clearly, *Christine, I don't love you for what you can do; I love you for you.*

'That was my turning point. I gave up striving and relaxed into God's plan for my life. Now, much as I desire to be well, I am at peace and believe that God will heal me in His own time.'

To which we say, Amen. We have seen enough miracles to know beyond a doubt that our God is capable of restoring Christine to full health. She and Stuart are unwavering in their own faith, as is evidenced by their story of the red shoes.

'It began in January '93,' Christine recalls. 'I was reading my

Bible one day when a verse from Jeremiah leapt off the page at me. It said, "Thou shalt go forth in the dances of them that make merry" - and I immediately took those words as a promise that I would dance again before the Lord. As I thought about this I decided that, when it happens, I'd like to be wearing red shoes.'

By now Christine could hardly walk and was using a wheelchair, but as they were driving back from a meeting one day, Stuart said, 'I think you should go and buy those shoes now.'

'So we stopped off at Ripon and went looking for red shoes. But this was winter and all we could see were black, brown, navy or grey. Then, at last, we found a pair. I was quite excited, but I don't think the assistant wanted to sell them to me because as she was trying to fit the right shoe my foot kept rolling over. She could see I was determined, though, and asked, "Are they for a special occasion?" She could never know just *how* special, and I smiled to myself as I replied, "Oh yes, a very special occasion".'

Driving home, their spirits were high, lifted by the step of faith Christine had just taken. She had no doubts that she would dance before the Lord again, and was looking to Him for a miracle. They were still rejoicing when they drove into a local supermarket for some groceries. Stuart parked in the disabled area before going to get the wheelchair from the boot, and while he was lifting it out he glanced at a small car parked next to theirs. 'It was a Nissan Micra,' he recalls. 'A special edition with a special name. Just one word, painted on the side toward the back. The word was "Miracle". I pointed it out to Christine and she just beamed.'

Back home, they found further encouraging signs. 'On the shoe box,' says Stuart, 'we noticed that the style name of the shoes was "Miriam".' As Christine points out, Miriam was one who danced before the Lord.

Inside the shoes they found further encouragement: 'A label bearing the single word "Vision".'

Coincidence or God-incidence? Time will tell, but in the meantime the fellowship is committed to standing with these dear ones in prayer. Members from the fellowship visit them and pray with them often. At our prayer meetings, we continue to lift them to the throne of grace as we seek God's healing touch. We are certainly believing, with them, for a miracle. We just don't know when it will be granted. Christine hasn't been able to visit Hollybush since December '97, but we are all looking forward to her next visit, and to rejoicing with her when she steps on to the platform in those red shoes and dances in praise to our miracle-working God.

Another of our good friends who has suffered over the past several years is evangelist David Willows. Dave is part of our leadership team and has been with us since 1976, when he first made Hollybush his base and ministered here at the fellowship, as well as travelling out to take missions and meetings across the country, and occasionally across the sea. He was a man with a full diary, a man well known and liked for his enthusiastic presentation of the Word, his ministry of healings and miracles, and his joyful leading of praise and worship. Always rejoicing in the victory of the cross, he preached that 'Christ is the answer to my every need' and believed it for his own life. He lived by faith, standing on the promises of God, and trusting in the power of Christ's blood for his protection.

Year after year Dave kept up the pace, sometimes travelling thousands of miles a month, and faithfully honouring every preaching engagement. His schedule was sometimes gruelling, but he trusted God to keep him going. He had no doubt that the Lord would take care of him and his family, meeting their every need.

But in 1992, after a meeting over in the Lancaster area, Dave felt exhausted. He put this down to the fact that he was getting over a virus, but a few days later, after taking a meeting down in Hampshire, he collapsed into bed at his lodgings, totally fatigued, his body trembling, his mind racing as fears came out of the darkness, tormenting him.

'I knew what to do,' he told me. 'Claim the promises, plead the blood, get the victory and praise the Lord.' But the formula only helped up to a point. 'Eventually I managed to sleep, but then I was at the mercy of all sorts of terrible dreams.'

A couple of days later, in no state to drive, he was taken home. Claiming health and wholeness by faith, Dave rested up and expected to be back on the road within a few weeks. But the symptoms continued and worsened. He visited the doctor, wondering if he was suffering from M.E., but the diagnosis was nervous exhaustion, chronic fatigue syndrome and clinical depression. He would need rest and medication.

Shaken, Dave went home to Dorcas, his wife, who got on the phone to cancel his preaching engagements for the next few weeks. 'And that made me feel awful,' he said. 'The guilt I felt in letting people down was bad enough, but then there was the embarrassment of owning up to my illness. I was an evangelist; a joy evangelist, a glory way evangelist, a healing evangelist. How do you tell people you've got clinical depression? How do you admit that you're a victory preacher who's on anti-depressants?'

Dave reminded me that he'd had a bout of this back in '84, when he was out of action for six weeks. 'But this time, as the weeks passed, I got worse rather than better. I couldn't drive, couldn't bear to meet people, couldn't go in a shop without holding Dorcas's hand, couldn't stand the sunlight . . .'

Unable to take meetings, Dave lost his income and, against his principles, went on to incapacity benefit. 'But friends pointed out that I'd paid my stamps and was entitled to the payments. Even so, I wanted nothing to do with the social security envelopes that dropped through the letterbox. Dorcas dealt with those; they just upset me. I would worry about filling in the forms, which seemed endless. Would I still get my benefit? If not, and I couldn't work, how would we live?'

More distressing, he says, was the fact that the Scripture verses he quoted, verses about the Lord delivering us from all our fears, seemed to have no effect. 'I'd recite the promises over and over and told myself I'll be better today, but the more I did it the worse I felt. All my strength was gone. Where was God in all this? I couldn't understand what had happened to me.

The weeks dragged into months, the months drifted into years, and still Dave was not getting well. Just now and then he was able to get down to the farm, and on one occasion I was giving him a lift home when I thought I'd put a suggestion to him.

'What would you think about seeing a Christian counsellor?' I asked, expecting him to react and reject the idea out of hand. The joy evangelist doesn't believe that a Christian would ever need medication or any kind of therapy. But, to my surprise, Dave said that counselling might be a good idea; his doctor had suggested it only the previous week.

'Good,' I said, 'because I've got the name of someone who might be able to help you.'

And he did. But it was a long haul. Dave's trouble continued for more than four years. During that time he was also helped by what he considers to be one of the best books on the subject: *A Practical Workbook for the Depressed Christian* by Dr John Lockley. It was recommended by another Hollybush member who had suffered a similar but more extreme condition and was rushed into hospital. There he met a Christian doctor who introduced him to the book.

Today, we're glad that Dave is back taking a few meetings, ministering at Hollybush, sometimes leading a praise service, and occasionally travelling out from here. It's good to see him in action again, and to know that he and Dorcas have been able to use the experience of those dark and difficult years to help other Christians who are going through the same thing.

'When I was so down,' he says, 'I would look at texts on the wall, texts about preaching the Gospel, and I'd say to Dorcas, "What's the point of living? I'm an evangelist; that's what I love.

What's the point of going on?"

'I used to wonder where God had gone - I couldn't understand why He was letting me go through this - but now I know He was there all along, and that He was working things out in His own way, for His own purposes.

'Best of all, I can tell anyone else who's suffering clinical depression that there's no need to feel shame or guilt. It's just an illness, and God will get you through it.

'But when you're low like that the enemy attacks, and when you're not strong enough to speak in tongues or plead the blood of Christ for yourself, that's when you need the body of Christ to be praying for you. In my case, I am so thankful for the prayers of the friends at Hollybush and many other Christians who have known me over the years. With the support of other believers, and the unchanging love of God, you can come through it; you can live again.'

Dave has got it right; at the end of the day we cope with change by placing our faith in an unchanging God. Without Him, we might well give up hope, as indeed some of my fellow farmers did in the late Nineties. With farming steadily becoming more demanding and more costly, and with returns falling as competition increased, many fell into despair as they faced up to financial ruin, along with the prospect of losing their homes. Over a period of time, in separate incidents, three men who felt the situation was completely without hope had taken their own lives.

I felt for them. The least I could do was to remind those who remained that God loved them and is ready and waiting to carry their heartaches and cares. Sharing my concern was fellowship member Derek Wheldon, who prepared a tract, declaring that there was some Good News amid the bad. Then I got on the phone to Robin Jessup, the head auctioneer at Northallerton Auctions, and asked to have a few minutes at the commencement of the next livestock sale to address my fellow farmers. This he kindly granted.

Now, farmers can be a hard-nosed bunch who'll not suffer fools gladly, but that day I was willing to be a fool for Christ so that those men might hear the Gospel. As the bell rang to indicate the start of the proceedings, I stood there in fear and trembling, but when I began to speak I found I had a boldness which only the Lord can give at such times, and I was able to tell them about God's power to save and keep, and to offer the tract, in which they could read about the love of Christ in the quiet of their own homes.

When the winds of change do their worst, and we've never felt so low, we need to be reminded that we have a Friend in high places. His love is deeper than any pit into which we might stumble, and He is able to lift us out or carry us through even the harshest of circumstances or the darkest depression. No matter how bleak the outlook, if we've placed our trust in Him, He will not let us fall.

THE STORY OF HOLLYBUSH CHRISTIAN FELLOWSHIP

22/Spadework

The couple were just visiting, as folk do, but I could tell that they had something on their mind. 'Tell us the true story,' the husband said at last.

'About what?' I asked, intrigued.

'We heard you'd sold up and gone to Singapore.'

I had to smile. We had been to Singapore but only for a holiday. Yet rumours that Jim and Cynthia were moving on from Hollybush seemed to have travelled far and wide. 'We're not going anywhere,' I said, 'unless of course the Lord tells us to, and even then we'd need to hear His audible voice…twice.'

The notion that we might leave Hollybush had begun to circulate in the mid-Nineties. There was never any truth to it, but people had got the wrong idea when we'd started to explore the possibility of handing on the baton. Cynthia and I were far from ready to be put out to grass, but since I'd reached the age of 65 we'd talked about easing up a bit. There was no rush; my health was pretty good, though a few problems in recent years had led me to realise that there was no sense in pushing myself unnecessarily. It made sense to think about bringing in a younger man to take on some of the load.

We'd shared this with the fellowship, of course, and there was no misunderstanding there, but evidently word had got out and the rumours had taken wings. No doubt those wings were embellished when we brought in a friend and fellow pastor, Ray Belfield, for discussions about the way forward. Ray had a good deal of experience in matters of leadership and we believed we would benefit from debating the situation with him. For some years Cynthia and I had been assisted by a very able leadership team and we wanted these folk to be present for Ray's visit, and to contribute to the discussion.

We reached no firm conclusions on that occasion, but our thoughts about the future of Hollybush did begin to take shape as a result of that meeting. In time, after much prayer, we started to look around for likely candidates - godly men who might have the necessary qualities we would look for in the person we would want to assist us. As a first step we invited two men, independently, to visit us for exploratory talks. It felt right to do this, but as discussions and prayers went on we felt the Lord giving us an amber light; neither red nor green. So we pulled back, unable to take the matter further at that point. Unfortunately, one of these men had already made it known that he was to be the new pastor of Hollybush, which of course was premature, to say the least. It also threw up a serious question as to his suitability. In the end, with no word from the Lord on either man, we thanked them for their time and moved on.

Some time later we were approached by two men from the fellowship who expressed a desire to assist in a leadership role. These were good men, faithful supporters of Hollybush, and capable, too. But they were rather anxious for Cynthia and me to respond to their offer without delay. At that point we were just about to leave for a holiday in America and I told them we would think about their suggestions while we were away. I certainly wasn't going to rush into anything - and, besides, I had my reservations. What they were proposing sounded pretty much like a takeover to me, and I said as much in a letter to them. In their response they did not acknowledge that to be the truth, but they didn't deny it, either.

Our break in the States gave us time to think, and on our return we declined their proposal. I genuinely believe those men had the interests of the fellowship at heart, but I simply felt uneasy about proceeding with a plan that would have given them the leadership. These good men subsequently left the fellowship, and at times I wondered if we'd missed out. But then we learned that, although these brothers had put forward a plan to work together for the benefit of Hollybush, in actual fact they had not been in agreement about the way in which the fellowship should develop. On balance, I think we were right to pass them up. Though I was sorry to see them go.

It's at such times that I'm glad that the Lord didn't call me to be a full-time pastor. I've seen what the pressures of leadership can do to a man whose life revolves around his church, and I'm thankful that I've always had the farm as the main focus of my time, and as the means of earning my living and keeping my family. Leading a fellowship of around 130 people is not without its pressures, even at the best of times, but those pressures are put into perspective when I get out on the farm and turn my attention to God's wonderful world of creation.

I love life on the land. I love the cycle of the seasons, the certainty and continuity of living things, the promise of a crop, be it hay, wheat, sugar-beet or lambs, and the dependability of Nature. God is a good God and His laws are written into His creation. When there have been pressures within the fellowship, the farm has provided the perfect antidote. It's there I've spent the majority of my time, and gladly so. If I've been 36 hours looking after people, I've been 60 hours looking after the farm and the livestock. One of the blessings is that, out there, nothing answers back. It's a wonderful place to recharge the batteries, to talk to the Lord, to let go of any stress.

The full-time pastor does not have this sort of escape. He can easily get into a place of striving, of having to perform, of needing to keep the flock happy, and even to justify his salary. I thank God that I haven't had to struggle with any of that.

Most of the big struggles I have had to deal with have been about the same thing: the work of the Holy Spirit. Embracing His activity in my life was the biggest hurdle I had to face way back when the fellowship was still taking shape, and determining what is and isn't His will has been at the heart of all the major challenges which Cynthia and I have faced since.

One of these challenges concerned what became known as the Toronto Blessing. At first I'd been excited to hear about the move of the Spirit across the pond, but as time went on and fresh stories reached us, I became concerned about what I was hearing. Some of our folk went to Toronto and came back bubbling with stories of what God was doing. One of them told me he'd had a revolving, head-shaking experience and assured me that it was okay because 'lots of people do it'. Then there were stories of people making noises, like barking dogs or mooing cows. It didn't much sound like the work of the Spirit to me. But I needed to keep an open mind, and when I heard that our friends up at Sunderland Christian Centre had connected with the Toronto Blessing and were enjoying something of a refreshing, I was not slow in joining others from Hollybush who made the journey to find out what was going on. If God is handing out blessings, I want to be there. And I was among many who were slain in the Spirit and had 'carpet time' with the Lord in that place. But for many, myself included, that was where the blessing ended. Curiously, there seemed to be a marked lack of joy resulting from the encounter at Sunderland. But more disconcerting was the fact that, in the ensuing weeks, I didn't see the sort of growth that's normally associated with a move of God.

My own experience had taught me that an encounter with the Spirit will naturally, or supernaturally, result in a deepening of our relationship with Him. In this case I saw folk getting blessed, but not following through. They weren't being drawn into a closer walk with Him and His children. If anything, the experience seemed to give rise to a little bit of elitism. Phrases like 'we're in the flow' or 'let's go swimming in the river of God' were heard. But from what I saw some folk must have jumped into a dry river bed because, even after a few months, the experience didn't seem to take them anywhere.

I'd also learned that any such encounter with the Lord should fire my spirit *and* enlarge my heart. Evangelism should follow. Elitism has no place.

So, while I remained in fellowship with our friends at Sunderland – lovely Christians whose company I enjoy - I had reservations about the Toronto phenomenon, and told our members so. I especially had misgivings about the animal noises associated with the 'blessing'.

'Hey, folks,' I said, as we began a worship service one evening, 'we want to worship the Lord freely and joyfully, but if there are any barking dogs around, or any mooing cows, we've got a dog kennel outside, and we've also got a cow byre where we can fasten the cows up.'

Some folk were not pleased, but God didn't call me to please man. Probably that marked the beginning of the stormy time which gave me and Cynthia some stress, and some heartache, and which rumbled on for the next six years. At the heart of that difficult time was a difference of opinion over the way Hollybush should go forward. Once I'd announced that Cynthia and I would be looking to ease up a little, folk stepped forward with their well-intentioned proposals, believing they had God's leading and were doing His will. Now, I've never shied away from a hearty discussion, but it's very difficult to argue with a man who says 'God has told me…' Who am I to say he is wrong? At the same time I must be true to what I believe God is saying to me. Hollybush is His, not mine, but He has placed it in my care, and I can do nothing other than try to hear Him and follow His leading for the fellowship.

Cynthia and I can't claim to hear God all the time. In fact, more often than not we hear nothing at all and have to fall back on the pattern for decisions as it's found in the New Testament, where the first Christians moved forward based on 'what seemed right to the Holy Ghost and to us'. That principle has served us well.

During those turbulent times, however, some felt we were wrong, and to them we had to say, We hope we can agree to disagree. For some this was good enough. Others, feeling we were way off beam and completely missing the move of God, decided to leave. We were sad to see them go. Some had been with us since the early days and we valued their friendship.

As I've said before, I don't always get it right. But I will always try to determine what is pleasing to God and stick with it.

Now, with the storms pretty much past, and sensing that God is beginning to refresh and rebuild at Hollybush, I am relieved but not complacent.

I admit to growing weary sometimes, but we can feel weary *in* well-doing without becoming weary *of* well-doing, and that's okay. We're only human (most of us, anyway!) and from time to time we'll feel the effects of our human frailty. We shouldn't be afraid of that; God can use even our weakness, and often does.

A while back, probably as a result of the stress we'd endured, I began to feel strangely lethargic about the fellowship. My usual bounce was missing, and I found I had no desire to attend the meetings. This had been coming on for about a month and now had lasted three weeks. Concerned, I turned to the Father. 'What's going on?' I asked. 'I don't understand why I feel like this.'

In response, He showed me two pictures. In the first I was on a treadmill, like a wheel in a hamster's cage. And, like the hamster, I was putting in a lot of effort but getting nowhere.

In the second picture I was still on a wheel, but this was a water-wheel, a wheel that was generating power. Since water is a symbol of the Holy Spirit, who moves in power, I was encouraged. *Keep going*, the Lord seemed to be saying. *I'm taking you off the treadmill and placing you on the water-wheel.* Sooner or later, I sensed, we would see the Spirit at work.

Certainly we're at a point in the history of the fellowship when we're ready for a new outpouring. The past six years have not been easy. We're six years older, six years further on, but are we six years nearer the foot of the cross? That's where we need to be. And it's to the cross that we want the person who eventually joins us as Assistant Pastor to lead us, then take us forward.

But if a fresh anointing fails to materialise, we shall not flinch. Born just up the dale from here, both Cynthia and I inherited the famous Yorkshire grit, and one thing we're good at is sticking with it. Spadework is no hardship to a farmer. As Cynthia reminds me from time to time, 'We are not of those that shrink back, but of those that persevere.'

We won't be short of inspiration, either. Despite the disappointing start to the Nineties, with no visible response to the various outreach programmes, we finished that decade with a result so encouraging that it more than compensated.

The Alpha Course was an evangelistic initiative which we embraced wholeheartedly, working in four groups to lay on meals and a short presentation to introduce our guests to Christianity. The total number of non-Christians who attended the course was 24. Out of those, 22 committed their lives to Christ, with a large number of them now attending Hollybush.

We've been encouraged by the increasing use of our camp facilities, too. In addition to our regular family and youth camps, more and more folk are coming to Hollybush for retreats or holidays, organising their own programmes and catering, and simply making use of the land and buildings.

For some years we've been pleased to host camps for, among others, the Northern Evangelical Trust, which organises three separate weeks for young people from urban schools in

Lancashire; for Northern Light, an Anglican group which visits each summer; and for the Christian Motorcyclists Association, which comes for the occasional weekend.

We welcome them all, and any who will come in the future. This is the Lord's place and we want to see it used. We'd rather the facilities wear out than rust out.

This book, too, is another exciting project which has inspired us to believe for a new work of God in our midst. How it came about has the stamp of the Lord's plan upon it.

It began several years ago when a family from Kent were taking a holiday in North Yorkshire and came across the original edition of *Miracle Valley* in the Christian bookshop at Pickering. Vic and Sheelagh Harvey and their son Matthew had never heard of Hollybush up to that point but they were gripped by our story and greatly blessed. 'It had a terrific impact on our lives,' Vic tells me, 'and was instrumental in our drawing closer to God, adding an exciting new dimension to our faith and lives.'

On a later holiday in the area, Vic, Sheelagh and Matthew looked us up and we got talking about Hollybush, and about the book which had so affected them for good. By then the original edition had been out of print for six years and Vic was eager that it should be reissued, so that others could be blessed by it. He also felt it would be a good opportunity to bring the story up to date, since the book had first appeared in 1984. The original publisher was approached but declined to reprint, yet Vic was undaunted. A former city businessman, he was used to getting projects up and running - and used to persevering when the prospects did not look encouraging.

The big question which needed to be answered was fairly obvious. Who would write the new portion of the book?

I toyed with the idea of writing up the story myself. I'd been doing a bit of journalism for the local newspaper, writing a 300-word sermon every month, and was in writing mode, sort of. And I did make a start. But the demands of the farm and the fellowship prevented me from getting very far, and it soon became clear that the job was more than I could handle at that time. So Vic set about trying to find the next most obvious person - the man who had ghosted the first book for me.

As it happened, the last address I had for Chris was within an hour's drive of Vic's home, but a phone call revealed that the ghost had disappeared. Vic visited Chris's former village near Maidstone in the hope of finding someone who knew where he was, but again drew a blank. Eventually, through a family who had attended the same church as Chris, Vic was able to get a letter to him, although at that point we still didn't know where he was. Nothing happened for a few weeks, until an email from Chris popped up on our computer screen here in the Hollybush office. He had been living in London but had now moved back to Kent, and was willing to discuss an updated version of the book.

After phone calls and an initial meeting down south, when Vic and Sheelagh met Chris, the four of us got together here for lunch in November 2000. What you're reading right now is the result of that meeting.

Also brought alongside to help us produce this new volume was graphic designer Merve Jones of Spring Graphics. Merve has created book jackets and other materials for various Christian publishers and we were glad he had a break in his normally heavy schedule and could join the team for this project.

I believe the timing of this new, updated version of the book is significant. I'm not alone in sensing a fresh wind of the Spirit beginning to move through this place. Arthur, my right-hand man on the farm, believes 'there's a new unity building'. Jen Raine, who's active within our women's group, says 'the love is coming back'. Ernest Allison, who plays cornet in our music group, believes we've been through 'a period of refining' but senses a new day dawning.

We have been through a dry time, a time of paring back, of taking stock, of listening, waiting and persevering. A time of turning over the earth, of harrowing the soil, of sifting out the stones. Now the shoots are beginning to grow again. There's a new song in our hearts, a new light in our eyes.

And a new face at Hollybush. Shortly before going to press, we appointed Andy Newlove as Assistant Pastor. He and his wife Tracey had agreed to join us for a trial period of six months. We believe the appointment is of the Lord - the fellowship voted 83% in their favour - and we are excited about this new development. Interestingly, and perhaps significantly, Andy is the same age as I was when Cynthia and I first moved up here from Sandhutton.

It may also be significant that he and Tracey have long had links with Hollybush. Both of them used to attend as young people back in the Seventies, and while they've been serving the Lord out in the Philippines for the past 15 years they have kept in close touch with us here, praying for us, as we have for them. Having them join us on the leadership team is, we feel, akin to them coming home. We welcome them, and their four children, who will be swelling the small group of youngsters who are livening up our Sunday school and youth work once again.

Yes, the children are returning to Hollybush. Young families are joining us. Growth is visible again. And this book will, without doubt, renew interest in Hollybush and the God who has made this place His own. The God we love and worship. The God of miracles. The God without whom this would be but a place of memories, of what was, of what might have been . . . but *with* whom anything is possible. And through whom the best is yet to come.

23/In search of revival

In all the years that Cynthia and I have been pastoring at Hollybush we've never received any remuneration. The hours we've put in, the words we've shared, the prayers we've prayed, and the love with which we've sought to serve our brothers and sisters in the Lord have all been given gladly and freely. And, because we're eager to emulate our gracious God, we've tried always to be generous in our commitment to the individuals who make up the fellowship.

The fellowship, on the other hand, has been generous to us, blessing us in a variety of ways, large and small. We are often touched and always grateful. Sometimes we are mightily surprised, too, like the time the folks decided to send Jim and Cynthia on a trip down to Australasia and the Pacific. Of course, they could have been sending us because they wanted a rest from us (!) but they said it was because they wanted *us* to have a rest. A good, *long* rest. Well, it would have been churlish to decline such a thoughtful offer! Besides, I had a very good reason for accepting.

I'd been studying up a bit about revivals - the move of the Spirit on certain areas at certain times - and a question had been quietly gnawing away at the back of my mind. While there was no doubting the intensity of the movement of God in, say, the Hebridean revival or the Welsh revival, why were they always so short-lived? From my understanding of the subject, the phenomenon rarely lasted more than a year or 18 months, yet the Scripture says that 'the promise is to you and your children, and your children's children, and to all that are afar off'. So what was wrong? I'd heard that in some places, such as the Republic of Fiji, revival had continued for generations, which was in line with the biblical promise. 'Let's go visit,' I said, 'and see if we can catch the wind of the Spirit.'

Joining us on the trip were long-time Hollybush members David and Jen Raine, who had been planning a similar holiday. It made sense for us to travel together, so we had company and fellowship along the way.

Our first stop was in Singapore, where, on a previous trip, I'd had the joy of preaching in an Anglican church, The Church of The Saviour, to a congregation which included a number of deaf folk and their interpreter. It thrilled my heart when six of those dear ones came forward with others to receive the Lord. And I rejoiced again when, at the close of the service, we were approached by a young woman, a Chinese national, who looked familiar.

'Remember me?' she asked, beaming. 'Chan Aik Hoon. I was at Hollybush a few years ago. You baptised me there.'

It never ceases to delight me that, over the years, we have made so many friends overseas, but there's a special thrill in travelling half way round the world to be greeted by someone we last saw at that distant Yorkshire farm.

This time our visit to Singapore was less eventful, but then we were supposed to be relaxing. Not even my questions about revival were exercised here, although we were glad to find that the witness of the Christian churches continued to shine, and that those who came to know the Lord during our previous visit were growing in the faith.

The next leg of our trip took us south to Australia, where we enquired about a reported move of the Spirit in Cairns before heading for Brisbane and then Sydney. There we were blessed in being able to attend the famous Hills Christian Life Centre, home of some of the most inspiring Christian music of the past decade and, more recently, the location for a Bible school. Later on, a couple from our own church, Colin and Carey Towers, would spend two years there in preparation for full-time ministry, and we would be hearing all about their experiences 'down under' when they returned to Hollybush during a break in the course. But during our own visit we learned enough of what is happening there - especially the outreach programmes - to be impressed and encouraged. It's good to know that this former penal colony, once the destination of so many British prisoners, is now a centre of liberty and new life in the Lord. Whether or not what is happening there is revival depends, of course, on your interpretation, but certainly the Lord is at work there in a mighty way, and joining them for a time of worship certainly refreshed our own hearts.

From Sydney we flew on to Wellington, New Zealand, where again we were blessed with warm fellowship and a wonderful sense of belonging to the family of God, but it wasn't until we moved on to Fiji that I found what I was looking for.

I'd long cherished a dream of visiting this Pacific island, a dream whose roots went all the way back to my childhood. As a young lad attending the Methodist chapel in Snape, I sometimes received literature from the Junior Missionary Association (JMA). Among the initiatives to encourage us to support this work was a sort of sponsorship card, as it would be called today. Fundraising was encouraged by the promise of a JMA badge and ribbon for every youngster who could collect donations - to be recorded on the card - to a total of £5. That was a great deal of money in the 1940s, but knowing it was going to missionary work spurred me on to fill the card and claim my badge.

This valuable work was being carried out under the auspices of the Methodist Missionary Society, and it was through one of their leaflets that I first read about the revival that was going on in Fiji. As I understood it, that work of God continued to this day, with 92% of the native Fijian population now committed Christians, so I was eager to explore this phenomenon and couldn't wait for our plane to touch down.

From the moment I stepped on to Fiji's sun-baked soil I felt blessed. Those who welcomed us off the plane seemed genuinely pleased to see us - in contrast to greetings I've received in other parts of the world, where I can't help feeling that I'm being 'welcomed' by someone whose greeting could be translated as, 'Let's get you off the plane as soon as possible and then we can go for a cup of tea.'

The warmth of the Fijian greeting, however, was genuine and was repeated by all the folks we met during our four-day stay. These were the happiest people on earth, as Demos Shakarian would put it, and we felt the joy of their faith reaching out to embrace us as their brothers and sisters in the Lord. I instantly felt at home, and even more so when I learned something of the islands' Christian history.

Interestingly, some sources list the principal religion here as Methodist, rather than Christian, which suggests that the Western Christian missionaries who arrived here in the 1830s were good Wesleyans.

I wondered about that remarkable 92% statistic and asked one of the Republic's officials. 'What about the other eight percent?' I was met with a bright white smile shining from a dark face. 'Well, there is always someone who's backslidden.'

At a youth festival, with a band pumping out lively tunes in the shade of a sun-canopy, we tasted the Fijian food and hospitality and had the joy of meeting four generations of Christians from one family - something I don't think I've come across in all our years at Hollybush. Maybe folk live longer in these parts; certainly life is taken at a slower pace. And life certainly seemed simpler there. But that didn't explain the joy of these good people. The secret - an open secret in this place that I can only describe as an open heaven - came from a familiar source.

In each of the villages we visited we found a meeting place, a large room where, four times a week, the folk gathered for Bible study. No comfy chairs here, just little desks with an inkwell at the corner, like those I remember from my schooldays. The leader of the group had few resources at his fingertips, but he had enough: the Bible, a concordance, and a copy of John Wesley's Journal.

And faith. Trusting the Father, praising the Lord, these uncomplicated Christians had learned how to enjoy their walk with the Lord, and revival had followed. And so it goes on.

We, on the other hand, have all the aids to building faith and encouraging prayer - videos, books, cassettes, seminars with high-profile preachers - yet we lack revival.

To put it another way, even the poorest of us is materially wealthy compared to our Fijian brothers and sisters, yet spiritually they are the ones who are blessed with riches. Digging into the Bible, they have uncovered seams of gold, and they haven't been slow to mine them.

I was intrigued to read in the tourist information that gold is among the commodities which Fiji exports. As we left that lovely place, our visit all too brief, I prayed that we might take some of their 'spiritual gold' with us as we headed back home.

At that point we could not have know that the Lord was about to move on His people with what was to become known as the 'golden glory' or 'the golden anointing'.

The first time I witnessed this phenomenon was when a piece of gold appeared on the forehead of one of our visiting speakers while he was ministering the Word. Hollybush had seen some strange sights over the years, but this one took some beating. What it meant was a mystery, but the gold was so real that, after the meeting, and with the speaker's permission, I was able to reach out and try to take hold of it with my fingers. Perhaps it was as well that I was unable to remove it, but I was simply intrigued by such an extraordinary manifestation and couldn't resist trying to capture it.

Our speaker, on the other hand, was not surprised by what had happened; apparently he'd experienced the 'golden anointing' on previous occasions, and in different forms, sometimes as flecks of gold on his cheeks - but he could offer no explanation.

We were granted a little insight, however, with the arrival of an email from Neal and Noreen Hall, the Australian couple who had visited Hollybush the previous summer and now wrote to tell us of an experience they'd had on the journey home.

Noreen had been reading a book containing testimonies from folk who had experienced the so-called 'golden glory' when she noticed that the palms of her hands were 'glittering with the tiniest specks of a very shiny substance'. This was barely visible, she said, so asked the Lord to increase it so that she could show Neal. 'It was so fine you had to have your glasses on to see the glimmer,' she wrote, 'but I eventually called his attention to it.'

When Neal moved Noreen's hand under the light, the little specks were seen to sparkle. It was, Noreen admits, only a tiny manifestation, but nonetheless it was a reminder that 'God is taking revival out into the world through the golden anointing'.

Cynthia and I witnessed the phenomenon again on a trip to the States. We'd been visiting our good friends Wilbur and Jo-An Jackson at their home in Cincinnati and had flown down to North Carolina to attend a convention. There, just as at Hollybush, gold appeared on the face and jacket of one of the speakers while he was preaching the Word. We heard from others that they had seen 'the anointing' on the backs of people's hands. Again, we don't know why, but God has His reasons.

As it happened, gold featured in an extraordinary miracle which we witnessed on that same trip. Along with Wilbur and Jo-An, we had motored north from Cincinnati to the town of Hamilton, where Cynthia and I were to share our story and some Scriptures at a small afternoon meeting. At the end of our time I invited people to come forward for prayer, and the first to respond was a woman who told us she wanted us to pray over a financial matter.

'I've had trouble with my teeth for years,' she explained, indicating the metal brace she was wearing. 'Never been able to shut my jaw properly, so my bite isn't right. Now my dentist says he can fix the problem but it'll cost me nine thousand dollars.'

Apparently the dentist required half the money up front, but our friend didn't have that sort of cash. Could the Lord help?

'Let's ask Him,' I said. And so we began praying about this lady's finances, at the same time laying hands on her.

When we'd finished praying, the woman looked at me and said, 'My face feels strange.'

'Open your mouth,' I said, 'and let's take a look.' I had a feeling I knew what I was going to find. Wilbur and Jo-An's son-in-law had received some gold fillings through prayer, and I thought perhaps the Lord had done the same for this lady. But to my amazement, and the amazement of those around me, we saw five completely gold teeth at the back of this lady's mouth - all on the bottom jaw, two on one side and three on the other.

'Can you shut your jaws now?' I asked, and after she'd removed the brace and tried biting a few times, she said she could. The smile on her face confirmed it.

But miracles sometimes need confirming, so I found a sheet of paper and asked her to bite on it. The teeth marks proved that her jaw was right at last.

Then we asked if there was a photographer in the house. And, yes, the Lord had arranged for one to be in the congregation that afternoon, and he 'just happened' to have his camera with him! He obliged by taking some shots of the new teeth as evidence that we weren't just dreaming.

Later, we heard, the woman's dentist confirmed that there was no longer a problem with her jaws, and that the new teeth were indeed gold.

Why does God do such things? We don't know. He is God

and He does what He thinks best. This woman wanted the Lord to touch her finances, but He had a better answer. A crooked jaw made straight. Five gold teeth added as a bonus. Whatever He does, He does well.

Flying home from that trip, I leaned back in my seat, looked out at the clouds, and thought back over our years at Hollybush. Yes, whatever He does, He does well. We had seen His magnificent, awe-inspiring handiwork time and time again.

Now, with the trials of the previous few years behind us, I longed for the wind of the Spirit to blow through the farm once again in revival power.

It never occurred to me that I might be too close to the situation to appreciate that the power had never left.

It was Andy Newlove who put things into perspective for me. He had first come to Hollybush back in the Seventies, when we were meeting in the big house, and he had continued to be part of the fellowship as the years passed. When, in 1983, he and Tracey married and went off to the mission field, they continued to regard Hollybush as their spiritual home. Throughout the next 15 years, most of which they spent in the Philippines, they watched Hollybush grow and thrive from afar.

'In the early days,' Andy told me, 'this place was in revival, and I got revived. But I determined then to never let it go. As far as I'm concerned, revival never left Hollybush, either. Some people think the move of God came and went, but I've always believed that it came and stayed. Revival only leaves if you let it go. But if you keep it in your heart, it will always be there.'

I'd not seen that before, and it put a completely different perspective on my question about revivals tending to last only a year or 18 months. If Andy's view was correct, and it certainly made good sense to me, then the work which God began here back in the Sixties continues to this day. That means the revival which first swept through Hollybush is still going on, more than 30 years later.

But what about the *evidence* of revival? Signs and wonders, such as the 'gold' phenomenon, were exciting to behold, but I longed to see the miracles flowing again. The incidents of supernatural healing had always been the clearest indication of the Spirit at work here, just as they had been the most dramatic part of Jesus' earthly ministry. 'Do it again, Lord!' was my constant prayer.

Some time later, He gave me His reply. And it came through a couple who were visiting Hollybush for the first time.

Peter and Elaine Bowden had been given a copy of *Miracle Valley* a few years earlier by a pilot friend of mine, Ian Ferguson, who had been visiting their area to speak at a Full Gospel Business Men's meeting. Peter had been quick to devour the book, but Elaine never got round to reading it until after their daughter, Katie, was born a couple of years later. Elaine was drawn to the book because their little girl was born with only one hip, a short femur, and a foot that was abnormally small. The doctors wanted to amputate the foot, but Peter and Elaine believed there was a better solution. As she read the book, and was inspired by the many healings in our story, Elaine sensed the Lord was telling her to bring Katie to Hollybush.

If she had been inclined to hesitate, her mind was made up when she read about the woman from South Africa who turned up at the farm because the Lord had told her, *Go to England, to Hollybush Farm*. Elaine is South African.

The family turned up here for the Sunday morning service, and over lunch in the cafeteria Cynthia and I got talking to them. Later that day, during our prayer time in the evening service, we called the family out and prayed for them, especially asking healing for little Katie.

But Katie was not healed. Elaine, however, was slain in the Spirit, and while she was lying there on the carpet the Lord spoke to her with a word for the fellowship; a word that thrilled our hearts.

'You have seen mighty miracles in this place, and for a season you have seen those miracles withheld; but the time is coming when the Lord will once again release mighty miracles in your midst.'

Elaine later told me that she believes the reason the Lord wanted them here was to deliver that message. I believe it. And, while we're waiting for the word to be fulfilled, we thank God for the miracles that He has promised to perform.

Meanwhile, the Bowdens are rejoicing in the miracles the Lord is doing for Katie. Although no healing appeared to take place during their visit to the farm, prayers have continued to go up, and Elaine tells me that Katie now has the hip she needed; her distorted foot is now the same size as her good one (apparently it grew three sizes overnight); and her femur has grown a little.

Our faith has grown, too. Our vision, once a little blurred, is back in focus. Revival is in our hearts.

Do it again, Lord. Do it again!

24/Milestones and memories

The Golden Lion Hotel was abuzz with farm talk. Local landowners had gathered in town for one of the Northallerton Estate Agency's occasional auctions, and I was there with a particular interest in two lots, one of 29 acres and one of 23. It was all reminiscent of the day, almost three decades earlier, when I had shown up here to bid for Hollybush Farm.

But on this chilly afternoon in November, 1996, I was selling, not buying. That acreage was part of The Limes and I had decided it was time to let some of it go. Farming in Britain had seen its best days; rising costs and falling returns meant it was no longer possible for the two farms to support four families. So, encouraged by the handsome price which one of my neighbours in Sandhutton had recently picked up for some of his land, I decided that now was a good time to test the market for myself. The result was a sale, one lot on that afternoon and the other a year later, for ten times the amount we had paid for the land. As it happened, this sale returned The Limes to the same acreage as when my dad bought it back in 1956.

Further changes were to follow a couple of years later. Edwin Gill, who had worked for me at The Limes for the past 30 years, came to see me with a proposition.

'I realise farming isn't so good at present,' he said, 'and it doesn't look like it'll pick up again, not for a long time, if ever, so I wouldn't mind if you wanted to lay me off early.'

Edwin was almost 64 at that time, with just over a year to go before he was due to retire, and his suggestion quite appealed to me. Later that evening I chatted it over with Cynthia and we decided it would make sense. In seemed only fair to offer the same arrangement to both our full-timers at The Limes, so we asked Ernest Allison if he too would be willing to take redundancy pay. It turned out that the arrangement suited everyone, so we went ahead and paid off our brothers in the Lord, one in December of 1999 and the other in the first month of 2000.

I say the arrangement suited us, but there was a sense in which I was reluctant to let the men go. Along with Arthur, who worked mainly at Hollybush Farm, Edwin and Ernest had become like family, and of course *were* family in terms of the fellowship; we both worked and worshipped together. Part of me didn't like having to make redundant two good men who'd worked hard for us and had become our friends. But as well as being concerned about what happened to my employees, I also had a responsibility to make the farm's figures add up. God had given me good sense as well as a caring spirit.

But where exactly *was* God in this situation? From the outset at Hollybush we had enjoyed the practical fulfilment of the promise He had given us: *You just be here and I'll prosper the land*.

Did the fact that we were now finding it wise to sell land and lay off men mean that the promise had at last failed? Not a bit of it. For a start, the Lord had never promised that He would prosper us for ever. And in any case, the fact that we had been *so* blessed down the years meant that we had been able to put some money away for leaner times, and that too had been God's provision.

If I could have planned things myself, I would have liked to keep Edwin and Ernest on till they reached 65. In fact I had planned to continue farming until they retired. But the Lord decided otherwise. And, as it turned out, this did the men a big favour because they were able to bank their redundancy money *and* continue working on a job-by-job basis for myself and other farmers, as the need arose. In fact, at the time of writing, both have more work than they can cope with.

Arthur, meanwhile, continues to work on both farms, as he has done for even more years than Edwin and Ernest. He was my first full-time employee at Hollybush and probably will be my last. To all who know the place, it wouldn't be the same without Arthur's cheery smile and infectious chuckle, not to mention his enthusiasm for what God is doing here, and in his own life.

A while back he got blessed on his first trip to Uganda, where he met up with his old pal John Mattison (of 'rabbits equals petrol' fame) and his wife Betty. The Mattisons were working out there with the Church Missionary Society, providing technical support to a vital water supply project. Arthur had been meaning to make the trip for some years and, once there, wished he'd not delayed so long. Africa simply captivated him, and for weeks after his return he continued to enthuse about the place, and how he would love to return. The colours, the sounds, the sights…he was mesmerised.

Some while later, Arthur had even more reason to be thankful for his eyesight. And, as it happened, this also centred on a holiday. It was a morning when Arthur and Jane, along with their children, were due to leave for a week's break down south. Before he could leave, however, Arthur had a job to do, marking the sheep which were destined for the trip to market later that day. He had done the job a hundred times before, and over the years had handled thousands of sheep without incident, but today, without warning, one of the animals rose up on its hind legs and butted him in the eye.

'It happened so fast,' he told me later, 'that I didn't have time to react.'

Jane took one look at the damage and drove him to hospital, where Arthur expressed his hope that they could see to him fairly promptly as he was due to leave for the family holiday. The doctor had a different view.

'You're not going anywhere,' she said. 'Your eye is deflated and we have to get the pressure back up. That means surgery.'

The injury required eight stitches and when Arthur came round from the anaesthetic he found himself focusing his good eye on a nurse, who asked if he wanted any painkillers.

'What for?' was Arthur's response.

These days, apart from sensitivity to bright light, Arthur's eye is as good as new. 'And I've never had a moment's pain,' he adds, 'not from the initial thump or at any other time. God was looking after me. He always does!'

God's loving care was a theme which had been ongoing in my own life, of course, and it was given sharp focus when I reached my 70th birthday.

'Jim Wilkinson, this is your life!' were words I'd never expected to hear, but they came complete with a flash of a red folder and a widely grinning master of ceremonies. No, I wasn't on the television, but I was certainly surprised, and pleasantly so. Family and friends had gathered at the church to celebrate with us as I had entered the ranks of the septuagenarians, and to mark the occasion Tom Walters had prepared a little jaunt down memory lane, reminding me and all present of many of the events and highlights which stand as markers along the course my life has taken.

Looking back these past 30-odd years, it still amazes me that we just came here, at the Lord's invitation, and that out of that simple step of faith has flown so much blessing, not just for Cynthia, Joanna and myself, but for all who have come to Hollybush with an open heart.

It amazes me as I reflect on how we came out of the house into the barn, out of the barn into the small church, out of the small church into a bigger barn for a while, then out of that barn into the present church. None of it was planned - not by us, anyway; we simply took the Lord at His word when He said, *You just be here, and I'll prosper you.* Everything good that followed has been His doing, and in His time. Even the café that was being built when we finished the first part of this book and, more recently, statutory approval for a caravan site on the farm . . . it's all dovetailed together beautifully.

And because the Lord does all things well, we remain excited about what might be next. Yes, we believe there is more to come! With the completion of the new 800-seater church it would have been easy to think we'd arrived as far as buildings are concerned, but the Scriptures warn us about building houses with ceilings in. In other words, it's the Lord who decides when the structure is complete, when the work is finished. So far He hasn't said 'stop', so we are listening and waiting, ready for the next step, whatever that may be.

Some visions are still to be fulfilled; for example, sending out live TV broadcasts of the meetings to people's homes. Advancing technology has brought the possibility of this much nearer and we await the Lord's directions. Meanwhile the video ministry continues, all of it now on the VHS system, and with much-improved recording quality.

And while we wait, we have much to be grateful for. With a full heart I thank the Lord for bringing us through. It's sometimes been a bumpy ride, and there have been one or two big blows, the pain of which we wouldn't wish on anyone, but, apart from that, as the Scripture says, the lines have fallen to us in pleasant places. In fact, so blessed have we been that if He chooses not to speak to me again audibly, or through His Word, or through a prophetic gift, and if I never see or receive another miracle until my last breath is breathed or He should come in the clouds, I have seen, heard and known sufficient love, joy, peace, gentleness, goodness, guidance and blessing to carry me through the rest of my days here on earth and on into that blessed eternity which He has promised for each one who has yielded their life to Him.

25/The greatest miracle of all

It was New Year's Eve, 1999. Just a couple of hours and we would be welcoming in the much-hyped, much-anticipated New Year's Day, 2000. At Hollybush the new church was buzzing with folk enjoying a meal at tables set on the balconies. More than a hundred of us had taken up the invitation to eat our last meal of the old century together, in the Lord's house.

Half an hour later I looked down and saw more members of the fellowship and a few visitors coming through the double doors, arriving early for the meeting we had planned for 11.00 pm. Well, what better way to see in the new millennium than to gather before the Lord, thanking Him for past mercies and trusting Him for future ones. Many prayers went up that night, but the prayer that was on my own heart was that this very evening, right at the outset of the new era, at least one person would have a life-changing encounter with the Lord of the years.

I was not to be disappointed. Just minutes after midnight, as we brought our meeting to a close and made an appeal for folk to place their faith in Christ, a young man, Tony, came forward. 'I want to go into 2000 as a Christian,' he told the counsellor who greeted him. His response brought tears of joy to his sisters, twins Michelle and Claire, who had been faithfully praying for this moment for a long time. They had also brought their mother that night and there was a double rejoicing as she joined Tony out at the front in a prayer of acceptance as both said 'yes' to Jesus. The previous month, Michelle had led her dad to the Lord as he lay dying in hospital. God was at work, honouring the girls' prayers, blessing their family, reaching down with saving power.

We rejoice in miracles of healing, of deliverance, of provision - we thank God for each and every one of them - but at the same time we acknowledge that, in time, all of these miracles will fade; all will come to an end when life itself ends.

But the miracle of a sinner finding forgiveness through the work of the cross...the miracle of a troubled life turned around by the power of the Holy Spirit...the miracle of a soul saved for all eternity . . .

. . . *that* is the greatest miracle of all.

Over the years it has been a privilege and a joy to help many cross over from spiritual death to eternal life, and to see the difference Christ has made to their lives.

People like John B, who came to us a slave to pornography but was set free by the power of God. We saw John a while back and were delighted to know that he was happily married, still free, and going on with God.

People like Doreen, a witch who arrived here needing release from the grip of Satan, and who was gloriously saved and baptised on the farm one camp week. The last we heard, she too was keeping close to the Lord and continuing to rejoice in the promise, 'He whom the Son sets free, is free indeed.'

People like Grace Elenor, whose story we told in the opening pages of the original book when it was first published 17 years ago. In those days she was known as Barbara, a woman who had suffered years of manic depression, and whose life was beautifully transformed by the love of Christ, healing her in that deep place where doctors and psychiatrists could not reach, setting her free as only He can.

Still free and at peace 21 years later, still rejoicing in the Lord who brought her out of darkness into light, her story is a wonderful testimony to the saving and keeping power of Christ.

'It's not always been easy,' she told me recently, when Cynthia and I had the joy of attending a little party at her bungalow home to celebrate her receiving a Diploma in Health Studies. 'Sometimes it's a rocky road, but the Lord always sees me through.'

And the change of name? 'Barbara means "a stranger or a foreigner", and for me it has unhappy memories associated with it, so, at the suggestion of a counsellor friend, I decided to change my name to one which reflects the happiness of the past 20 years. John, my husband, was in agreement, so I wrote out a list of ten names and asked him to choose one. "Grace," he said - which was the one I'd hoped he would choose.'

And so Barbara became Grace. I had the joy of conducting a little service at Hollybush when she 'officially' made the change. It was a wonderful moment, a moment which more or less summed up what the work of Hollybush has been about down the years, and continues to be to this day:

There *is* hope in this hopeless world.

His name is Jesus.

Postscript

While I've been working on this second part of the book, during the spring of 2001, the farming community in Britain has been staggering beneath devastating blows from one of the worst epidemics ever to ravage our land. Here in North Yorkshire we were blessed to be free of 'foot and mouth' disease for quite a while, but eventually it reached the area, the nearest affected farm being about six miles away at Danby Wiske.

At Hollybush Farm we were concerned for our 100 ewes and their lambs, and because of the risks involved in having so many people coming on to the farm for the fellowship gatherings, we decided to move the meetings to a local hotel, the Sundial in Northallerton. We were grateful that our livestock remained clear, and at the same time sought to support other farmers who had a more difficult time. We particularly felt for those whose livestock was destroyed.

Some people said, so what? They're only sheep, or they're only cattle. But farmers are not without feelings and we become attached to our animals. It was different with the pigs I lost to swine fever all those years ago; pigs, generally speaking, don't have a tremendous amount of character, and they're only with you for a few months. Sheep and cattle, on the other hand, can be with you for ten years or more, so you get to know them; you get to know the way they walk, their progeny, the number of lambs or calves they've had. You care what happens to them, to the point of calling out the vet, if need be, at a cost which might exceed the animal's market value. Only this spring we summoned the vet when a ewe could not lamb, and his help in delivering the young resulted in a bill for more than £35, while the sheep and lamb together would not fetch more than about £30 when fully grown. But the shepherd cares for his sheep.

Which made it all the more painful for farmers like our friends John and Denise Dent, who told us their heart-wrenching story when they visited the fellowship recently. Still a little shaken, they shared with us how the Ministry vets had arrived one morning and ordered them to round up all the sheep for slaughter.

Reluctantly, John moved round the back of the sheep to herd them forward, while Denise shook an empty feed-bag to get their attention. The sheep were familiar with the routine and duly followed Denise as she led them to a corner of the field where the Ministry men had decided the animals would die.

'I felt like a traitor,' she told us, 'luring them with the promise of food but knowing I was leading them all to their death.'

Yes, the sheep will follow the shepherd. Jesus referred to Himself as the Good Shepherd, and said, 'The sheep hear the shepherd's voice and come to him. He calls his own sheep by name and leads them out.'

If we follow Him, we can be sure that He will have only our good at heart; that He will take us on a path that leads not to death, but to everlasting life.

But He leads only those who know Him.

Do you really know me?

The question which came to me all those years ago, when I was a young man chasing about the Dales with the Mission Band, leading services and delivering other people's sermons, changed my life for ever and led to blessings beyond my wildest dreams. Now it echoes down the years and resonates from these pages, five simple words packed with the promise of God's love, forgiveness, mercy and grace. Precious gifts, purchased at a great price, flowing from the throne of heaven to my heart's door by way of Calvary's cross. All I could need to carry me through this life; all I will need to gain entry to the next.

Meanwhile, the story of Miracle Valley continues. And *you* could be part of that which is yet to be written.

The Good Shepherd beckons. His sheep hear His voice.

And there's still room in the fold for one more...

Can We Help *You*?
If through reading our story you have been blessed and feel that we could be of further help, please contact us. We will be only too pleased to pray for you or to offer counsel in the Lord.

Yours in the love of Jesus.

Jim and Cynthia Wilkinson
    Hollybush Farm
    Newsham, Thirsk
    North Yorkshire YO7 4DH

Tel: 01845 587386
Fax: 01845 587103
Email: HollybushCF@aol.com
       miracle_valley@hotmail.com
Web: www.hollybushchristianfellowship.co.uk
       www.miraclevalley.co.uk